The Encyclopedia of Unsolved Crimes

OTHER BOOKS BY DANIEL COHEN

The Encyclopedia of the Strange
The Encyclopedia of Ghosts
The Encyclopedia of Monsters
Carl Sagan: Superstar Scientist
The Great Airship Mystery
The Far Side of Consciousness
Masters of the Occult
Mysterious Places
Voodoo, Devils, and the New Invisible World

FOR YOUNGER READERS

Ghostly Terrors
Creatures from UFO's
America's Very Own Monsters
America's Very Own Ghosts

The Encyclopedia
of
Unsolved Crimes

Daniel Cohen

Illustrated

Dorset Press
New York

To Sherlock Holmes, who would have made
short work of most of these cases.

This edition published by Dorset Press
a division of Marboro Books Corporation.
1989 Dorset Press

ISBN 0-88029-443-4

Printed in the United States of America
M 9 8 7 6 5 4 3 2 1

Contents

6   Getting Away With It

The Encyclopedia of Unsolved Crimes

Introduction

Wherein the Writer Justifies Himself

Do you feel a little guilty reading "true crime" stories? I know I do. I always feel a bit like a voyeur, or the sort of person who muscles up to the front of the crowd at an accident in order to see the body more clearly.

And yet, guilty or not, a lot of us read this sort of material. Every major crime is likely to be the subject of at least one popular book, with a film or TV "docudrama" to follow. This is not a new phenomenon, not another sign of the decline of morality in the late twentieth century. From the days of the Newgate Calendar and the broadsides sold at public hangings, crime writing has always been a major industry.

There are lots of reasons for writing about crime—or reading about it for that matter. Accounts of a crime can illuminate important parts of our society or of the human condition that we rarely think about. True crime accounts have been used to right a wrong, either historical or current, to free the innocent, punish the guilty, or simply set the record straight. On the other hand, lots of people read about crime because they like all the gory details.

I have no such high or low aims. In fact, I have left certain cases out because I felt that in this format they could not be given the sort of serious attention they deserve—the Sacco and Vanzetti case comes to mind, and there are others.

Most of the crimes covered in this book are murders, and so it's quite obvious that gory details cannot and should not be avoided. But I confess to being somewhat squeamish, and I don't dwell on the blood and brains splattered around the room, and the exact pattern of the mutilations on the corpse.

What I am primarily interested in is the mystery. Whodunit? Why? Was anything done at all?

Much of my career as a writer has been spent in recounting a variety of mysteries—everything from UFOs to ghosts. I love the feeling that one gets when confronted with something genuinely unknown, the sort of story you can puzzle over and argue over but can't really solve. I have approached the subject of unsolved crimes in the same spirit. Here are mysteries for which there are no solutions. I hope that you enjoy speculating over them as much as I did. The appeal of accounts like these is that they involve a certain amount of reader participation; you may make up your own mind as to what really happened. From these accounts I draw no major conclusions as to the nature of crime, punishment, justice, or the persistence of evil in the world.

Obviously no one could possibly hope to compile a complete account of "unsolved crimes." Even the definition of "unsolved" is a little unclear. There are genuinely unsolved cases like that of the San Francisco mass killer known as the Zodiac. There are other cases where we have a pretty good idea who did it, but the individual was never convicted, and so the case remains officially unsolved. The Lizzie Borden case is an example, though there are some who still believe Lizzie didn't do it. There are other cases where the guilty party is known, but the motive or the means remain quite mysterious. And there are accounts where there is a real question of whether any crime was committed at all.

Right now there are several fascinating cases that I wish I could have included—the assassination of Arizona reporter Paul Bolles, or the suicide or perhaps murder of two Italian bankers who may (or may not) have been connected with the Vatican. But these are the subject of ongoing investigations, and it is entirely possible that between the time I write up the events and the book reaches your hands a whole new set of facts will have emerged that will render my accounts dated and obsolete. I've tried to avoid that by sticking to cases that are more settled. If I had written up the trial of Claus Von Bülow in 1984, I would have said that he had been found guilty of attempted murder. Now, of course, the verdict has been reversed and the whole case looks very different.

A word about Jack the Ripper. In a previous book in this series, *The Encyclopedia of the Strange*, a collection of "miscellaneous" mysteries, I had an article on Jack the Ripper. At the time, I had no thought of doing a book of unsolved crimes. When I did decide to write this particular book, I thought I would not include Jack the Ripper, because I would be repeating myself. But the deeper I got into the research, the more I realized that compiling an *Encyclopedia of Unsolved Crimes* without including Jack the Ripper was a lot like doing *Hamlet* without the Prince of Denmark. Besides, this book is being published in the centenary year of the Ripper crimes. So Jack is back. I have rewritten my original article to include new material—no, there is no final solution as to the identity of the Whitechapel murderer, but there are some intriguing new theories.

Now suppress your guilty feelings, and though you are about to embark on a journey filled with human pain and suffering, with tales of murder, horrible injustice, and real evil—enjoy yourself.

1

Whodunit?

1870

BENJAMIN NATHAN   When Benjamin Nathan was killed, the New York Stock Exchange flew its flag at half-staff. That was one measure of the respect and affection that members of the financial community felt for one of their own. Nathan was not only an extremely wealthy man, he was regarded as a good citizen and a charitable man within the Jewish community and in the society at large. He had no known enemies. Yet, at around 2:30 A.M. on Friday, July 29, 1870, someone brutally beat the fifty-seven-year-old financier to death in the fashionable brownstone he owned on Twenty-third Street in Manhattan. The great mystery of this case is that no one heard what was happening.

Those who could afford to escape the July heat in New York City by going out to what was then the country did so. Most of the large Nathan family were in their summer home in Morristown, New Jersey. Benjamin Nathan had returned to New York on business on Thursday the twenty-eighth. He apparently had not been expected to stay the night, for the Twenty-third Street house was being redecorated. The Nathan housekeeper, Mrs. Kelly, had to make a temporary bedroom for him on the second floor. Also in the house at the time were two of Benjamin's sons, Frederick and Washington, and Mrs. Kelly's twenty-five-year-old son, William, who acted as sort of a messenger and general helper.

Frederick and Washington spent the early part of the evening with their father, and then went their separate ways, not returning to the Twenty-third Street house until after midnight. Both Frederick and Washington said that before they went to their respective rooms on the third floor, they looked in on their father, and found him peacefully asleep. The two Nathan sons reported hearing nothing unusual to disrupt their sleep that night. Mrs. Kelly and her son also apparently slept peacefully though a violent killing was taking place within the same house.

Benjamin Nathan
(*Leslie's Weekly*)

Benjamin Nathan and his sons had agreed to go to a nearby synagogue in the morning, so Washington rose early and went down to wake his father. He found his father's body, in the doorway between the temporary bedroom and a room that served as an office and study. Nathan was still clad in his nightclothes. The financier had been horribly beaten with an iron bar, a tool commonly called a carpenter's "dog," found near his body. There had clearly been a violent struggle. In the office a small safe stood open, and atop a pile of mattresses in the bedroom was an empty cash box. Washington Nathan called for his brother, and when he appeared, they both ran outside crying and shouting for the police who soon arrived.

The brutal murder of one of New York's wealthiest citizens created a sensation, pushing news of the Franco-Prussian War right off the front pages.

What remains astonishing about this case is that no one seemed to be aware of what had happened. A man had been brutally beaten to death in a house in which there were four other people. It was a hot night, windows were open all over the neighborhood, yet only one neighbor reported hearing anything unusual—the sound of a door slamming at about 2:30 A.M.

Suspicion centered first on Washington "Wash" Nathan. He was, by all accounts, the playboy of the family, and had argued with his father over money, and his "habits." Though there was no evidence that any of the family quarrels were of unusual bitterness, and there was no other evidence against him, Wash Nathan remained under a cloud of suspicion for the rest of his life. Some believed that the rumors about Wash were started by a newspaperman he had offended.

Frederick, a more dutiful son, was not suspected, nor was Mrs. Kelly the housekeeper. William Kelly, however, was given a very thorough going-over by investigators. Kelly seems to have been a weak and rather unstable fellow, who from time to time had friends who lived on the fringe of the law. The police wanted to know if Kelly had let some of his criminal friends into the Nathan house in order to commit a robbery. Even if William Kelly had criminal friends, it seemed unlikely that he would have let them into the Nathan home on the one night Benjamin was in residence.

There is also uncertainty as to whether there was a robbery at all. Though an open safe and cash box were reported on the scene, very little if anything of value seemed to have been missing. It's also uncertain how the killer got into the house, if indeed he was not already in the house. Everyone agrees that the Twenty-third Street house had been securely locked up that night, but Wash Nathan said that when he came downstairs the next morning he found the front door open. He assumed that it had been opened by Mrs. Kelly, who was up early and going about her chores.

In the days and weeks that followed the murder, there were a number of leads in the Nathan case. They came from people who claimed that they had seen a suspicious person on Twenty-third Street on the night of the murder, and they came from convicts who confessed to the crime or claimed that they knew who had committed the murder. Confessions of this sort are quite common from prisoners who are looking for some way to lighten their sentence by striking a deal with the authorities, or simply looking for a way to break the monotony of prison life. A California prisoner named John T. Irving was brought all the way to New York, but was unable to convince police he knew anything at all about the murder, and was returned to California to serve out the remainder of his term.

A more convincing story was told by George Ellis, who was serving time in Sing Sing prison in upstate New York. He implicated a burglar named Billy Forrester. He said that Forrester had merely intended to rob the house but was surprised by Nathan and had killed him. Forrester himself was finally located, in Texas, and brought to New York. Forrester denied even being in New York at the time of the murder. The district attorney said he was satisfied that Forrester was in New York at the right time, but since there was no solid evidence to connect him with the crime, and simply being in New York is no crime, Forrester had to be let go.

There were more exotic stories, like the one about a beautiful Spanish prostitute who had a key to the Nathan house, supposedly given to her by Wash. She told a friend, "There was a murder done in that house last night. What shall I do about it?"

Her friend's advice was "Keep your mouth shut."

The Spanish beauty, if indeed she ever existed, was never identified.

Aside from Benjamin Nathan himself, the one who suffered most from this tragedy was Wash Nathan. Every time he got into a scrape with the law, which was fairly often, the newspapers raised all the old suspicions about his father's murder. Wash became morose and finally left America entirely to live in either London or Paris. Creditors began suing him for unpaid bills and he died in 1892 when he was only forty-two. It was said that his hair had turned entirely white. Was this premature death the result of a guilty conscience? Probably not. It was more likely the result of the extra pressure on a weak character.

The murderer of Benjamin Nathan has never been found.

1891

OLD SHAKESPEARE   The crimes of Jack the Ripper made headlines on both sides of the Atlantic. In New York City, the bumptious chief inspector of the Police Department, one Thomas F. Byrnes, had been scathing in his criticism of his British counterparts. If Jack the Ripper committed a murder in New York City, Byrnes had confidently declared, he would be behind bars within thirty-six hours.

On April 24, 1891, the corpse of an aging and alcoholic prostitute was found mutilated in Room 31 of the squalid East River Hotel off the Bowery. The woman had registered as "Carrie Brown," one of several names that she used. She was best known as Old Shakespeare, because she had a reputation for quoting snatches from the Bard when she got drunk.

Under normal circumstances, such a case would have been a routine one that would not have attracted much attention. But the press seized upon the killing so they could headline the "arrival" of Jack the Ripper in New York. The Ripper murders had been carried out in 1888, and of course the murderer was never apprehended, so it was not completely unreasonable to assume he might still be alive and active in 1891. There was some similarity between the killings, since the Ripper had also killed and mutilated prostitutes. But the idea that the Ripper had come to New York was more of a journalistic fancy than anything else. Still, Byrnes was stuck with his boast and he had to arrest somebody for the crime. The unlucky fellow was a man named Ameer Ben Ali, a French-speaking Algerian, who was generally known as Frenchy.

Frenchy had rented the room directly across the hall from Room 31, and police said that bloodstains had been found on both sides of the door of his room. That was good enough for a jury, and despite Frenchy's protestations of innocence, he was convicted of second-degree murder and sentenced to life imprisonment.

Still, there were many who were not at all satisfied with the verdict and dug up evidence that severely damaged the case against Frenchy and implicated another man. Witnesses were found who testified that there had been no bloodstains on Frenchy's door until many hours after the murder. Old Shakespeare's room had been locked but no key had been found in Frenchy's possession, and the police made no efforts to find the missing key. Old Shakespeare had a client who had come with her to her room the night of the murder, but no effort had been made to locate him, either. This missing man had actually been recognized, through newspaper descriptions, as a man who lived in a New Jersey boardinghouse. The man had disappeared shortly after the murder, but when his room was searched a bloody shirt was found in the drawer, and along with it was the key to Room 31 of the East River Hotel.

This evidence did not come completely to light for eleven years, but it clearly demonstrated Frenchy's innocence. He was pardoned, and upon leaving prison he immediately booked passage on a ship to his native Algeria. The missing New Jersey boarder was never found.

The entire miscarriage of justice might not have taken place had it not been for the chief inspector's intemperate boast about Jack the Ripper.

See also: *Jack the Ripper.*

1908

OSCAR SLATER   On the evening of December 21, 1908, an eighty-year-old woman named Marion Gilchrist was beaten to death in the dining room of her flat at 15 Queen's Terrace, Glasgow, Scotland. A man named Oscar Slater was arrested, tried, and ultimately convicted for the crime, which he absolutely did not commit. Slater's case became a *cause célèbre* largely due to the persistence of Sir Arthur Conan Doyle, creator of Sherlock Holmes; Slater was released from prison after having served nineteen years. The case is one of the most famous miscarriages of justice in history. What is often overlooked is that it remains a mystery, for if Oscar Slater didn't kill Marion Gilchrist, who did?

From the very beginning, there were oddities about the murder. Miss Gilchrist, who had no apparent means of support, lived alone, save for a servant girl named Helen Lambie, and kept thousands of dollars worth of jewels hidden in her wardrobe. She was a badly frightened woman who had extra locks on her doors, and had arranged a signal with the Adams family, who lived downstairs. She would knock on the floor if she required assistance.

On the night of the murder, the servant had gone out "for ten minutes," and during that period the Adams family heard "a noise from above and then a very heavy fall and then three sharp knocks." Mr. Adams went upstairs and rang the bell. There was no answer, but there was a sound "as if someone were chopping sticks." Adams returned to his own apartment, but loud noises from above continued, so he went back upstairs just as the maid returned. She unlocked the door with two keys, and she and Adams entered.

At that moment, they saw a stranger coming out of the bedroom. He acted "quite pleasantly," but as soon as he got out of the door he rushed down the stairs. Lambie did not seem surprised that there was an unknown man in the apartment, and moved around the house in a rather casual way. Only after Adams asked,

"Where is your mistress?" did the maid go into the dining room and find Miss Gilchrist's battered body on the hearth rug, and the fireplace splattered with blood. In the bedroom, the wooden box in which Miss Gilchrist had kept her private papers had been broken open and the contents scattered about. Diamond and other rings, a gold bracelet, and a gold watch and chain were in plain view on the dressing table. According to Lambie, the only item missing was a diamond crescent brooch, which had also been in plain view.

William Roughead, who wrote this case up for the volume *Famous Trials*, observed:

"It has often struck me how strangely certain features of this murder resemble the circumstances of that other most famous one in Dostoyevski's *Crime and Punishment*. The scene: the staircase, the empty flat—here above, there below; the victim: the strange old woman, Alyona Ivanovna; the situation of the murder: Raskolnikov waiting breathless behind the bolted door, while the violent pealing of the bell rings through the silent house. I have sometimes wondered whether, had Lambie returned alone, she might not have shared the fate of hapless Lizaveta."

But Roughead points out that the parallels do not extend to the investigation of the crime. In the novel, Porfiry Petrovich, the Petersburg police official, is an expert in detection and criminal psychology. The police officials of Glasgow completely bungled the real case.

Adams and Lambie actually saw a man, presumably the murderer, leave the apartment. Down in the street a young girl named Mary Barrowman saw a man rush from the house at the time the murder was committed. The descriptions given by Adams and Lambie differ markedly from that given by the girl Mary, and neither bears any resemblance to the description of Oscar Slater, who was soon to be arrested for the crime.

Slater first came to the attention of the police when, on December 25, he was reported to be trying to sell a pawn ticket for a diamond crescent brooch. When the police went to look for him, they found he had left Glasgow for Liverpool, and when they went to Liverpool it was discovered he had departed with a lady friend on the *Lusitania* for New York.

The case against Slater collapsed, or should have, almost at

Oscar Slater in 1908 (*RTHPL*)

once. The brooch that brought him to the attention of the police had been in pawn since November 18, five weeks before the murder, and could have had nothing to do with it. Though it may have seemed that Slater was trying to flee from justice, he did his traveling quite openly, under his own name. Indeed, he had announced his intention to go to America months earlier, long before the murder, and he was really just carrying out previously made plans with no idea that the police were looking for him.

But Slater was the sort of person who police thought *should* have committed the crime. He was a foreigner, a German Jew, though he had lived in England for some twenty years. A man of "irregular" life, he appeared to exist on the fringes of the law, as a dealer in jewels perhaps stolen, and as a "friend" of many different women. It was suggested (though never proven) that Slater lived off the earnings of prostitutes. Slater was extradited from America, and on May 3, 1909, was finally brought to trial at Edinburgh.

Much of the case rested on the identification of the witnesses. The two girls, Lambie and Barrowman, unhesitatingly pointed out Slater as the man they had seen. It turned out that these young and impressionable girls had been carefully coached by the police. Adams, who was older and less susceptible to influence, made only a highly qualified and uncertain identification of Slater. He noted that his eyesight was poor, and he really didn't get too good a look at the man who had left the murder scene.

The police produced a few other bits of "evidence." They found a hammer among Slater's belongings, and suggested it might have been the murder weapon. A very common sort of raincoat he possessed was said to be the very one he had worn on the night of the murder. All in all, it didn't amount to much, but Slater was convicted anyway, because the jury, like the police, thought he was the sort of person who would have committed this sort of crime. So therefore, evidence or not, he was guilty. Oscar Slater was sentenced to death.

Slater was scheduled to be hanged on May 27, but just two days before the execution, the Scottish Secretary, Lord Pentland, commuted his sentence to life imprisonment. Lord Pentland had just not been satisfied with the evidence presented at the trial.

Then began the long struggle, led and largely financed by Sir Arthur Conan Doyle, a fierce enemy of injustice, to get Slater freed. He finally was, in July 1928, though on a technicality. This was not the full vindication Slater partisans had hoped for and deserved. "However, it is done now," wrote Conan Doyle, "and we must be thankful for what we have got." For his nineteen lost years, Slater was given an inadequate compensation of £6,000.

Slater married, and lived quietly and respectably in the town of Ayr, until January 1948, when he died at the age of seventy-six.

So who did kill Marion Gilchrist? The police never paid sufficient attention to the victim herself. Who was she? Where did her money come from? Whom did she know? And why was she living in such fear? It's more than likely that the murder was an inside job, done by someone with whom Miss Gilchrist was acquainted, and had allowed to enter her securely locked apartment. Helen Lambie probably knew the murderer as well, which would explain why she didn't seem at all surprised to see a strange man in the apartment on the night her mistress was killed. Most who have followed the case closely believe that the maid held the key

to the solution, but that the police were so involved in getting
Slater that they never pressed her hard enough. Roughead was
convinced that two different men were involved, "one of whom
either made off between Mr. Adams's visits to the door, or
waited—like Raskolnikov—in the empty flat above until the coast
was clear." This, he feels, would resolve some of the difficulties
created by the different descriptions of "the man" and what he
did.

At all events, "the man" was not Oscar Slater.

1911—1919

THE NEW ORLEANS AXEMAN   Between the years of
1911 and 1919, there were a series of bloody axe murders and
attacks in New Orleans. Though there were many similarities between the various crimes, it has never been determined whether a
single killer was responsible for them all, or if several unrelated
cases were linked together in the public's mind and attention became focused on a theoretical unknown killer who was dubbed
the Mysterious Axeman. Though a father and son were convicted
for one of the attacks, they were almost certainly innocent, and
they were ultimately released.

The first wave of Axeman murders took place in 1911. The
victims were three Italian grocers and their wives. The pattern of
the murder was always the same: a back door was chiseled open
and the victims were attacked with an axe. The bloody weapon
was then discarded near the scene of the crime. These first murders
were investigated, though apparently not very closely. The general
impression was that the murders were the result of some sort of
vendetta within the Italian community, and the police did not seem
overly concerned with the problem. After the six murders, the
killer stopped, and the cases were nearly forgotten until 1918, when
the horrors began once again.

Mr. and Mrs. Joseph Maggio were hacked to death in the
apartment above the small grocery store they owned. A bloody
axe was found near the back door. The police first suspected two
of Maggio's brothers, who had been living with the grocer and his
wife, but the brothers were able to produce alibis. The press,
recalling the earlier murders, announced that the Mysterious Axeman had returned.

The next attacks, which took place on June 28, were somewhat different. The victims were grocer Louis Besumer and Mrs.
Harriet Lowe, a woman he had been living with. Both victims

survived the attack, but Mrs. Lowe received serious head injuries. The newspapers first assumed Besumer was another Italian grocer. When it turned out he was not Italian at all, but Polish, that gave the press something new to get worked up about. In 1918, America was involved in World War I and the country was swept by an anti-German hysteria. Many in New Orleans made no particular distinction between Poles and Germans, and it was rumored that Besumer was not only the Axeman but a German spy as well. Mrs. Lowe, who was delirious much of the time, died about a month after the attack. In her delirium, she mumbled something about Besumer's hitting her with an axe, and he was arrested.

On the very night Besumer was arrested, someone attacked the pregnant wife of Edward Schneider with an axe. She survived and described her attacker as a tall, heavyset white man. On August 10, Joseph Romano, an Italian barber, was killed by an axe-wielding assailant.

There was panic, particularly in the Italian sections of New Orleans. For about eight months the crimes subsided; then, on March 10, 1919, there was an attack on grocers Charles and Rosie Cortimiglia and their two-year-old daughter. The Cortimiglias survived, but the child did not. Mrs. Cortimiglia identified the attackers as a couple of rival grocers from down the street, Frank Jordano and his father, sixty-nine-year-old Iorlando. Charles Cortimiglia vehemently rejected his wife's identification, but the Jordanos were arrested anyway.

At this point, New Orleans was gripped by a virtual Axeman craze, which ranged from genuine dread in the Italian community to black humor in the rest of the city. There were Axeman parties, and "The Mysterious Axeman's Jazz" became a local hit tune. A rumor that the Axeman would stalk the city on the night of March 19 but would spare any house or club playing jazz was floated in the *New Orleans Times Picayune*. That night the city echoed more loudly than usual to the sound of jazz. Incidentally, there were no Axeman murders on that night of March 19.

The Jordanos were brought to trial in May 1919. The only evidence against them was Mrs. Cortimiglia's testimony, and that was thoroughly disputed by her now estranged husband. They were convicted anyway. Frank Jordano was to hang; his elderly father was given a life sentence.

The police were relieved, and some of them may actually have believed that the Axeman rampage was now over. But they were wrong. In August, another Italian grocer, Steve Boca, was attacked. A few weeks later, the home of an Italian druggist was invaded, but the assailant was frightened off when the druggist fired a shot at him. A young woman was attacked by an axe-wielding man but survived.

The final known attack in the gruesome series occurred on October 27, 1919. Italian grocer Mike Pepitone was hacked to death in his own bedroom. His wife said she had actually walked into the room while the Axeman was still there, and when she screamed he rushed out past her.

Clearly the Jordanos, who were in jail, could not have been responsible for the later outrages. Mrs. Cortimiglia emotionally confessed to reporters that she had lied when she accused them, and the unlucky father and son were released.

The final act in the Mysterious Axeman case took place, not in New Orleans but, in Los Angeles. A man named Joseph Mumfre was shot to death by a woman who turned out to be Mrs. Mike Pepitone, widow of the final Axeman victim. She said that Mumfre was the Axeman and she had recognized him and killed him in revenge. Mumfre was a man with a long criminal record, and he had spent a lot of time in prison. Yet the dates checked out fairly well—for he seemed to have always been out of prison when the Axeman killings took place. The Los Angeles police, however, were not convinced by Mrs. Pepitone's story. She got ten years for his murder, but was paroled after three. The New Orleans police, who had thoroughly bungled the Axeman case, refused to say if they believed Mumfre's death would close the book on the killings.

The mystery remains. Was Joseph Mumfre the Mysterious Axeman, and if he was, what was his motive for all the slaughter? Was there just one Axeman, or many who simply copied one another? Was the basis for the killings some sort of extortion plot within the Italian community of New Orleans? Or did a mad, mass axe murderer simply get away with it?

1920

JOSEPH B. ELWELL   It was said that "everybody really knew" who had killed millionaire card wizard Joseph B. Elwell. The trouble was that "everybody really knew" that somebody else had killed him. Though somebody, probably a fair number of people, actually did know who killed Elwell, no one ever stepped forward with evidence.

Elwell was basically a card hustler who managed to parlay that skill and his personal charm into a fortune. His biggest stroke of luck was to marry socialite Helen Darby. She not only introduced him into society, she actually ghosted the books *Elwell on Bridge* and *Elwell's Advanced Bridge* that made him famous. Bridge-table arguments were usually settled with "Elwell says . . ." In his day, he was *the* bridge expert. The couple divorced after ten years, but not before Elwell had made himself a rich man, the owner of a large racing stable, a yacht, an art collection, and several cars. And there were women—loads of them. Elwell was a notorious womanizer.

In 1920, at the age of forty-five, Joseph B. Elwell seemed to be at the peak of his career. With wavy hair and flashing teeth, he was considered a handsome, youthful-looking man. But like so much else about the card hustler, his appearance was phony. He was quite bald, and had a collection of forty wigs. He also wore false teeth. Elwell never appeared in public and rarely in private without his wig and teeth. His real appearance was a well-guarded secret.

On the night of June 10, Elwell dined with friends at the Ritz, went to see a show, and somewhere around 2:00 A.M. returned home alone to his elegant house on Manhattan's West Seventieth Street. At 2:30 A.M., he received a call from a friend. Late-night calls were not unusual, for Elwell was a chronic insomniac and all his friends knew it. During that night, Elwell made a couple of calls of his own.

22

At 6:30 A.M., the milkman deposited two bottles on Elwell's doorstep. They were gone an hour later when the postman arrived. At about 8:00 A.M., Elwell's loyal housekeeper, Mrs. Marie Larsen, arrived. The front door was ajar, which surprised her, and when she looked into the living room, there was Elwell without his wig and teeth—at first, the housekeeper didn't recognize him. More alarming was the fact that he had been shot in the head and was near death. In his hand was a letter that had been delivered that morning, indicating that the shooting had taken place sometime between 7:30 and 8:00 A.M. The crime was a very public one, for that was a time of the morning when the street outside was filled with people. No one reported seeing or hearing anything suspicious.

The newspapers had a ball with the Elwell case. He kept what the reporters called a "love index," a list of fifty-three attractive, socially well connected, and often married women he was involved with. Even as Elwell lay dying, his loyal housekeeper tried to hide from the doctors a pink kimono she had found in the bedroom. Later, investigators found all kinds of flimsy underclothes left behind by women who had visited him, hidden in Elwell's bedroom.

A host of theories were advanced as to who killed the card hustler. A favorite candidate of the press was a "jealous woman." However, most of the women on Elwell's "love index" had alibis. The police did not favor a female suspect. They speculated that the .45-caliber gun used in the murder was too large a weapon to be used by a woman. That wasn't really true, since most women would be physically capable of using a .45, but it is still unlikely that in 1920 a woman would have chosen or had easy access to a gun of that size. Another fact weighing against the *cherchez la femme* theory was that Elwell was not wearing his wig and false teeth. He was far too vain to admit a woman to the house while appearing bald and toothless. It's unlikely that he would have willingly admitted anyone while in that condition.

A "jealous husband" was a possibility—there were many to choose from. Elwell was a gambler, not a profession in which one often makes close friends. Sometimes gambling companions can become violent. His ownership of racehorses could easily have brought him into contact with people willing to kill. There were even rumors that Elwell had served as a government agent during the war and had been killed by spies he had exposed. There were too many possible killers, too many possible motives.

Despite the rumors that the police really knew who the killer was, the case officially remains unsolved.

1922

WILLIAM DESMOND TAYLOR   In 1922, Hollywood was
in the midst of its biggest scandal ever, the "Fatty" Arbuckle affair.
Throughout the country, morality groups were screaming for censorship and box-office receipts were hurting. The studios were
scared. Then Hollywood was confronted with another crime and
potential scandal.

On February 1, 1922, the well-known silent-film director and
former actor William Desmond Taylor was found shot to death in
his Los Angeles bungalow. There was no sign of robbery or forced
entry, and every indication that Taylor had known his killer. Worse
yet, from a publicity standpoint, the last person to have seen Taylor
alive was Mabel Normand, a talented actress, and the now notorious Fatty Arbuckle's best-known costar.

Newspapers throughout the country, and particularly in Los
Angeles, covered the case extensively. The stories contained all
sorts of tantalizing tidbits of information and gossip. It was said
that several hours passed between the time Taylor's body was
found and the police were called to the scene. When the police arrived, the stories continued, they found that a number of Taylor's
associates, including Mabel Normand, were already on the scene.
Studio employees were said to be burning piles of paper in the
fireplace. The smell of cover-up was thick in the air.

There were reports that love letters and pornographic photographs showing Taylor with a number of leading actresses had
been discovered and destroyed. Taylor was supposed to be carrying
a bunch of mysterious keys for which no locks could be found.
There was also a story that in Taylor's bedroom were found scores
of women's panties and other underwear, each carefully tagged
with a name and date, presumably souvenirs of the director's sexual
conquests. The only item specifically mentioned in the stories was
a silk nightgown embroidered with the initials MMM, which stood

for Mary Miles Minter. She was a pretty young star (though at age twenty she was not nearly as young as she looked) who had been brought in to take the place of the aging and increasingly independent and expensive Mary Pickford, "America's Sweetheart." Minter had been a popular child star on the stage, and her first few films as a Pickford-type romantic lead were successful, but despite an extensive publicity campaign, Minter never really made it. It is often said that her association with Taylor and the murder killed her career. In fact, her career was on the skids before the murder. The Taylor case might have been the final straw.

Taylor himself, a suave man about town, was a rather mysterious character. He had been born in England in 1867 with the name William Deane Tanner. His family was Irish Catholic, though his father was a major in the British Army. Very much against his family's wishes, the boy became an actor and wound up in America. His career was up and down, and at the age of thirty-four he married a young singer who came from a wealthy family. The girl's family set Tanner up as part owner of a very successful antique shop in New York. The couple had a child and seemed to get along reasonably well for about seven years. Then Tanner began acting oddly and drinking heavily. On October 23, 1908, he simply disappeared. Four years later, he wound up in Hollywood, first as an actor and then director. By this time he had changed his name to Taylor. During the missing four years, he seems to have traveled a good deal and held a variety of jobs. Tanner, now Taylor, did, however, get in touch with his wife and daughter, and one of his brothers came out to Hollywood to work for him.

Though Taylor had been married, and his name was often associated, in the press, with that of Hollywood beauties, privately there were rumors that he was really a homosexual.

At the time of his murder, there were suspicions that he was being blackmailed, for he seems to have taken a large sum of money out of his bank the day he was killed. It was suggested that he might have been killed by someone out of his murky and mysterious past. Before his death, a chauffeur named Strange had robbed Taylor and forged some checks, then disappeared. It was thought Strange might really have been Taylor's brother and that is why the director refused to press charges. Could the brother have also

Mabel Normand

been a murderer? A witness appeared who claimed he heard a couple of tough ex-Canadian Army men say that they were going to revenge themselves on their former officer "Bill" because he was responsible for having them "sent up." Taylor had served briefly in the Canadian Army. A Hollywood chauffeur named Kirby, who actually had served in the Canadian Army under Taylor, was arrested but released when he was discovered to have an airtight alibi and no reason to hate the director.

Drugs also entered into the story. Cocaine was common in Hollywood during the twenties, and Mabel Normand was known to be a heavy user. It was suggested on the one hand that Taylor was a dealer who had been killed by his associates, and on the other hand that the drug dealers killed him because he was trying to break Normand's habit and thus rob them of one of their best customers. (The Taylor murder and her drug habit doomed Normand's promising career, it should be noted.)

There were the usual confessions by publicity seekers, loonies, and prison inmates trying to break the boredom of prison life with a little notoriety. There were "hot tips" from all over the country, indeed all over the world. They led nowhere. Though the case had attracted an enormous amount of attention, and there were the usual hints that the police really knew the identity of the killer, no one was ever officially charged with the murder.

The case, of course, was not forgotten. Rumors continued to circulate, and there were endless retellings of the details and speculations in the press. In the 1930s, Mary Miles Minter and her mother, Charlotte Shelby, who had always been popular suspects, demanded that the police reveal any evidence that they might hold against them. Minter and Shelby said they wanted to end the speculation and what they believed was harassment by the press. The police said they had nothing—but the speculation continued. In 1967, Minter unsuccessfully sued TV producer Rod Serling for the way that she was portrayed in a dramatization of the Taylor murder.

Late in 1966, the film director King Vidor was looking for a new project, and decided that the unsolved Taylor murder would be a good one for him. Murder and scandal in Hollywood were always popular with the public and, besides, Vidor had been around Hollywood a long time and personally knew many of the people who had been involved. He began researching the murder, and his investigation occupied him for the better part of a year. In the end, he believed that he had solved the case, but for reasons that are not entirely clear he put the results of his research away and never attempted to make a movie about the murder.

After Vidor's death in 1982, his biographer, Sidney Kirkpatrick, came across all the evidence the director had compiled during his year of research. He pulled the information together in a popular book called *A Cast of Killers*, which once again revived interest in the sixty-year-old murder case. Vidor had not found a great deal that was new or startling, and there was no "smoking gun," but his research did confirm some long-held suspicions and help to dispel others.

In comparing official police records with the press accounts, Vidor found that the facts surrounding the case had been wildly distorted and sensationalized by the press. For example, the police had actually arrived less than half an hour after the murder was reported, not several hours later. Mabel Normand was not at Taylor's bungalow. There were a few people there—Taylor's neighbors and some studio employees who had been notified and arrived just ahead of the police. There was no mass burning of love letters or any other incriminating evidence. In fact, Vidor found that the stories about the women's underwear, the pornographic photos, and the mysterious keys had all been planted by studio publicity people. Why would they have done such a thing, particularly in that morally sensitive time? One of Vidor's informants said that Taylor was a homosexual and the studio was doing everything it could to cover up that fact, which would have been far more shocking to the movie-going public, and to public moralists, than gossip about affairs with numerous Hollywood beauties. But there was no evidence at all that Taylor was being blackmailed because of his alleged homosexuality, or anything else in his life. He was a careful man with his money, and there seemed to be no unusual drain on his finances that would indicate blackmail payments. His brother was not the elusive chauffeur Strange, and no one from his past seemed to be stalking him. Taylor was a drinker, but had no involvement with drugs, and there was absolutely no reason to believe that he was shot by angry drug dealers.

Well, then, who did it? According to King Vidor, and many others who had been close to the case, the person who shot Taylor was Charlotte Shelby, Mary Miles Minter's mother and manager. In Kirkpatrick's book, Shelby comes across as a monstrous, though rather shadowy, character—a sort of demonic stage mother, intent on controlling every aspect of her daughter's life and incidentally squeezing every cent that she could out of her daughter's career. Later, Minter spent years suing her mother for money she believed had been stolen from her.

It's well established that Minter had what might be called a crush on the older, but still handsome and elegant, director. Her love letter found in his bungalow was apparently genuine, as was the nightgown initialed MMM. Hairs from her blond head were found on the dead man's lapel. Whether the relationship with the apparently homosexual director was also a physical one is impossible to determine. She certainly regarded him as her mentor.

Charlotte Shelby tried to keep her daughter away from all men. She had already broken up one possible love affair. In 1921, Minter attempted suicide after a violent argument with her mother, probably over Taylor. She locked herself in her bedroom and tried to shoot herself with her mother's .38-caliber revolver, but the gun misfired. Taylor was killed with a .38, though the weapon was never found. The night of the Taylor murder, Vidor believed that Minter had slipped away from her mother's surveillance and Shelby was searching for her. She found her with Taylor and shot him.

The reconstruction of events is a compelling one, for a lot of people who knew Charlotte Shelby regarded her as a violently possessive and unstable woman who was quite capable of murder. But neither Vidor nor anyone else was able to come up with solid evidence, the sort that would stand up in court. Minter herself later said that she and her mother and several other members of the family were at home the evening of the murder.

Though the case was officially still open when Vidor examined the Los Angeles police files, he felt there were large gaps in the evidence that had been saved. (Technically, all the evidence should have been saved.) One investigator who had worked on the Taylor murder said that he had been pulled off the case just as he had started to develop a promising line of inquiry that might have led to Charlotte Shelby.

Vidor believed that three successive Los Angeles district attorneys had been bribed by Shelby to suppress evidence against her. The record shows that the police barely questioned Shelby and her daughter, though they were clearly prime suspects. The police also did nothing to correct the wild rumors about scores of women's panties and pornographic pictures and blackmail that swirled about Taylor—though they knew such stories were completely untrue. Indeed, there is little doubt that the William Desmond Taylor murder case was badly handled.

But Vidor could produce no solid evidence of bribery, and one of the district attorneys, a tough, politically smart former California lieutenant governor named Byron Fitts, was still alive in 1967 when Vidor was doing his research. Fitts may have been one reason why Vidor decided to abandon the plan to make a movie about the Taylor murder. However, in 1973, Fitts committed suicide, shooting himself with an old .38-caliber Smith and Wesson, the same sort of gun used in the Taylor murder. But by that time Vidor himself had gone on to other projects.

There are big holes in King Vidor's case against Charlotte Shelby. Why did she hate Taylor so much? Why did her daughter provide an alibi? One certainly wonders if Shelby had enough money and influence to silence three successive district attorneys. But still, *A Cast of Killers* presents a compelling and far from implausible reconstruction of one of the great unsolved Hollywood crimes.

See also: *The "Fatty" Arbuckle case.*

1928

ARNOLD ROTHSTEIN   He was Mr. Big, The Big Bankroll, The Man to See, The Brain, The Man Uptown, or simply Mr. A. Those who really knew him called him A. R. He was Arnold Rothstein, gambler, loan shark, fixer, and financier for everything from bootlegging to smuggling. He was one of the real financial geniuses of the underworld.

He was also a dapper Broadway charmer with friends in politics, sports, and the press. Rothstein was the model for Damon

Arnold Rothstein

Runyon's gentleman gambler Nathan Detroit in *Guys and Dolls*. In real life, Arnold Rothstein was nowhere near that gentlemanly. The character Meyer Wolfsheim, in Scott Fitzgerald's *The Great Gatsby*, was also based on Rothstein.

Rothstein masterminded the fixing of the World Series—the infamous "Black Sox" scandal. He abandoned his close friend Jules "Nicky" Arnstein (husband of Fannie Brice of *Funny Girl* fame) to the cops after a Wall Street robbery he had financed was uncovered. Though A. R. was generally an independent operator, he was also an associate of the likes of Mafia bosses Johnny Torrio and Frank Costello and helped to set up the nationwide organized crime network that began during Prohibition and persists to this day.

By 1928, the forty-six-year-old Arnold Rothstein was a millionaire many times over. He was rumored to be one of the most powerful men in America, certainly one of the most powerful in New York City. The word on the street was that no one went to jail in the city unless A. R. approved. That is probably an exaggeration, but there is no doubt that Rothstein was extremely rich and extremely powerful.

In 1928, however, Rothstein ran into a string of bad luck. He made investments and loans that didn't pay off, or payed off very slowly. He lost bets for huge sums of money. On Memorial Day alone, he dropped a hundred and thirty thousand dollars at Belmont Park racetrack. It's possible that A. R.'s acute mental powers were slipping.

Rothstein was accustomed to playing high-stakes poker in games that lasted for several days, but a two-day game from September eighth to tenth was unusual and possibly fatal. The game was held in the apartment of Jimmy Meehan, and among the players were a couple of West Coast gamblers, Alvin "Titanic" Thompson and Nate "Nigger Nate" Raymond. The game had been set up by George F. "Hump" McManus.

The usually careful Rothstein was betting and losing with uncharacteristic abandon. His cash ran out quickly and he started writing IOUs totaling hundreds of thousands of dollars. By the end of the game Raymond held more than three hundred thousand dollars in Rothstein's markers, and others held lesser amounts.

Rothstein marched out of the apartment saying, "I'll pay off in a day or two. I don't carry that kind of dough under my fingernails." At one time, though, Rothstein had carried hundreds of thousands of dollars in cash.

The out-of-town gamblers were upset, but McManus, who knew Rothstein well, said, "That's A. R. Hell, he's good for it."

But as the days and weeks passed, Rothstein didn't pay up, and the rumor got around that The Big Bankroll was going to welsh on a bet—an unimaginable event just a few months earlier.

Friends advised Rothstein to pay, but A. R. complained that the game had been fixed and that he wouldn't pay a cent. The advice was to pay even if the game had been fixed. If A. R. had been played for a sucker, there was no point in publicizing that fact.

Rothstein told some associates that he was going to pay, but just wanted his creditors to "sweat a little." What Rothstein was really angling for was a chance to pay his debts off at a discount. Raymond and Thompson were anxious to get back to the West Coast, and Rothstein reasoned that in their anxiety they might settle for less.

The man in the middle of this squeeze play was Hump McManus. He had set up the game and was held responsible for the debts. McManus's friends were pressing Rothstein to get him off the hook, but Mr. Big still resisted. Whether it was because he was still trying to beat down the amount of the debt or because he really didn't have the money is unclear.

Matters came to a head on the night of November 4, 1928— the night of the presidential election. Rothstein was sitting at his customary table in the Broadway restaurant Lindy's taking bets on the election. Rothstein was backing Herbert Hoover heavily, and he stood to win a bundle, because Hoover won. Rothstein, however, did not live to collect.

At about 10:00 P.M., Rothstein got a phone call. He told one of his flunkies that "McManus wants to see me" and that he would be right back. He headed for the Park Central Hotel, a few blocks uptown.

Approximately forty-five minutes later, an elevator operator at the Park Central found Rothstein on the floor near the servants' entrance to the hotel off Fifty-sixth Street. The gambler was clutching his stomach and was obviously in great pain.

"I've been shot," he groaned. "Call me a taxi."

The elevator operator called the police instead. When the police arrived, they asked Rothstein who shot him. Rothstein wouldn't say. "Never mind," he replied. "Get me a taxi."

There was a taxi across the street, and driver Abe Bender was sitting in it when something hit the roof. The "something" was a .38-caliber "Detective Special" Colt revolver that apparently had been thrown from a window of the Park Central Hotel. The police were already on the scene, and the gun turned out to be the one that had been used to shoot Rothstein.

A. R. was rushed to the hospital by ambulance still insisting he wanted a taxi to go home. He clung to life for two days. The police repeatedly asked him who had shot him, but Rothstein said nothing. "I won't talk about it," he told Detective Patrick Flood. "I'll take care of myself." Rothstein died on November 6, 1928.

Room 349 of the Park Central Hotel had been rented by Hump McManus, and the police calculated that the murder weapon had been thrown to the street from a window in that room. McManus was indicted for murder, but never brought to trial, allegedly for lack of evidence. McManus also had some pretty powerful political connections in New York City. All the gamblers to whom Rothstein owed money were questioned, but everybody had an alibi.

The general assumption has been that Mr. Big was killed for trying to welsh on a bet. He wasn't big enough to get away with that. However, some believe that the gambling debts were only a cover for the real motive: Syndicate bosses wanted to get rid of him, perhaps because they felt that his powers were slipping and he might become a problem.

Investigators were no more successful in locating the bulk of Mr. Big's presumed fortune than they were in finding his murderer.

1941

ABE "KID TWIST" RELES   The most productive informer on organized crime in the history of United States law enforcement was a murderous character named Abe Reles, better known as Kid Twist.

As far as the police were concerned, Kid Twist was just another small-time hood from Brooklyn when he was picked up for questioning in a murder case in 1940. He had a long arrest record for a variety of crimes, including murder, though he had never been convicted of a major crime and had spent only brief stretches in prison. He had never shown any signs of becoming an informer.

Reles was arrested along with Buggsy Goldstein and Dukey Maffetore for questioning in the murder of a young hood known as Red Albert. Once in custody, Reles got the impression that somebody on the outside wanted him dead; he also began to fear that Dukey was about to talk and implicate him in several murders. So, on the promise of immunity from all prosecution, Kid Twist agreed to talk first.

What he told the police over the next two years was a shocking, almost unbelievable tale of organized mass murder. Everyone knew that mobsters frequently killed off others who threatened or opposed them. But few had suspected that there was a regular organization of professional killers who served as the enforcement arm for the mob and had been responsible for four hundred to five hundred murders during the 1930s. Reles himself had taken part in at least thirty of them. The group was known as Murder, Inc. The killers often didn't know their victims. Sometimes they used guns, but usually they didn't want to be caught carrying weapons, so they used whatever they found close at hand—an axe, an ice pick, a rope.

Reles's testimony introduced new underworld slang to the general public—the "contract," the "hit," the "mark," and the "bum." He also popularized the colorful nicknames of his associates, such characters as Happy Maione, Dasher Abbandando, Chicken Head Gurino, Blue Jaw Magoon, and, the worst of them all, Pittsburgh Phil.

With Phil, said Reles, killing wasn't just a business, it was a real pleasure. "Phil never could get enough hits. He talked about them all the time."

After strangling a small-time mobster named Puggy Feinstein, Phil threw the body in a car, drove out to an empty field in Brooklyn, poured gasoline over the corpse, and lit it. " 'Puggy makes a nice fire don't he?' " Reles quoted Phil as saying, "What-taya gonna say to somethin' like that. Huh? Phil is nuts."

A number of Reles's associates, including Pittsburgh Phil, were convicted and ultimately executed on the basis of his testimony; others were given long prison sentences. Since Reles stood fairly high up in the crime organization, he was able to implicate some of the big-time mobsters like Albert Anastasia, Lucky Luciano, and Louis "Lepke" Buchalter, as well as the professional hit men of Murder, Inc.

Reles was in and out of courtrooms for over a year. It was common knowledge that a lot of powerful mobsters were willing to pay a lot of money to stop Reles from singing. It was said that Lepke alone had a fifty-thousand-dollar contract out on Kid Twist. Reles was kept in protective custody on the sixth-floor wing of the Half Moon Hotel in the Coney Island section of Brooklyn. The place was supposed to be a veritable fortress. There were six policemen in the room with the informer at all times. Yet, on the morning of November 12, 1941, Kid Twist went out the window and was killed.

His guards insisted that he must have tried to escape by climbing out the window. Several sheets tied together were found dangling from the room window. But there were serious problems with the escape theory. Where would Reles go? Once out of police custody, he wouldn't have survived for a day. And then there was the fact that his body was found a good twenty feet away from the wall of the hotel building. There was a suggestion that he committed suicide by jumping. But if that was the case, what did he need the rope for? The only reasonable explanation is that Reles was thrown out the window with the aid of crooked cops.

Years later, an ailing and exiled Lucky Luciano recalled that

Frank Costello had arranged the murder and that the fifty thousand dollars had been distributed within the police department to have Kid Twist thrown out the window.

His immediate destruction was deemed necessary because he was about to give information in the case being built against two important mob leaders, Albert Anastasia and Bugsy Siegel. William O'Dwyer, then Brooklyn district attorney and later mayor of New York City, dropped the Anastasia prosecution saying that the case "went out the window" with Kid Twist. O'Dwyer was heavily criticized for failing to proceed with the prosecution.

There were other rumors about Kid Twist's testimony. One Brooklyn reporter said that there was evidence that some of the information was being used by crooked cops to shake down mobsters. A lot of criminals breathed easier when Kid Twist "went out the window."

1943

SIR HARRY OAKES   Was the blunt-speaking, self-made millionaire killed by his oily but aristocratic son-in-law, or was he bumped off as part of a Mafia plot to build a gambling empire in the Bahamas? Did everybody from Thomas E. Dewey, a New York prosecutor with a reputation for racket busting, to the Duke of Windsor, in unhappy exile as governor of the Bahamas, have something to do with covering up the real story behind the death of Sir Harry? In the case of every mysterious murder of a rich and powerful person, rumors abound—they certainly do in this case.

Sir Harry had been born in the United States but went to Canada to make his fortune, which he did after many years by prospecting for gold. He then moved to the Bahamas and became a Bahamian citizen. He made the move partially for the climate and because the Bahamas were still part of the British Empire and he could buy himself a title, but mainly because Bahamian tax and other financial laws were laughably lax. Oakes could save huge sums in taxes and he could make deals that might be illegal in other parts of the world.

When Harry Oakes moved to the Bahamas in the 1930s, the islands were not the gambling and tourist magnets they are today. They were still undeveloped backwaters of the British Empire. The Duke and Duchess of Windsor were sent there because they were an embarrassment to the British government and the Bahamas were far out of the mainstream. Oakes soon established himself as the colony's richest man, and one of its greatest benefactors. He had started a number of extensive land projects designed not only to increase his own fortune, but to benefit the people of the Bahamas. In addition, he had donated some £50,000 to a hospital in London and in July 1939 was rewarded with a baronetcy—which gave him the right to call himself Sir Harry Oakes.

Oakes was known as a rather rough-hewn, straightforward

Sir Harry Oakes (*UPI*)

man, who said what he thought, and thought that his self-made fortune meant he was smarter than practically anyone else he met. No one could make the kind of money that Sir Harry Oakes made without picking up some enemies along the way. Yet it would be misleading to say that Oakes had a lot of enemies in the Bahamas and that when his murder was discovered the authorities had a wealth of possible suspects to choose from. Indeed, there seemed to be relatively few people who would have benefited from Sir Harry's sudden death.

That is why there was great surprise when, on July 3, 1943, the sixty-nine-year-old Sir Harry was found dead in his bed at Westbourne, his house near Nassau overlooking the ocean.

Initially the murderer had been rather unlucky. He (it has always been assumed that the murderer was a man) had killed Sir Harry with several blows to the side of the head. He then dragged the body to the bed, poured gasoline over it and other parts of the room, and set a match to it all. The murderer had even put an electric fan on the floor near the bed in order to fan the flames. Before the fire could really do its work, a freak thunderstorm with high winds had sprung up and quenched the flames. Sir Harry's body was partially burned, but there was enough left so that the cause of death was clearly visible.

In the morning, the body was discovered by the Honourable Harold Christie, a close friend of Oakes and one of Nassau's most successful real estate dealers. Christie had been visiting Oakes, and was asleep in an adjoining bedroom. He often spent the night at Westbourne. There were no servants in the house at the time of the murder.

Immediately after the murder was discovered, the governor of the Bahamas, the Duke of Windsor, was informed, and announced that he would take a "personal hand" in the investigation. He knew Sir Harry well; the circle of wealthy on the islands was small. The duke's first act was to forbid any information about the murder to be published. The order wasn't entirely effective, but it did slow the flow of information.

Next, the duke decided that the Bahamas' own Criminal Investigation Department, under experienced British officers, should not be allowed to investigate this particular crime. Instead he telephoned the chief of police in Miami for two policemen, Captain James Barker and Captain Edward Melchen, to handle the murder.

Barker and Melchen were described as fingerprint experts, but they were not nearly as experienced as they liked to lead people to believe. Indeed, they both had rather checkered careers, and why the Duke of Windsor chose them is far from clear. The Florida policemen conducted an investigation of almost monumental incompetence. When they first arrived in the Bahamas they didn't bring any special fingerprint equipment with them. They delayed the search for fingerprints, while they allowed visitors from all over the island to roam around the murder house. They didn't even conduct a search for the murder weapon. Once they decided they knew who the murderer was, they started to destroy any conflicting evidence.

In less than twenty-four hours they announced they had their man, thirty-three-year-old Alfred (Freddy) de Marigny, Oakes's son-in-law. Marigny, who had been born on the island of Mauritius and was holder of a minor French title, had the reputation of being something of a playboy and an international fortune hunter. After failing in a number of careers, the twice-married Marigny had taken up chicken farming in the Bahamas; he was apparently making a modest profit on the venture, but it was certainly not what he expected from life. Then he met and captivated Oakes's seventeen-year-old daughter Nancy. Sir Harry and his wife did not approve of Freddie Marigny at all, but Nancy was headstrong, and on her eighteenth birthday, she married him in the United States, without her family's permission or knowledge.

Oakes wasn't happy, but just how angry he really was is far from clear. Indeed, he may have been quite reconciled to the marriage, for he gave his new son-in-law a five-thousand-dollar check for Christmas 1942, and promised to help him in future business ventures. Throughout the trial, Nancy stood firmly by her husband, proclaiming his innocence.

The most damning piece of evidence against Marigny was that his fingerprints had been found on a Chinese screen in the murder room. Marigny insisted that the prints must have gotten there in the hours after the murder, when he and many others visited the house.

Marigny felt that there was a conspiracy building against him, though he could not understand who was behind it or why. Many of his friends who could possibly have provided information on his whereabouts at the time of the murder were visited by police and threatened. His driver, who insisted that he had not driven Marigny anywhere on the night of the murder, was beaten up by the police. A colonel in the police force who said he was with Marigny when he visited the bedroom after Sir Harry's murder, and when he presumably left the incriminating fingerprints, was suddenly transferred to Trinidad and would be unavailable for the trial.

Nancy Marigny countered by hiring a celebrated American private detective, Raymond C. Schindler, to try and prove her husband's innocence. Schindler was able to uncover evidence of massive bungling and perhaps worse on the part of the Florida cops, Barker and Melchen. When Marigny was finally brought to trial in October of 1943, what had once seemed an open-and-shut case against him began to crumble and finally to collapse.

But if it wasn't Marigny, who killed Sir Harry Oakes? Writer James Leasor suggests that the killing may have had an organized crime connection. It's well known that organized crime figures like Charles "Lucky" Luciano were very interested in opening gambling casinos in the Bahamas once World War II ended. They already had extensive business interests and influence in Cuba.

However, there were some stumbling blocks: there was a war on, Luciano was in prison, and Sir Harry Oakes, the richest man in the Bahamas, was not at all enthusiastic about opening the islands to gambling or to the mob.

Leasor suggests that these stumbling blocks were not insurmountable, for though Luciano was an inmate of Dannemora Prison, he was still able to exercise a great deal of influence beyond its walls. During the war, Luciano became a valuable property to the United States government. In return for favors granted with the agreement of supposedly racket-busting New York prosecutor and later governor and presidential candidate Thomas E. Dewey, Luciano used his influence with the Sicilian Mafia to smooth the way for the Allied invasion.

According to Leasor, Luciano and other crime figures were trying to get a foothold in the Bahamas and wanted to crush Oakes's opposition. They had not originally planned to have him killed, but rather to blackmail him because of connections he had with financier Axel Wenner-Gren, a shadowy figure who allegedly had Nazi ties. But during a meeting on a yacht there had been a scuffle and Oakes had been accidentally killed. His body was then taken back to his house and partially burned in an abortive arson attempt. Stuck with the murder of a prominent man, the mob then had to use its considerable influence to cover up the killing and frame someone else. Any honest investigation of the killing might have revealed a sinister web of corruption and influence that would have endangered many careers and even lives.

Leasor's speculations are fascinating, but they are just that—speculations. The freedom of action given to Luciano in return for his wartime services in Sicily is well known. So is the move by organized crime into the Bahamas in the years following World War II. But no solid evidence is presented to connect the mob with the murder of Sir Harry Oakes, or the subsequent bungled murder investigation.

There are even those who still believe that Freddie de Marigny really did kill his father-in-law after an argument, and because of a clever hired investigator, a good attorney, and remarkable stupidity on the prosecutors' side, simply got away with it.

1945

THE BLACK DOG MURDER   On February 14, 1945, an apparently harmless old man was found brutally murdered in a quiet English village near William Shakespeare's birthplace. Two days later, some of the details of the murder were run in the *Stratford-upon-Avon Herald*:

"On Wednesday night, following a search, the body of a seventy-four-year-old farm labourer, Mr. Charles Walton, of Lower Quinton, was found with terrible injuries in a field on Meon Hill, where he had been engaged in hedge-laying.

"A trounching hook and a two-tined pitchfork are said to have been embedded in his body.

"Mr. Walton, who lived with his niece, was a frail old man.

Stratford-upon-Avon H

AND SOUTH WARWICKSHIRE ADVERTISER

I wish no other Herald. No other speaker of my living actions.—Shakespeare.   FRIDAY, FEBRUARY 16, 1945   Registered at the Gen

CHEME: COUNTY RVE JUDGMENT

MPARE WITH THAT OPTON BRIDGE?

"I have been in this thing for the last 20 years," said Alderman T. H. RYLAND, amid laughter.

He recalled that 21 years ago the County Council agreed on a scheme for widening Clopton Bridge and it was decided that it could be done. Then, unfortunately, societies came along and intervened, causing differences between the County Council and Stratford-on-Avon. All the way through there had been two issues—whether to widen the existing bridge or to have a new one—but the main question had been one of finance. He thought it only reasonable that before they sanctioned any

OLD MAN'S TERRIBLE INJURIES

Inflicted with Billhook and Pitchfork

TRAGIC DISCOVERY AT QUINTON

Warwickshire police are investigating what may prove to be a murder of a particularly brutal character.

On Wednesday night, following a search, the body of a 74-year-old farm labourer, Mr. Charles Walton, of Lower Quinton, was found with terrible injuries in a field on Meon Hill, where he had been engaged in hedge-laying.

A trouncing hook and a two-tined pitch fork are said to have been embedded in his body.

Mr. Walton, who lived with his niece, was a frail old man. He suffered

TWO LOADS FOR SHOREDITCH

Miss Melville (local W.V.S. organiser) states that two loads (eight tons) of household goods have been sent from Stratford-on-Avon and district to Shoreditch, and she hopes that another will be despatched next Tuesday. So far the only other place to send two loads is Sutton Coldfield. Gifts are still being received. A crate of china, worth £74, has also been bought and sent direct from the Pottery district, and this will be added to Stratford and district total.

Miss Melville has received a letter from Miss Gammon (the W.V.S. organiser for Shoreditch) in which she says: "Your two loads have arrived and are just marvellous. I think it is amazing of people to send us all this lovely stuff, which they must need themselves, but I cannot tell you how we appreciate it here and what a joy

He suffered considerably from rheumatism and walked with the aid of two sticks . . .

"Mr. Walton spent his whole life in Quinton, and was known to everyone. The tragedy has shocked the locality. A neighbor told the *Herald* that he was a quiet, inoffensive old man, 'one of the best you would meet in a day's march,' and he was not likely to have had any enemies in the village. 'He always had a cheery word for everyone,' she said. It seems impossible to impute any motive for the murder."

The first impression left by the newspaper account is that this was an act of random violence carried out by an unknown lunatic. However, the following week the *Herald* added some details that made the murder seem a lot less random and a good deal more sinister.

The old man had apparently been knocked down and his body pinned to the ground with the pitchfork. The hook was then used to slash a cross in his chest. The case was sufficiently baffling for the local police to call upon Scotland Yard. Detective Robert Fabian was put in charge of the investigation. Later he was to become famous as "Fabian of the Yard," one of England's most successful detectives, but solving this murder lay beyond even Fabian's considerable powers.

As Fabian talked to the locals, he began to build up a picture of Charles Walton. He was not the cheery, well-loved old man of the *Herald* article. He was isolated, with no real friends, and there were hints that people believed he possessed some sort of supernatural powers.

One day, while Fabian was examining the site of the murder, a large black dog ran by. A few moments later a boy passed, and Fabian asked him about the dog. The boy suddenly became confused and sullen.

That evening in the pub, Fabian again mentioned the black dog. A wall of silence and hostility was raised. From that point on, people in the village were no longer willing to cooperate with the investigation. Fabian now began to suspect that the roots of the crime may have lain in some of the old customs and beliefs of the villagers. In researching the folklore of the area, Fabian came across a book by Harvey Bloom entitled *Folk Lore, Old Customs and*

Superstitions in Shakespeareland. There was a story in the book about a black dog in the vicinity of Lower Quinton in 1885. On nine successive evenings, the dog was seen by a young ploughboy. On its last appearance, it changed into a headless woman. The next day, the boy's sister died.

What intrigued Fabian most of all, however, was the name of the ploughboy: It was Charles Walton. The ages fit. The old man would have been about fourteen in 1885. So Walton had been the subject of an eerie legend in the previous century.

The more digging the police did, the more strange parallels they uncovered. In 1875, a somewhat similar murder had taken place in the same vicinity. An old woman named Ann Turner had been killed by James Heywood. Like Walton, she had been pinned to the ground with a pitchfork and had been slashed in the form of a cross. Heywood, who was described as "more or less the village idiot," claimed that the old lady was a witch, and by spilling her blood he could undo the spells she had cast. Some years later, a police constable had his throat slashed, and once again there was talk of the supernatural.

Legends of black dogs abounded in the region and, ominously, during the investigation a police car hit and killed one. This did not endear the police to the locals.

The Walton case, with its hints of black magic and ritual killings, attracted a great deal of attention throughout Britain. There was all sorts of speculation about witch cults and ritual killings. There were attempts to connect the day of the murder with old Druid festivals.

The police rejected any complex explanations, but were convinced that a simple rural belief in witchcraft probably did contribute to the murder. The year had been a particularly bad one for the village. Walton, a solitary eccentric with the reputation of being able to influence nature, may have been blamed for putting some sort of curse on the village. Perhaps the old man even gloried in the reputation for having such power and had boasted of cursing the crops or animals. Such fears, along perhaps with a personal grievance against Walton, may have pushed one of the more simple and violence-prone among the locals to act. It would not even have to have been a premeditated murder. The weapons, the pitchfork and the hook, were Walton's own tools. Perhaps there was an argument, and the murderer, in the heat of the moment, may have remembered what he had heard about witchcraft killings long ago.

Many police also believed that the identity of the murderer was known to others in the village. Indeed, the police themselves probably had a suspect in mind, but since the villagers would not cooperate in the investigation, the authorities had little in the way of hard evidence.

One of the detectives on the case, Alex Spooner, returned each year on St. Valentine's Day to the spot where the murder had taken place. He believed that one day the killer would come up to him and confess. Spooner retired without ever hearing that confession, and the case remains unsolved.

See also: *Murder by Magic.*

1947

THE BLACK DAHLIA   Twenty-two-year-old Elizabeth Short was one of the many rootless young girls who was attracted to the glamour of Hollywood in the post-World War II years. She hung around the fringes of the movie world and was, some said, willing to sleep with anyone who had any connection with the studios, no matter how tenuous.

Elizabeth Short also had a gimmick, a trademark, something that she hoped would make her stand out just a bit from the rest of the crowd of eager hopefuls. She always dressed in black. People began calling her the Black Dahlia. A popular film of 1946 was *The Blue Dahlia*, ominously a murder mystery starring Alan Ladd and Veronica Lake.

Whatever hopes she might have had for a movie career ended on January 15, 1947. Elizabeth Short was viciously murdered, her corpse mutilated and then crudely cut in half at the waist and dumped in an open Los Angeles field on South Norton Avenue near Thirty-ninth Street. The initials BD, presumably for Black Dahlia, had been carved into the victim's thigh. It took the police some time to identify the mutilated corpse as that of Elizabeth Short.

This was a horrible crime, but not, unfortunately, a unique one. Yet, somehow this murder seemed to capture the attention of the American public like few crimes of that time. Perhaps it was the sheer brutality of the act, or the catchy nickname of the victim that grabbed the headlines. Most likely it was the setting, the sleazy underside of glamorous Hollywood.

This killing may have set some sort of record for attracting crackpot confessions. Every notorious murder excites a certain number of people, from publicity seekers to the genuinely insane, to confess to the crime. In the Black Dahlia case, there was the fellow who confessed because his wife left him. He hoped that by

Scene from the 1946 film *The Blue Dahlia*.

becoming notorious and getting his picture in the paper, she might be induced to return. There was the woman who walked into a Los Angeles police station and said, "The Black Dahlia stole my man, so I killed her and cut her up." Someone calling him or herself "Black Dahlia Avenger" sent a letter made up of pasted-up words cut from magazines in which the writer offered to meet the police and give them important information. The meeting never took place.

Among the masses of nut letters was one that might actually have come from the killer, or in the very least someone who knew something about the murder. In the envelope was a message that read: "Here are Dahlia's belongings. Letter to follow." The envelope contained Elizabeth Short's Social Security card, birth certificate, and her address book, with a page torn out. No letter ever followed.

The police thought they had some promising confessions, but in the end they all turned out to be the fantasies of disturbed minds.

There were no solid clues, nothing except the crazy confessions, and to this day the case of the Black Dahlia murder remains unsolved.

The case, however, has been turned into at least one fairly decent made-for-television film, so the Black Dahlia attained by her brutal death a measure of fame that had escaped her in her brief life.

See also: *The "Fatty" Arbuckle Case, William Desmond Taylor, Thelma Todd.*

1955

SERGE RUBINSTEIN   The problem with finding the murderer of financial finagler Serge Rubinstein is that there were too many people who had a reason to kill him. Rubinstein was a White Russian emigré who made a fortune on Wall Street in the years before World War II. Many of his deals skirted the edges of even the financial community's laissez-faire morality.

It wasn't financial dealings that first got Rubinstein in trouble with the law; it was draft dodging. In order to stay out of the army during the war, he falsely claimed that he was a citizen of Portugal. When the government found out that he wasn't, that earned him two and a half years in the federal penitentiary and a great deal of public condemnation.

The experience didn't change Rubinstein's style, for he returned to Wall Street and started his slick financial maneuvering all over again. In 1949, he was indicted for a variety of charges, including stock fraud, mail fraud, and violation of the Securities Act. The charges involved Rubinstein's handling of stocks of Panhandle Producing and Refining. He bought the stock at an average of less than two dollars a share. It was charged that he then drove the price up with phony rumors that the company was about to pay dividends. He sold his shares before the investors found out the truth and the bottom dropped out of the stock price. It was said that he made some three million dollars on the deal. Rubinstein's lawyers fought the charges, and after a two-year battle through the courts, he was acquitted.

Serge Rubinstein ostentatiously enjoyed his wealth, living the life of a Manhattan playboy, and was generally seen in public with a beautiful woman at his side. Early on the morning of January 27, 1955, Rubinstein returned to his home with one of these women. After she left, he called another woman whom he knew and asked her to come over, but since the hour was so late, she declined.

Serge Rubinstein (*Wide World*)

That was the last that anyone, willing to talk about it, ever heard from the flamboyant financier.

At 8:00 A.M., Rubinstein's butler entered his bedroom with his customary breakfast tray. Rubinstein was on the bed wearing elegant black silk mandarin pajamas—but the rest of the scene was not elegant. Rubinstein had been tied hand and foot with venetian-blind cord. Strips of thick adhesive tape covered his mouth and were wound around his throat. He was dead, and the first suspicion was that the death had been inadvertent; that kidnappers or robbers had come in and tied Rubinstein up, and that he had strangled on the tape while struggling to get free. The autopsy indicated, however, that there had been nothing accidental about the death, that Rubinstein had been deliberately strangled by someone with very powerful hands.

The financier's personal notebooks provided a wealth of suspects. He seemed to have written down the name of everyone he met, along with personal comments about them. He was a suspicious man who often had his girlfriends shadowed, and sometimes had their bedrooms bugged. Said one of the women coolly, when confronted with this information by newspaper reporters, "Now everyone in New York knows my bed squeaks."

Aside from the kidnapping or robbery-gone-wrong theory, there was a suggestion that, for unspecified reasons the financier had been killed by the mob. He had made plenty of enemies in business who would have been happy to see him dead. There were angry women, their angry husbands and lovers, and old prison associates. There were, in short, a wealth of suspects, but a poverty of evidence.

Despite intensive investigation and even more intensive publicity, the Rubinstein case remains unsolved. Like many other celebrity murders, it is quite possible that a number of people actually do know who did it and why. But they're just not talking.

ROGER "THE TERRIBLE" TOUHY   Roger Touhy was a
Prohibition-era bootlegger and hood who was really no more "terrible" than others in his profession. He never used more violence than absolutely necessary to maintain his control over the saloons and speakeasies in the Chicago suburb of Des Plains. He relied primarily on providing a superior product, paying off crooked police and politicians, and on maintaining an appearance of toughness.

One of Touhy's business competitors was Chicago mob boss Al Capone. There are so many apocryphal tales and legends around Capone and other gangsters of the time that it is difficult to separate fact from imaginative reconstruction. Hawk-faced and beady-eyed, Touhy looked like the killer that he wasn't, but it was said that Capone genuinely feared him and that he was one of the few who was ever able to back Scarface Al down in a confrontation.

According to one story, the Capone mob bought eight hundred barrels of Touhy's superior brew. But when time came to pay, Capone said that fifty of the barrels were "leakers" and offered to pay for only seven hundred and fifty. Touhy had his own cooperage for making kegs, and was very proud of the fact that he didn't produce any bad barrels. "Don't chisel me, Al," he said. "You owe me for eight hundred and I expect to get paid for eight hundred." Capone paid in full.

Touhy was popular with many of the residents of Des Plains, not only because he provided a better, if illegal, brew, but because he was credited with keeping brothels out of churchgoing, working-class neighborhoods. Capone's men came to ask about setting up prostitution operations and Willie Heeney, one of the Capone henchmen, allegedly uttered the too-good-to-be-true line that Des Plains was "virgin territory for whorehouses." Touhy nixed the offer, figuring that the operations would turn the locals against him.

Touhy claimed that he conned Capone into thinking that he had more of a mob than he really did. He borrowed machine guns and other heavy firepower from the very cooperative local police. He even had some of the biggest cops pose as his gunmen. One of them lumbered into Touhy's office while he was talking to some of Capone's men, walked over to a closet, and took out a couple of machine guns. "Me and Louie are going to give those bastards a good scare—or maybe worse, boss," the burly cop growled.

Touhy kept picking up the phone and ordering imaginary hits on his enemies. The Capone men were impressed, and frightened. They ran back to Al in Chicago and told him that Touhy had a huge and dangerous operation. Of course, these stories were based on Roger Touhy's own recollections, which may have been self-serving.

Eventually, though, Al Capone got tired of being opposed by Touhy; he kidnapped Touhy's partner, Matt Kolb, and Touhy had to pay fifty thousand dollars for Kolb's release. The feud between the two mobsters went on for years.

It was a kidnapping charge that finally brought an end to the career of Roger Touhy. First, Capone arranged to have Touhy and three other men charged with kidnapping William A. Hamm, a wealthy brewer. That frame-up failed, but Capone tried again. This time Touhy was accused of kidnapping another gangster— Jake "the Barber" Factor. Witnesses for the prosecution lied shamelessly, but the Chicago police and the district attorney co-operated and the result was that Touhy was found guilty and sentenced to the Illinois State Prison in Joliet for 199 years, an astonishing sentence.

Touhy kept protesting his innocence and saying that the whole thing had been arranged by the Capone mob so they could grab his bootlegging interests. After a decade of trying to get out of jail legally, Touhy decided to break out. He was one of seven convicts to scale the walls at Stateville and jump into a car that was waiting for them. It was a futile gesture. All were recaptured the next day and two were gunned down trying to resist arrest. "Terrible" Touhy went back to jail meekly.

However, efforts on his behalf sparked by newspaper publicity continued, and in the 1950s Touhy won a rehearing on the original conviction. Judge John H. Barnes looked into all the evidence surrounding the original indictment and trial and declared that the Factor kidnapping was a "hoax." Judge Barnes said Factor had faked the kidnapping in order to avoid being extradited to England, where he would have to stand trial for a major swindle. Not only had the Capone mob been in on engineering the frame-up, the mobsters had gotten considerable help from Chicago district attorney Thomas J. Courtney, and from a Chicago police captain, Daniel A. Gilbert, whom the press later dubbed "The World's Richest Cop." Gilbert had convinced one witness to lie during the Touhy trial on the promise that he would receive a reduced sentence on a burglary charge.

Moreover, Judge Barnes noted that although the FBI had classified Touhy as a major criminal, he had never been linked to a capital case. Despite his reputation, despite his nickname, Roger Touhy was very much the businessman, the middle-class bootlegger, and not a desperate or dangerous criminal. He wasn't "terrible" at all; he just crossed the wrong people.

It still took several years of legal maneuvering before the old bootlegger was finally released from prison, on November 25, 1959. He had spent a quarter of a century behind bars, and he was allowed to live in freedom for exactly twenty-two days. On December 17, he was going into his sister's home when he was cut down by several shotgun blasts. On the way to the hospital, he mumbled to an attendant, "I've been expecting it. The bastards never forget." He died four hours later.

No one was even indicted for Touhy's murder, but the general opinion was that the hit had been carried out by Murray "the Camel" Humphreys. Eight months later, Humphreys collected forty-two thousand dollars in profit on a shady stock deal that had been set up by Touhy's old foe, Jake Factor.

1968

ZODIAC   Some criminals have taunted the police with letters or other clues to their identity. It's risky, for the more that is known about a criminal the more likely he is to be caught. But in the case of the California mass murderer known only as Zodiac, the publicity seeking may have helped to provide a cover. The case became so sensational, so widely publicized, that it brought out hordes of loonies, copycat killers, phony letter writers and callers, false accusations, and false confessions. In addition, the pressure to catch Zodiac was so intense that it created rivalries between the various law enforcement agencies that were investigating the crimes, and timely evidence was often not shared promptly and effectively. It may have been the confusion (and a good deal of luck) rather than any diabolical cleverness on the part of the killer that has allowed him to escape detection.

No one is sure how many Zodiac victims there have been—estimates range from five to forty. Though Zodiac has actually been seen several times, no one is really sure what he looks like. Millions have been spent on investigations, thousands of witnesses have been questioned—there have been at least two thousand actively investigated suspects. Yet after twenty years, the identity of Zodiac remains a mystery.

This is what we do know. The first known Zodiac victims were a teenaged couple, found on December 20, 1968, near their parked station wagon in a "lover's lane" area in Riverside, California, near San Francisco. The boy had been shot behind the ear; the girl had been shot several times in the back, apparently while trying to flee the killer. There was no obvious motive for the killing. The boy's wallet had not been stolen; the girl had not been sexually assaulted.

At 12:40 A.M. on July 5, 1969, a gruff-voiced man called the Vallejo, California, police department, and said, "I want to report a double murder." He described where the bodies could be found and added, "They are shot with a 9-mm Luger. I also killed those kids last year. Good-bye."

Actually, the scene of the attack had already been discovered, and just two minutes before the call was made, one of the victims, Darlene Ferrin, had been brought to the hospital, dead. The other victim, Michael Mageau, was seriously wounded.

There is a possibility that this was not a random attack and that Darlene had known her killer. Darlene was driving, and Mike reported that it seemed as if they were being followed. They had driven to a golf-course parking lot when a car pulled up beside them.

Mike asked, "Do you know who it is?"

Darlene's reply was ambiguous. "Oh, never mind. Don't worry about it."

The car pulled away, but was back ten minutes later. This time someone shone a strong light through the open car window and started shooting, without saying a word. After the attack, Mike, though badly wounded, got a good look at the killer, whom he described as stocky, about five foot eight, round-faced, with wavy light brown hair. The age he estimated as being between twenty-five and thirty. Witnesses nearby heard the shots and saw the killer's car drive away. They called the police.

The killer made his own call to the police from a phone booth within sight of Darlene Ferrin's house. It is unknown whether this was deliberate or accidental. Several of Darlene's relatives reported receiving "breather" phone calls within two hours of the shooting, well before the news had gone out over radio or TV. It is also unknown if the calls were related to the murder.

On August 1, a newspaper in Vallejo and two in San Francisco received similar letters from the killer. All contained details about the crimes that were not available to the general public. Each letter also contained one part of a strange-looking cipher or coded message. It was made up of a mixture of Greek letters, Morse code, weather symbols, astrological symbols, and so on. The killer wanted the papers to print the cipher "on the front page . . . In this cipher is my identity." If the papers didn't print the ciphers, the killer insisted he would go on a rampage. The signature on the letters was also a symbol, a circle with a cross inside it.

Section from the Zodiac cipher from the *Times-Herald*.

The cipher turned out to be a fairly simple one made more difficult by the fact that there were numerous mistakes, deliberate or otherwise, in the coding and spelling.

The message began, "I like killing people because it's so much fun . . ." It rambled on about how the victims would become the killer's slaves after death, but it did not contain the killer's identity.

Even before the police announced the code had been broken, the killer wrote to the papers again. The letter began: "This is the Zodiac speaking . . ." It was the first time he ever used that name. Once again he provided details about the killings that were not known to the general public. The letter said that when the police cracked the code, "they will have me." But they had cracked the code and they didn't have him.

What may have been Zodiac's most bizarre crime took place on September 27, 1969. Cecelia Ann Shepard and Bryan Hartnell, students at Pacific Union College, went to the park at Lake Berryessa, near San Francisco. They felt that they were being followed by a heavyset man, but were not too concerned at first. Then suddenly the man reappeared quite close, and there had been a change. He had put on a black hood, and was wearing a biblike garment with a cross enclosed in a circle—the sign of Zodiac—sewn on the front. He was brandishing a pistol, and a large knife in a holster dangled from his belt. For a few moments, it seemed like a robbery. The man asked for money and the car keys. "I want your car to go to Mexico," he said. Then he tied the students up and announced, "I'm going to stab you people." He did so, repeatedly and viciously. Hartnell, though seriously wounded, survived the attack. Shepard did not.

The attack had taken place at 6:30 p.m., before it was completely dark. The killer had apparently loitered around the area for several hours and was seen by a number of people. His car was also observed driving away after the crime. One hour and ten minutes after the attack, the killer phoned the police to report what he had done. Actually, the police had already been notified and were on the scene. The call was traced to a phone booth twenty-seven miles from the scene of the attack. A clear palm print was lifted from the receiver, but it was never related to any of the Zodiac suspects.

At Lake Berryessa, police found that the killer had written a message on the door of Hartnell's car in a black felt-tipped pen— the same sort of instrument used in all the Zodiac letters. The message read:

Vallejo
12-20-68
7-4-69
Sept 27-69-6:30
by knife

The numbers referred to the dates of the other Zodiac killings. Above the message was the killer's symbol, a cross in a circle.

Two weeks later, on October 11, the killer struck again. This time the victim was cabdriver Paul Lee Stine. The cabbie picked up a fare in the San Francisco theater district and drove him to the fashionable Nob Hill district. There, the passenger pulled out a gun, put it to the cabbie's head, and fired. The weapon used in the attack was the same as the one used to kill Darlene Ferrin. The killer then walked around to the front of the cab, took the driver's wallet, and cut off a portion of his bloodstained shirt.

From the time the killer went to the front seat, his actions were witnessed by a group of teenagers who were having a party in a building across the street. They had an unobstructed view from about fifty feet away. They saw the killer, a heavyset man, apparently wipe his fingerprints off the cab door and dashboard, and then walk away. The police were called and went to the scene immediately.

At this point, there was an incredible police blunder. Somehow the description that went out to police was of a black male —but the killer was white. A police patrol unit near the scene actually saw a stocky white man "lumbering" along in the fog. He was almost certainly Zodiac, and if the police had stopped him they would have found his clothes covered with blood. The police shouted to the man, asking if he had seen anything unusual. He responded that he had seen someone waving a gun and running in the opposite direction. The police sped off in chase of a wild goose. Soon the neighborhood was flooded with police accompanied by dogs. It was too late. Zodiac had escaped.

Three days later, the *San Francisco Chronicle* received a letter from Zodiac. He admitted to Stine's murder and chided the police for not being able to catch him. In order to prove that this was indeed an authentic letter from the killer, he enclosed a piece of the cabbie's bloodstained shirt. Most ominous of all, the letter also contained a threat:

"Schoolchildren make nice targets, I think I shall wipe out a school bus some morning. Just shoot out the front tire & then pick off the kiddies as they come bouncing out."

Zodiac's threat produced a near panic in the San Francisco area. A whole range of protective measures were instituted for school buses, but the killer never attempted to carry out this plan. Indeed, the murder of cabdriver Stine is the last killing generally attributed to Zodiac. But there was plenty more to be heard from him, or from people claiming to be him.

On October 21, a caller claiming to be Zodiac contacted the Oakland police and indicated that he would be willing to give himself up if he could be represented by a famous lawyer. He wanted F. Lee Bailey or Melvin Belli. He said that he would contact one of them if he appeared on a popular early-morning television talk show. Bailey declined, but the colorful Belli agreed to go on the show. During the show, someone with a soft, boyish voice called and identified himself as Zodiac. The caller, who said his real name was "Sam," made repeated brief calls—probably assuming the short calls could not be traced. "Sam" talked about the murders he committed and about the terrible headaches he suffered from. He agreed to meet Belli in front of a store in Daly City. Belli showed up, followed by a huge crowd of reporters and police—the caller did not.

Three people who had actually heard Zodiac—a policeman, a switchboard operator, and one surviving victim—listened to recordings of "Sam's" voice. They didn't think the voice sounded like Zodiac. They were right. Eventually the caller was discovered to be a patient in a state mental hospital. He could not possibly have been Zodiac.

Two months later, however, Belli received what was almost certainly a genuine communication from Zodiac, a letter containing another scrap of Stine's bloody shirt. The killer now claimed eight victims, and warned that he would kill again. But the old bravado seemed to be gone. The letter ended: "Please help me, I cannot remain in control much longer."

Newspapers, police organizations, and prominent individuals received many, many other "Zodiac letters." Some of them looked authentic, but there is no proof that any of them were. Some writers claimed an ever-increasing number of victims, and in one letter the writer indicated that he had "changed his way of collecting slaves," and that many of his murders would in future be listed as accidents or "ordinary" murders. As a result, practically every suspicious accident or unsolved murder in the San Francisco area during the 1970s was suspected of being a Zodiac murder.

Author Robert Graysmith, whose book on the case is one of the most complete available, definitely attributes two additional crimes to Zodiac—the murder of a young woman in 1966, before the Zodiac spree is believed to have begun, and the attempted murder of another woman in March 1970.

It is generally agreed that Zodiac is no longer active. What happened? It is possible the killer is dead, a suicide, the victim of an accident, or he may have been killed while committing another crime, or by someone who knew what he had done and wanted to get rid of him. Zodiac may have died of natural causes—a brain tumor that also triggered his murderous behavior is a possibility. He may be in prison for some other crime or in a mental institution. Or he may still be out there. Graysmith says that his prime suspect, and the suspect favored by many of the police who have investigated the case, is a man he calls Robert Starr—though that is not the suspect's real name. According to Graysmith, Starr has been under observation for years, but police have never been able to find enough evidence to indict, much less convict, him of the Zodiac crimes. Yet they are convinced that this hulking ex-mental patient is indeed the killer.

If the police couldn't get Zodiac in real life, Clint Eastwood could get him in the movies. In the Eastwood hit *Dirty Harry*, Detective Harry Calahan ignores the rules to catch up with a hooded killer known as "Scorpio." The film either uses or exploits the Zodiac case, depending on your point of view. But *Dirty Harry* is only one of many films and books based loosely on Zodiac. Zodiac has not achieved the mythic proportions of Jack the Ripper, but he is probably America's best-known unknown murderer.

1978

GEORGI MARKOV   There is something James Bondish about the assassination of Georgi Markov. Markov was a Bulgarian defector who was granted political asylum in Britain in 1969. Markov worked for the Bulgarian unit of the BBC, and also for Radio Free Europe, which was at that time funded by the CIA. His satirical broadcasts had made him a very unpopular figure with the government in Sofia. Markov's wife said that he often spoke of his fear of the Bulgarian secret police, the *Dazjavna Sigurnost*.

On the morning of September 7, 1978, Markov drove from his home to work at the BBC. Because of the heavy traffic in central London, he had parked his car near the Waterloo Bridge and walked the rest of the way. He was working late, so at 6:00 P.M., when traffic had cleared, he went back to his car and moved it closer to his office. He was walking along the Strand when he felt a stinging sensation in the back of his right thigh. He had the impression that the pain had come from a prod with an umbrella held by a man waiting for a bus. The man apologized, in what Markov recalled was a distinctly foreign accent. He then hailed a taxi and disappeared.

Markov's leg began to stiffen, and he showed a colleague at the BBC the wound, a bright red spot. Markov stayed at work for a while, but he began feeling worse and worse, so at 11:00 P.M. he went home.

The next day he was so sick that his wife Annabella took him to the hospital. He had a high temperature, and his white blood count had soared. The doctors didn't know what was wrong with him, nor could they explain the red mark on his leg, which didn't seem to be the result of an insect bite or a hypodermic injection. No treatment worked, and on September 11, Georgi Markov was dead.

From the beginning, the authorities suspected that Markov

probably had been killed by Bulgarian agents—but how and with what? The best guess of the experts was that he died from a poison called ricin, which is made from the seeds of the same plant that gives us castor oil. A rarely used poison, there is no known antidote for ricin, which destroys vital enzyme systems in the body.

Forensic scientist Dr. Robert Keeley found a tiny metal sphere smaller than the head of a pin embedded in Markov's leg. The sphere had two minute holes in it and a larger hole in the center that could have served as a reservoir for the poison. The pellet was not the sort of object that could have been fashioned by an amateur or in an ordinary jewelry shop. Sophisticated political assassination seemed a reasonable deduction.

Dr. Keeley had seen this sort of poison pellet before. One had been removed from the back of another Bulgarian defector, Vladimir Kostov, who had been attacked on August 24, 1978. Kostov had survived the attack. He said that he heard a muffled sound, something like an air gun being fired, then he felt a stinging sensation in his back. The pellet, which apparently did not contain a lethal dose of poison, was recovered.

No direct evidence was ever brought against the Bulgarian government, and technically the Markov case remains unsolved.

1981

KENNETH REX McELROY   On July 10, 1981, a local bully named Kenneth Rex McElroy was shot to death while sitting in his pickup truck on the main street of Skidmore, Missouri. There were anywhere from twenty to sixty witnesses to the shooting, yet no one would admit that they had seen a thing, and investigations were not pursued vigorously. The case remains unsolved.

Skidmore is a not very prosperous farming community of a few hundred inhabitants, a little over a hundred miles from Kansas City, Missouri. It is almost typically Middle America with its family-oriented, churchgoing, conservative population. But Skidmore is also a town where everybody has a gun and knows how to use it. Farmers usually ride around with a shotgun or rifle in the cab of their pickup truck. It is a town where some of the "good ol' boys" (the town is not really southern, but the term still applies) gather on weekends to drink beer, talk loudly, and sometimes fight. Violence was certainly not unknown in the region. In 1931, in nearby Maryville a young black man named Raymond Gunn, who was suspected of raping and killing a white woman, was dragged from the county jail and burned alive.

Kenneth Rex McElroy (known by practically everyone as Ken Rex) was a product of the region. He was the twelfth of thirteen children born to a poor farm family in the middle of the Depression. Ken Rex was a poor student. As was the custom in rural schools, he was just passed on from grade to grade until he dropped out in the sixth grade. He never really learned to read or write. He had always been big for his age, and very early in life he had earned the reputation of being a troublemaker and a bully. During his teenage years, Ken Rex suffered two serious head injuries, which made people wonder if brain damage did not contribute to his outbursts of temper and general meanness. Sometimes he would just pass out, for no apparent reason. After his death, there were

66

rumors that he had a steel plate in his head. That rumor was not true.

Ken Rex had a reputation with women. Before he was forty he had gone through several "marriages," and he often had more than one woman at a time living at his scruffy farm outside of Skidmore. He had a flock of children. Ken Rex's most notorious conquest was a girl by the name of Trena McCloud. In the early 1970s, Ken Rex, who was then pushing forty, fastened his attention on Trena, who was barely into her teens. He used to hang around the schoolyard waiting for her to get out of school. He intimidated her parents, who totally lost control of their daughter. She was placed in a foster home, and Ken Rex intimidated the foster parents, in fact a whole string of foster parents.

Finally, Trena's stepfather decided to stand up to the bully. He went down to the courthouse and filed a rape charge against Ken Rex—Trena was, of course, under age. Mysteriously his house burned down, and Trena's mother and stepfather fled the state, leaving Trena behind. There was no charge of arson against Ken Rex, because the possible witnesses were gone. Ken Rex found an out-of-state judge who would marry him to teenaged Trena, and so the rape charge, too, was dropped. Ken Rex brought Trena to his farm, where there was already another woman who stayed on and a house full of children from previous "marriages." Whether Trena genuinely loved Ken Rex, or was simply brutalized into submission by him, is unknown, but she stayed with him, and she was sitting beside him in the pickup truck the day he was shot. After his death, she defended him as an all-American husband and father who had simply been misunderstood and persecuted.

There was always a good deal of speculation as to where Ken Rex got his money. As far as anyone knew, he had never worked a steady job in his life. He made some money raising and training coon dogs—he had the reputation of being an excellent dog trainer. But there wasn't much money in that. His prime source of income was probably theft, mostly rustling hogs and cattle from his neighbors. People didn't want to testify against Ken Rex for fear of what he might do to them.

Ken Rex seemed to have more money than could be made simply from cattle and hog rustling and small-time robbery. There were rumors that he worked as a hit man for a north Kansas City mob. Indeed, Ken Rex often bragged of being a hired killer—but there is no evidence that such boasts were true, since he was a notorious braggart and liar. It was hard to separate fact and legend in the life of Ken Rex McElroy.

Ken Rex began having brushes with the law when he was only thirteen, but he always seemed to know just how far he could go, for he never spent a single day, not even a single hour, in jail. He was also lucky, and he had a good, high-priced Kansas City lawyer named Richard Gene McFadin, who through a series of clever maneuvers was to keep his client from winding up behind bars where he belonged. People in Skidmore also wondered how a small-time goon like Ken Rex could afford a lawyer like McFadin.

The lawyer's skills can be seen in how he handled one of Ken Rex's more serious problems. In 1976, Ken Rex got into an argument with farmer Romaine Henry, and he shot Henry twice, at point-blank range with his shotgun. The gun was loaded with buckshot, so the wounds weren't mortal and probably not meant to be, but they were extremely painful. Ken Rex's lawyer got a change of venue, to a county where he was not known. He found a couple of witnesses who swore that Ken Rex was with them at the time of the shooting. But the biggest coup was to find that Henry had once been convicted of fighting when he was a teenager, and Ken Rex had no convictions on his record. The many times he had been arrested but released could not be mentioned in court. Whom was the jury to believe, the "convicted criminal" or the apparently law-abiding Ken Rex? Ken Rex was acquitted, much to the horror of the people of Skidmore.

Ken Rex's next serious confrontation with the law came after he got into an argument with Ernest Bowenkamp, the elderly owner of the local grocery store. Ken Rex apparently brooded over the dispute for days and then shot the old man on July 8, 1980, on the loading dock behind his store. Ken Rex had spent the day drinking and muttering threats. Once again the weapon was a pellet-loaded shotgun, dangerous and painful but not really deadly. Ken Rex was arrested but was able to post the thirty-thousand-dollar bond immediately.

What with one legal delay after another, the case didn't actually come to trial for nearly a year. Ken Rex's defense was that the old man had attacked him with a knife. The jury didn't buy it—Ken Rex was convicted of second-degree assault and given a two-year sentence. That wasn't the sort of long sentence that the people of Skidmore had hoped for, but it was the first conviction the bully had ever received, and it promised that he would be taken off the streets, at least for a while. But it wasn't going to be that simple.

Lawyer McFadin filed an appeal of the conviction, and Ken Rex was freed pending appeal—he had still not spent a single hour in jail. The members of the jury who found him guilty reported receiving ominous phone calls.

Four nights after his conviction, Ken Rex walked into Skidmore's only tavern, where a number of the local men were drinking. He was followed by Trena, who was carrying an M-1 rifle with a bayonet. He made some threatening remarks about "Old Man Bowenkamp" and took the gun from her. With that act he violated the terms of his bond, and everybody in the tavern knew it.

Some Skidmore residents petitioned the court to have Ken Rex arrested immediately—but once again his lawyer arranged for a delay. By July 10, 1981, it began to look to some of the residents of Skidmore, Missouri, that Kenneth Rex McElroy was never going to go to jail. That morning, a large group of Skidmore's men met at the local American Legion Hall to decide what to do next. There was a great deal of frustration and anger expressed during the meeting. Then word went around that Ken Rex had come into town and was in the tavern. Many of the men decided to go over to the tavern and confront him.

They found Ken Rex and Trena at the end of the bar; they just stared at him, trying to intimidate him as he had often intimidated them. And perhaps they did frighten him, for Ken Rex soon steered Trena out the door and into their pickup parked in front of the tavern. The men of Skidmore followed him out and stood around the truck.

Then, just as Ken Rex was reaching for the ignition key, someone standing behind the cab with a high-powered rifle sent two slugs into his head. At the sound of the shots, everybody dropped to the ground. Then they scattered. Though the street had been crowded before the shooting, within a few minutes it was completely empty. Ken Rex's body remained slumped over the wheel of his truck for more than an hour until the authorities finally arrived. Trena had fled to the bank and ultimately was taken home by relatives.

The story made national news, and when reporters descended upon Skidmore they found very few residents expressed any regret about what had happened. "Whoever did it did everyone a favor" was the common attitude. But no one would tell who did it. Trena saw only the barrel of the gun in the rearview mirror; she did not see who was holding the weapon. There were some perfunctory investigations by local authorities and by the FBI. No evidence as to the identity of the killer was turned up.

Is it possible that no one in the crowd actually saw the killer? Perhaps they were all so intent on staring Ken Rex down that they didn't see someone raise a rifle at the back of the truck. After the shot, everyone hit the ground, and thus the killer could have escaped. But such a scenario is highly unlikely. Bob Lancaster and B.C. Hall, whose book *Judgment Day* covers the case in detail, write:

"But anyone who has spent time in the community will come away with the sense that most of the townspeople know, all right, who the killer is. And one gets the impression that those who don't know have deliberately avoided finding out: the knowledge would be a burden they'd rather not have to live with. Nobody in Skidmore will flat out tell you any of these things, but they can be picked up from many small intangible signs."

A couple of other questions remain about the events in Skidmore that day. Was the killing actually planned by the men in their Legion Hall meeting? It seems unlikely that they planned the killing as it happened, because no one could have known that Ken Rex was coming into town that morning. But it is possible that some sort of violent retribution against the bully had been discussed, and an unexpected opportunity to carry it out presented itself.

A second question is, why did Ken Rex come into town when he did? He certainly knew that feelings were running high against him. He may have even known that there was a meeting called to discuss him. Lancaster and Hall speculate that the bully actually sought out some sort of confrontation, possibly even a confrontation that would end in his death. He was forty-seven years old, and well past his fighting prime. He had grown fat and flabby, and people just weren't as frightened of him as they once had been. He was also in poor health; high blood pressure and other assorted conditions associated with middle age had landed him in the hospital several times, and he wasn't the sort of person who would have been able to change his way of living. He was also, for the first time in his life, facing jail. That prospect may have frightened him. Death may have seemed preferable.

We shall never know.

2

Historic Mysteries

????

BODIES IN THE BOGS   A couple of Danish farmers digging peat in a bog on May 8, 1950, came across a body buried a few feet below the surface. The body was so well preserved that the farmers assumed that they had stumbled on a recent murder, and they called the police. The police, however, had heard of such bodies before and they asked representatives of the local museum to accompany them to the site.

The men from the museum confirmed what the police suspected: the body unearthed in the Tollund bog was not that of a man murdered recently but that of one who had died some two thousand years ago. Because of the peculiar chemical makeup of the bogs of northern Europe, bodies that have fallen or are buried in them can remain astonishingly well preserved for thousands of years. The bodies take on the dark color of the surrounding peat, and they are somewhat shrunken, but no inexperienced observer could come upon such a body without assuming it was fresh. Tollund man was the most remarkably well preserved of these bodies found to date. Professor P. V. Glob, who was present at the excavation, described the body in his book *The Bog People:*

"The man lay on his right side in a natural attitude of sleep. The head was to the west with the face turned to the south; the legs were to the east. He lay fifty yards out from the firm ground, not far above the clean sand floor of the bog, and had been covered by eight or nine feet of peat, now dug away.

"On his head he wore a pointed skin cap fastened securely under the chin by a hide thong. Round his waist there was a smooth hide belt. Otherwise he was naked. His hair was cropped so short as to be almost entirely hidden by his cap. He was clean-shaven, but there was a very short stubble on the chin and upper lip.

"The air of gentle tranquillity about the man was shattered when a small lump of peat was removed from beside his head. This

Tollund man

disclosed a rope, made of two leather thongs twisted together, which encircled the neck in a noose drawn tight into the throat and then coiled like a snake over the shoulder and down across the back. After this discovery the wrinkled forehead and set mouth seemed to take on a look of affliction."

Medico-legal experts who examined the body concluded that the man was well over twenty years old at the time of his death, that he appeared to be in generally good health, and that he had been hanged with the leather rope that was still around his neck.

Examination of the contents of Tollund man's intestines and stomach indicated that somewhere between twelve and twenty-four hours before his death, he had eaten a meal of gruel made from barley, linseed, and other grains. In 1954, a couple of distinguished archaeologists ate a gruel patterned after the one eaten by Tollund man, two thousand years ago. They pronounced the taste to be absolutely awful. One of the archaeologists commented that it would have been punishment enough for Tollund man to have been compelled to eat this gruel for the rest of his life, however terrible his crime might have been. One common assumption at that time was that Tollund man was a hanged criminal.

Two years later, a bog near the village of Grauballe about eleven miles east of Tollund was the site of the discovery of another beautifully preserved body, called, naturally enough, Grauballe man. When police first examined the remarkably preserved hands of Grauballe man under magnifying glasses, they found the fingerprints to be so clear that they could not believe that the body was nearly two thousand years old, as the scientists had said.

A short-lived controversy over the age of Grauballe man erupted when an old farmer's wife in the village said that she recognized the body as that of a peat cutter named Red Christian who had disappeared from the district in 1887 or thereabouts. It was said Red Christian was a known drunk, and probably just fell into the bog and drowned, or perhaps had been murdered and dumped there. The controversy raged for a while, with some local people insisting that the scientists weren't as smart as they thought they were; but carbon-14 laboratory dating of the remains proved conclusively that Grauballe man was over 1,650 years old. Whoever he was, he wasn't Red Christian.

Grauballe man's death was no accident. His throat had been cut, perhaps after being knocked unconscious by a blow to the head. Tollund man had been hanged. But there were some similarities between the two bodies. Both were naked, and the intestines of both contained the same sort of mixture of grains.

Combining information gathered at these sites, and other similar finds, plus what was known about life among the peoples of northern Europe fifteen hundred to two thousand years ago, led scientists to come up with a theory about what had happened to many of those found buried in the bogs. The bodies, they said, were not murder victims, strictly speaking; they were sacrificial victims.

Roman writers, who knew something of the lives of the people of this region two thousand years ago, indicated that they worshiped a fertility goddess, and that after the main annual ceremony, slaves or others who had participated in it were sometimes killed. "Hence a mysterious terror and an ignorance full of piety as to what that may be which men only behold to die," wrote Tacitus.

Those who have examined the bog bodies believe that most of them were not slaves, but priests or other individuals specially selected to play the part of the king or husband to the goddess in an annual rite.

Says Glob, "Here one thinks of the special stamp of many of the bog people—delicate features and neat hands and feet, not worn by heavy work as those of soldiers and peasants must have been."

Glob also notes that the contents of the dead men's last meal is significant. "It consisted of an abundance of just those grains and flower seeds which were to be made to germinate, grow and ripen by the goddess's journey through the spring landscape. . . . there has not been the slightest trace of summer or autumn fruits." There was also no sign that the victims had recently eaten meat, though meat was surely available.

Hanging, a common method of death, was also significant. "The rope nooses which several of the bog people carry round their necks, and which caused their deaths, are a further sign of sacrifice to the [fertility goddess]. They are perhaps replicas of the twisted neck-rings which are the mark of honour of the goddess, and a sign of consecration to her."

Not all of the bodies found in the bogs were those of sacrificial victims. At least one was a genuine murder victim—though the murder took place some six hundred years ago. This body was found in 1936 in a bog at Bocksten on the west coast of Sweden. The body was fully clothed in trousers, a tunic, cape, and hood.

The man, who was over six feet tall—very tall for that time —had been killed by a blow to the side of the head and thrown face downward into a shallow hole scraped in the peat. To stop the murdered man from getting out of the grave, his murderers had driven wooden stakes through his back and side and a specially cut oak stake through his heart. This treatment, which in popular legend is reserved for vampires, was given to the corpse of anyone, murder victim, suicide, notorious evildoer, who was thought to possess a restless spirit. Peat was then simply raked over the body, but in the course of time the overlying peat had reached a depth of over two feet.

The murdered man's clothing was distinctive, and it fixed the year of his death at about 1360. There was a war going on in the region at that time, and the Swedish scholar Dr. Albert Sandklef speculated that the murdered man might have been an agent sent out to rouse the peasants against their king. The mission may have failed and the agent was murdered. "He was then hidden in the Bocksten fen; and by burying him in this spot the peasants ensured themselves against his taking revenge upon them. The bog is the meeting place of four parishes and, according to old beliefs, he would not be able to escape such a spot and revenge himself on his murderers. The fact that the body was carefully and firmly pinned with wooden stakes indicates that they sought extra protection."

148?

THE PRINCES IN THE TOWER   Richard III has the worst reputation of any king in the history of England and quite possibly the world. That is, of course, because William Shakespeare made him the archvillain, the cold-blooded murdering monster of his play *Richard III*. Among the many crimes Shakespeare attributed to Richard is ordering the murder of the twelve-year-old King Edward V and his ten-year-old brother Richard, Duke of York, who had been imprisoned in the Tower of London. It is considered the worst of Richard's many crimes. "The most arch deed of piteous massacre, that ever yet this land was guilty of."

Most people have tended to accept Shakespeare's version that Richard was responsible for the death of the princes. (Though Edward V was really a king at the time of his death, he was uncrowned, and because of his age he is generally referred to as a prince. The young Richard of York, who was also in line for the throne, was also called a prince.)

The princes disappeared in the late fifteenth century. Shakespeare wrote his play a little over a century later. He certainly had no firsthand knowledge of the event, and the sources available to him were not necessarily more reliable than those available to modern historians. Besides, the playwright had a very good reason for portraying Richard III as a monster. The reigning monarch was Elizabeth of the House of Tudor. Henry VII, the first Tudor king, had overthrown Richard and then worked very diligently at establishing his own dubious legitimacy by blackening the name of the king he replaced. The Tudor version of history was the official history of Shakespeare's day. Besides, it would not do for a mere playwright to insult the monarchy. When Shakespeare came to write a play about the Tudor monarch Henry VIII—he of the many wives—the playwright portrayed the monarch as a good-hearted fellow. The beheading of a couple of wives and numerous other crimes were passed over quickly.

So Shakespeare was no objective historian. For example, Richard was not a deformed cripple, a "poisonous hunch-backed toad." Contemporary portraits indicate that while Richard III was not a particularly handsome fellow, he was not the twisted fiend of the play. Richard was a brave soldier, who had loyally supported his own brother King Edward IV so long as he was alive. He was a diligent and competent administrator, austere and serious in his personal habits. He might have made a good monarch, had not events gone against him. Richard certainly had a reputation for being cold and ruthless. He was perfectly capable of murder, but so was everyone else who aspired to the throne in that violent age.

Richard III

The question is not whether Richard might have ordered the murder of the two princes; the question is, did he?

In April 1483, King Edward IV died suddenly, at the age of forty-two. He left the kingdom in the care of his brother, Gloucester, as Richard was then known. Gloucester was to govern as Protector until the young King Edward, then about twelve, came of age. This was not an unusual arrangement, but it was always a dangerous one, for an ambitious man might not want to give up the power once he possessed it, and Richard of Gloucester was certainly an ambitious man.

Richard had never been fond of his brother's wife, Queen Elizabeth (not the Queen Elizabeth of Shakespeare's day, or obviously of our own). She, too, was ambitious and probably thought of herself as exercising the power during her son's minority. As Elizabeth was bringing her son to London for his coronation, she heard of the arrest and execution on trumped-up charges of her brother and one of her sons by an earlier marriage. There were also rumors that she was going to be accused of witchcraft. Facing all manner of unknown dangers, Elizabeth agreed to allow her sons Edward and Richard, Duke of York, to be lodged in the royal apartments of the Tower of London. Though the Tower is best-known as a prison and place of execution, it was also a formidable fortress and sometimes a refuge for beleaguered royalty.

The coronation was delayed, and in the interim the story spread that the children of King Edward IV and Elizabeth (they had nine) were really illegitimate because Edward had been pre-contracted to marry a French princess. This was a flimsy technicality, and, besides, the circumstances of Edward's marriage had been well known for years. Richard was probably responsible for making the precontract an issue, and he used the excuse to have himself declared King Richard III on June 26, 1483.

The two princes were still alive in the Tower at the time Richard grabbed power. In July, and perhaps later, they were seen in the gardens and at the windows; then they were seen no longer, and stories began to circulate that they had been killed on Richard's orders. But the rumors are all we have, for the exact fate of the two princes is unknown. During Henry VII's reign, a young man claiming to be the Duke of York rescued from the Tower appeared on the scene. Predictably, he turned out to be an impostor.

Writing some thirty years later, Sir Thomas More gave what was the prevailing opinion in his day. Richard encouraged Sir James Tyrell to do away with the princes, and Tyrell employed two brutish men, named Forest and Dighton, to smother them and bury the bodies, "at the stair foot, meetly deep in the ground under a great heap of stones." The remains were later supposed to have been moved to a more respectable burial place. This was the same version of events later used by Shakespeare, but it must be remembered that More, like Shakespeare, was living under a Tudor monarch.

Still, this view of Richard as the instigator of the murders remained the prevailing opinion of historians until the early twentieth century. But in history there are always revisionists, and, beginning in 1906 with Sir Clements Markham's biography of Richard III, there has been a movement to revise Richard's awful reputation and place the blame for the murder of the princes on the first Tudor monarch, Henry VII. Richard was killed in 1485 after a reign of a mere two years. If the princes had still been alive when Henry VII took over, they would have presented an even greater threat to his claim to the throne (which was very dubious) than they had to Richard's. Like Richard, Henry was cold, calculating, and ruthless. He, too, would have been perfectly capable of killing off a couple of royal children if they stood in his way.

When Henry VII ascended the throne, he never accused Richard of the murder of the princes. He treated James Tyrell's alleged confession casually, and he never made any attempt to find the bodies of the princes and give them a proper burial. One would assume that he would have portrayed himself as the avenger of the princes, if Richard really had them killed.

In one of her finest mysteries, the writer Josephine Tey fictionally takes up the case of Richard III, and exonerates him.

Another popular candidate for murderer of the princes is Henry Stafford, Duke of Buckingham. Buckingham also had a good claim to the throne, and as Constable of England he would almost certainly have had access to the royal apartments in the Tower. If Richard and the princes stood in his way, he could get rid of the princes and place the blame on Richard, he would not only have eliminated two potential rivals, he would have blackened the name of the third. Buckingham did plot against Richard, and there is some evidence that he was suspected of the murder of the princes at the time.

In July 1674, workmen in the Tower of London unearthed an old wooden chest containing the skeletons of two children. They were generally assumed to be the remains of the two princes, and they were reburied with honor.

In 1933, the urn containing these bones was reopened for examination by experts. The remains turned out to be in a deplorable condition. Some of the bones were missing, and those that remained were mixed with animal bones. Obviously, the urn had been tampered with. From what was left, the experts decided that the remains belonged to children about the same ages as the princes, but they could not even positively determine the sex of the children. There was also no way of telling how old the bones were.

Modern experts could probably learn more. We might, for example, discover whether the bones really were those of the princes. But it is doubtful if even modern science could determine whether the princes were killed in 1483, which would probably make Richard responsible—or after 1485, which would point the finger at Henry VII.

As matters now stand, Richard III still is the best suspect. There is no convincing evidence that the boys were still alive after 1485. Indeed, as early as 1483, there were many rumors that they had been killed in the Tower. Richard had the motive, and he had the opportunity.

Still, we can't be absolutely certain.

1514

RICHARD HUNNE   In 1514, Richard Hunne, a respected
merchant tailor from London, discovered that his child, who was
being cared for in Middlesex, had died and was buried in the parish
of St. Mary's Matfellow, in Whitechapel. The curate of the church,
one Thomas Dryfield, claimed possession of the child's winding
sheet as a professional perquisite of the burial. Hunne thought this
unfair and refused. From this minor, and to us, arcane squabble
came one of the most curious cases in English history, resulting
in probable murder and the trial of a corpse for heresy.

The curate wanted the case to be settled before an ecclesiastical
court, feeling that as a man of the Church he would receive more
sympathetic treatment. Hunne, for the same reason, wanted the
case to go before the civil courts. The monetary value of the goods
was insignificant, but the principle at stake was not, for Hunne's
suit essentially challenged the legitimacy of all ecclesiastical courts
in England. The Church was thoroughly alarmed by this action
and retaliated by having Hunne charged with heresy. Under the
direct orders of the Bishop of London, the tailor was imprisoned
in Lollards' Tower under such close guard that no one was allowed
to see or speak to him.

The Church's reaction to Hunne's perfectly legitimate chal-
lenge seems extreme, and indeed it was. However, we must remember the times and realize the Church felt under attack from
many sides. Less than twenty years later, King Henry VIII broke
with Rome and seized the vast ecclesiastical wealth. This move
brought the king more popularity than censure from the English
public. In the Hunne case, the Church clearly felt it was necessary
to exert the full measure of its power over a restless laity—and to
make an example of Richard Hunne.

On December 2, at the request of Dr. Horsey, the Bishop of
London's chancellor, Hunne was examined by the bishop himself

and was said to confess to some of the charges of heresy brought against him and to ask for forgiveness. Later, it was discovered that Hunne's written confession was not in his handwriting.

The tailor was taken back to Lollards' Tower, and two days later it was announced that he had committed suicide in his cell. When his food was brought to him in the morning, he was found hanging by a silken noose from a ring in the wall. The death seemed straightforward enough. After all, if Hunne had actually confessed to being a heretic, his future was bleak. But custom required that a coroner's inquest be held in all such cases.

The following day, the coroner and twenty-four London citizens went to Lollards' Tower to examine the scene of the death and inspect the body. Nothing was to have been touched since the death was discovered. Almost immediately, the coroner's men began to notice that there were some very odd things about the scene. The rope was not really tied securely to the ring. There was evidence that Hunne's wrists had been bound at the time of his death. There was a pool of blood, not where Hunne had been hanged, but on the other side of the cell. The dead man's jacket had been folded over to hide it. The candle had been carefully extinguished, yet it was placed eight feet from the body. There were other inconsistencies in the physical evidence and in the stories told by those who had been in charge of the prisoner. There was a strong suspicion among the twenty-four jurors that Richard Hunne had not killed himself, but had been murdered.

News of this development alarmed the bishop and Dr. Horsey, for if it was decided that Hunne had been murdered under their care, they would be held responsible. The Bishop of London countered with a decision to carry through the trial of the dead man for heresy. This decision, though it turned out to be nearly disastrous, had a certain logic to it. They reasoned that if it was proved Hunne was a heretic, then it was also probable that he had committed the abominable crime of self-murder—suicide. As a heretic, he was to be burned anyway, so there should be no excessive interest in the manner of his death.

The trial was given the full backing of Church authorities, with the Bishops of Durham and Lincoln joining the Bishop of London on the bench when the inevitable guilty verdict was announced. Heresy trials usually resulted in guilty verdicts, and in this case, where the accused was dead and there was no defense, the guilty verdict was inevitable. Richard Hunne's body was burned at Smithfield for heresy on December 20, 1514.

The trial was carried on with such awesome solemnity that it was assumed, or at least hoped, that no one would dare take up the cause of a heretic—but the clergy had badly misjudged the mood of the people. The sight of poor Hunne's body burning infuriated Londoners. If imprisonment, murder, and burning were the penalties for suing a cleric in a perfectly legal manner, then no one's life or property was safe. The coroner's inquest was revived, and both the king and some prominent justices took an interest in the case.

The affair broke wide open when Charles Joseph, who was Hunne's guard on the fatal evening, confessed first that he had written the confession of heretical sentiments supposedly written by Hunne. Then he confessed that he and a simple-minded bell-ringer named John Spalding had actually killed Hunne under the personal direction of Dr. Horsey. Dr. Horsey himself hung up the body and faked the appearance of suicide. The inquest brought back a verdict of murder against Dr. Horsey, who then fled to the archbishop's palace at Lambeth to escape being arrested and brought to trial himself.

The Hunne case had now become a major political issue. Parliament restored Richard Hunne's estate to his heirs, as it had been seized for his heresy. It then specifically approved of the verdict of the coroner's jury, calling the members of the jury "honest men." The Bishop of London thundered against the action, but Parliament went ahead anyway.

However, the king was not yet ready for a full-scale confrontation with Church authority, which surely would have resulted from any attempt to try Dr. Horsey for murder. A compromise was worked out wherein Horsey was allowed to leave London and would not be prosecuted so long as he did not try to return. The people of London were outraged by this arrangement, and officially, at least, the murder of Richard Hunne has never been solved.

1560

AMY ROSBART   Did Amy Rosbart, beautiful daughter of the wealthy knight Sir John Rosbart of Norfolk and wife of Sir Robert Dudley, really accidentally fall down the stairs of her manor house in Oxfordshire and break her neck, as a coroner's jury declared, or was she pushed, as practically everyone believed?

The key to the alleged crime was Robert Dudley. He had married Amy in 1549, but they couldn't have spent much time together. A few years after the marriage Dudley was thrown into the Tower of London in the belief (probably justified) that he had taken part in his father's conspiracy to place Lady Jane Grey, his sister-in-law, on the throne of England. That plot cost Lady Jane her life, but Dudley escaped relatively unscathed. After he was released, he served with the English forces in France. His fortunes really rose with the accession of Elizabeth I, whom he had known earlier. Robert Dudley was a good-looking, charming man, very ambitious and quite able, and he soon won the queen's favor and, in the opinion of many, became her lover. But his ambition, power, and pretensions aroused a great deal of jealousy at court. It was suggested that he planned to become prince consort, and that Elizabeth favored the plan. There was only one thing that stood in the way—Dudley's wife, Amy Rosbart. Even before her death, there were rumors that he planned to get rid of her somehow.

So when Amy was found mysteriously dead at the foot of the stairs of her manor, Cummor Palace, on September 8, 1560, it seemed just too convenient to Dudley's many enemies. How could a healthy twenty-eight-year-old woman have taken a fatal fall down a wide, low-tread staircase? It was said that five days before Amy's death, Elizabeth had already discussed the death with the Spanish ambassador. The coroner's jury was supposed to have been specially picked for loyalty to the queen rather than honesty.

Suspicion for the actual murder fell on one of Dudley's servants, Richard Verney, who was later made a knight.

There is no evidence that Amy Rosbart actually was murdered. The case can and has been argued both ways. But if it had been Dudley's and Elizabeth's intention to get rid of the inconvenient wife so that they could marry, things did not work out as planned. Indeed, Amy proved a greater obstacle dead than alive. Suspicion of, and hostility toward, Dudley was running so high at court that the queen was forced to distance herself from him. He had never been popular (no favorite of the queen could have been), but the too-opportune death gave his enemies yet another charge to bring against him.

After Amy's death, while the queen's favor did not diminish, the possibility of marriage seemed to gradually recede. In 1564, the queen even suggested Dudley as a possible husband for Mary Stuart, and probably to further this project she created him Earl of Leicester. That marriage never took place, but in 1571 Dudley secretly married a wealthy widow, and a few years later cast her off to marry, secretly once again, the widow of the Earl of Essex. This time there were unpleasant rumors about how Essex had died.

Since Dudley managed to retain the queen's favor, and successfully negotiated the treacherous currents of Elizabethan politics for many years, he was able to die of natural causes on September 4, 1588.

During his lifetime, Dudley became known as an enemy of the Catholics, and in 1584 a celebrated attack containing a whole raft of charges, including the murder of Amy Rosbart, was written by Jesuit Robert Parsons. The work was officially suppressed, and the queen declared that it was her certain knowledge that the charges were untrue. Suppressed or not, the attack was still widely read and it was used by Sir Walter Scott when he wrote an account of Amy Rosbart in his novel *Kenilworth*.

1678

SIR EDMUND GODFREY   In 1678, religious feelings ran high in England. There were widespread rumors that the Roman Catholic Church was attempting somehow to recapture the monarchy and the influence in the country that had been lost when Henry VIII broke with Rome. Actually, the reigning monarch Charles II had strong Catholic sympathies, but the easygoing and very diplomatic Charles really didn't care much about religion one way or the other.

Stirring the pot of religious hatred was a despicable character by the name of Titus Oates. He was a lifelong informer and liar who had studied briefly in Rome and had picked up just enough knowledge of church affairs to be able to concoct a credible-sounding tale of a vast Catholic conspiracy to murder Charles II and place his staunchly Catholic brother James on the throne. The affair became known as the "Popish Plot."

Oates and his associates brought their bogus information to Westminster magistrate Sir Edmund Berry Godfrey, a respected justice of the peace. Whether Godfrey actually put any stock at all in Oates's tale is unclear. Although he did indicate that he felt threatened, he seemed to take no special precautions for his own safety. On the night of October 12, 1678, Godfrey left his home on Hartshorn Laine in London and disappeared. Five days later, his corpse was discovered in a ditch on Primrose Hill, Hampstead. He apparently had been strangled and run through with a sword.

Oates and his associates loudly insisted that the magistrate had been murdered by the Catholics because of his part in the investigation. Two months later, a man named Miles Prance confessed, under torture, that he had been present when Godfrey had been murdered in the courtyard of Somerset House in London by three servants—Robert Green, Henry Berry, and Lawrence Hill —all secret Catholics. An added detail was that priests had looked on while the murder was committed.

Given the overheated atmosphere of the time, the fate of the three men was sealed as soon as the accusation was made, though Oates and his associates failed in their attempts to have more prominent people also convicted of complicity in the murder. The murder did much to fan the flames of the "Popish Plot" hysteria.

Who did kill Sir Edmund Godfrey? In his fictionalized account of the murder, mystery writer John Dickson Carr builds an intriguing case against the Earl of Pembroke, an alcoholic, violent brute. Pembroke had once stamped a man to death, and was convicted of manslaughter before Magistrate Godfrey. He was certainly the sort who would carry a grudge and commit a murder to revenge himself. Others have suggested that Pembroke or someone else had been inspired to kill Godfrey by Oates himself in order to whip up anti-Catholic hysteria. It is even possible that the men who were beheaded for the murder actually did commit it. The truth is that the murderer or murderers of Sir Edmund Godfrey are unknown, and almost certain to remain so.

1811

THE RATCLIFFE HIGHWAY MURDERS   During the month of December 1811, two households, a total of seven people living in the vicinity of Ratcliffe Highway in the East End of London, were clubbed and slashed to death with unbelievable ferocity. The crimes both frightened and fascinated the British public as no others did until the Jack the Ripper murders eighty years later.

Like the Ripper murders, these crimes were not only brutal but audacious, committed almost under the noses of witnesses and the authorities. At the time, it was widely assumed that the identity of the murderer was known. However, a closer examination of the facts indicate that the person believed to be the murderer was most probably innocent, and that the story may be even more shocking and mysterious than people thought.

The area around Ratcliffe Highway had an evil reputation in Regency London. It was a waterfront district of narrow streets and alleys filled with pubs, brothels, and cheap lodging houses that served the needs and desires of men who spent the bulk of their time at sea under harsh and brutal conditions. There was plenty of violence, but it was usually limited to drunken brawls between the sailors themselves. What happened in December 1811 was way beyond the bounds of the usual Ratcliffe Highway violence.

Timothy Marr was a young former sailor who had opened a small linen draper's shop on Ratcliffe Highway. He primarily sold canvas for seamen's trousers and serge for their jackets. Marr was hardworking, and appeared to be making a modest success of his business. He lived above his shop with his wife and three-and-a-half-month-old son. He also employed a shop boy, James Gowen, and a servant girl, Margaret Jewell.

At about ten minutes to midnight on December 7, Marr sent

his servant girl out to buy oysters for supper. This seems a bit unusual, for while it was quite common for Marr and other tradesmen of the time to work until midnight, it seemed unlikely that any oyster sellers would be open. And indeed, that proved to be the case. Margaret Jewell spent about twenty fruitless minutes in search of oysters. When she returned to Marr's shop, she found it shut and dark. She rang the bell and listened. From inside she heard footsteps on the stairs and a single low cry from the baby. Then there was silence, and no one came to the door. It was another half hour before the watchman came around, and his knocking and shouting roused the neighbors. Some neighbors climbed over the back fence and entered the open back door of Marr's shop. What they found was a scene of unrivaled horror. Just inside the door was the body of the shop boy, James Gowen. His head had been beaten to a pulp. Mrs. Marr was lying face downward toward the back of the room. She, too, had been battered to death. Timothy Marr's battered body lay behind the counter, also face downward. One of the shocked neighbors called out, "The child, where's the child?" The child was found in its cradle in the basement. Its throat had been slit and the side of its face crushed with a blow.

On the counter lay a large metal object called a carpenter's ripping chisel. Marr was having his shop altered by a carpenter named Pugh. Earlier, Pugh had insisted his ripping chisel was missing, and Marr had searched unsuccessfully for it. The chisel could have been a murder weapon, and it was now set in the middle of the bloody scene. But it was perfectly clean.

It wasn't until the following day that the police ventured upstairs. There they found a heavy iron mallet or maul, a sort of tool often used by ship's carpenters. It was covered with blood. A later examination of the maul showed that it had a broken end, and the letters J. P. were crudely etched into the top. Nothing seemed to have been taken from the house or shop. There was money in the till downstairs. Marr had money in his pocket, and in the upstairs bedroom where the maul was found was a drawer containing £152 in cash—a considerable sum. If robbery had been the motive, the robber or robbers fled without taking anything. Perhaps they had been frightened off when Margaret Jewell rang the bell.

FIFTY POUNDS
REWARD.

Horrid Murder!!

WHEREAS,

The Dwelling House of Mr. TIMOTHY MARR, 29, Ratcliff Highway, Man's Mercer, was entered this morning between the hours of Twelve and Two o'Clock, by some persons unknown, when the said Mr. MARR, Mrs. CELIA MARR, his wife, TIMOTHY their INFANT CHILD in the cradle, and JAMES BIGGS, a servant lad, were all of them most inhumanly and barbarously Murdered!!

A Ship Carpenter's Pæen Maul, broken at the point, and a Bricklayer's long Iron Ripping Chissel about Twenty Inches in length, have been found upon the Premises, with the former of which-it is supposed the Murder was committed. Any person having lost such articles, or any Dealer in Old Iron, who has lately Sold or missed such, are earnestly requested to give immediate Information.

The Churchwardens, Overseers, and Trustees, of the Parish of St. George Middlesex, do hereby offer a Reward of FIFTY POUNDS, for the Discovery and Apprehension of the Person or Persons who committed such Murder, to be paid on Conviction.

· *By Order of the Churchwardens, Overseers, and Trustees,*

JOHN CLEMENT,

Ratcliff-highway,
SUNDAY. 8th, DECEMBER, 1811.

VESTRY CLERK.

SKIRVEN, Printer, Ratcliff Highway, London.

In the backyard of the linen draper's shop were two distinct sets of footprints, and the impressions contained traces of blood and sawdust. The carpenters had been at work in the shop that day.

The second outrage took place a mere twelve days later, on the night of December 19. The scene was the King's Arms pub on New Gravel Lane, a short distance from Ratcliffe Highway. The victims were John Williamson, owner of the pub, his wife Elizabeth, and their servant Bridget Harrison. This time the murders had very nearly been witnessed. A young lodger named John Turner was in his room on the top floor. Around eleven-thirty, he heard suspicious noises and crept downstairs just in time to see a tall heavyset man in a long gray coat bending over the Williamsons' bloody corpses. Williamson had complained about a man fitting that description who had been hanging around the King's Arms earlier in the day. Terrified, Turner ran back to his room, knotted a few sheets together, and lowered himself out the window. But the rope of sheets was not long enough to allow him to reach the ground, so he just hung there, half-naked and hysterical, shouting "Murder! Murder!" until a crowd gathered.

This time the ferocity of the killer or killers had been even greater. The primary weapon was an iron bar found near Williamson's body. All three victims had been horribly beaten, and their throats had been cut; Bridget Harrison's head had very nearly been cut off. Miraculously, the Williamsons' fourteen-year-old granddaughter, who had been asleep in the upstairs room, was unharmed. Williamson's watch was missing; the lodger had seen the man in the gray coat remove something from the corpse. But nothing else of value seemed to be missing, though as in the Marr murders, there was money around for the taking.

The murders produced a panic in London's East End, and the authorities were in a near frenzy to find someone responsible for the crimes. Law enforcement in Regency London was not of a very high quality. The first reaction was that the bestial deeds had been committed by a "foreigner," and several Portuguese seamen were arrested, for no better reason than that they were not English. The next to be arrested were Irish seamen. Aside from the general anti-foreign prejudice of the authorities, there was little evidence against any of the suspects.

The first real break in the case came when the source of the maul used in the Marr killings was identified. It belonged to John Peterson, a German-born ship's carpenter. Peterson was away at sea, and could not be considered a suspect in the crimes. But he had left the maul and other tools at the Pear Tree lodging house, where he often stayed between voyages. The tools were crudely marked with his initials, J. P. Peterson's tools had not been well looked after; they could have been taken by any of the other Pear Tree lodgers. Indeed, they could have been taken by practically anyone who entered the Pear Tree. The owner's young nephews

often played with Peterson's tools. The maul seemed to have disappeared about a week before the Marr murder. At the time, no
one had been very concerned about it.

After the Pear Tree was identified, the prime suspect became
a young seaman named John Williams, a lodger. Later, it was
suggested that his real name was Murphy, and that he was Irish,
but no evidence was ever advanced to support this suggestion.
Aside from being a resident of the Pear Tree, witnesses said that
Williams had come in late on the night of the Marr murders and
had acted strangely. He knew the Williamsons and had been in
the King's Arms early on the night of the murders. Williams was
known to be hot-tempered, and frequently got into fights, though
he wasn't much of a fighter. He had no solid alibi for the night of

VIEW OF THE BODY OF JOHN WILLIAMS
the supposed Murderer of the families of Marr and Williamson, and Self-destroyer, approaching
the hole dug to receive it, in the Cross Road, at Cannon Street—Turnpike.

either murder. So John Williams was arrested and thrown into jail to await further interrogation. At first it did not appear as if the evidence against Williams was any stronger than the evidence against half a dozen other suspects, some of whom were languishing in the same prison. Williams himself was reported as being quite cheerful, and confident that his innocence would soon be proven.

However, before the case was even formally brought before the court, the news came that John Williams had hanged himself in his cell just after Christmas—a holiday barely celebrated in England in 1811. As far as the authorities were concerned, that settled the matter—Williams's suicide was as good as a confession—and no further investigations were carried out.

Outrage over the brutal murders was so great that only a public hanging would have satisfied people; now that spectacle was denied them. In order to appease the mob, authorities arranged another sort of public spectacle. Four days after Williams's death, his corpse was tied to a platform and, surrounded by the maul and other presumed murder weapons, was taken in a cart along the Ratcliffe Highway to a crossroads. There the corpse was tumbled into a small hole, and a stake was driven through its heart with the fatal maul. (Burial at a crossroads with a stake through the heart was considered proper for a suicide victim.) Lime was then poured into the hole and it was covered with earth and the paving stones replaced. The grisly ritual was carried out in full view of a large and appreciative crowd.

Nearly three weeks after Williams's death, a blue jacket with a bloodstained inner pocket was found by one of the lodgers at the Pear Tree. A further search turned up a bloodstained clasp knife hidden in a hole in the wall. It was suggested both items belonged to Williams. Why it had taken so long to find them remains unexplained.

After this, the investigation of the Ratcliffe Highway murders was, for all practical purposes, finished. The public concluded that Williams and Williams alone was the murderer. Musing on the subject of murder years later, Thomas De Quincey wrote:

"Mr Williams made his debut on the stage of Ratcliffe Highway and executed those unparalleled murders which have procured for him such a brilliant and undying reputation. On which mur-

ders, by the way, I must observe that in one respect they have had
an ill effect, by making the connoisseur in murder very fastidious
in his taste, and dissatisfied by anything that has since been done
in that line. All other murders look pale by the deep crimson of
his."

De Quincey simply relied on the popular opinions of his day;
he did not bother to recheck the evidence. In 1971, however, the
British crime writer P. D. James, and T. A. Critchley, who had
written on police matters, did reexamine the whole case in their
book *The Maul and the Pear Tree*. A surprising amount of original
documentation concerning the murders had been preserved. The
authors concluded that not only was Williams probably innocent,
but he may well have been a murder victim himself. They note
that even at the time there seems to have been more uncertainty
about the conclusion that Williams was the murderer than generally
recognized.

Williams had never been convicted, tried, or even formally
charged with anything. He was just one of many who have been
arrested. The evidence against him was flimsy and had never been
tested in court. The most damning evidence—the bloodstained
jacket and knife, neither of which had conclusively been shown to
belong to Williams—only turned up after his death and could easily
have been fabricated by witnesses trying to collect part of the large
reward offered for information on the murders. In fact, they did
collect part of the reward. The murderer probably used a razor,
not a knife, anyway.

The most telling bit of evidence that Williams was not the
guilty party was the description given by Turner of the murderer
as a tall and heavy man in a long gray coat. This is the same
description as that of the man seen hanging about the King's Arms
before the murder. Williams was not large and did not own a long
coat of any color. His build was rather slight and his wardrobe
meager.

More intriguing still is the suggestion that Williams did not
end his own life. Up to the time of his death, he did not seem at
all depressed or suicidal. On the contrary, he seemed convinced
he would be freed. He left no note, confession or otherwise. The
sketchy records of the condition of Williams's body raise questions
about whether he really hanged himself or was strangled in his cell.

"No single feature of this mysterious case is stranger than the extraordinary abruptness with which the investigation ended," write James and Critchley. "Few who had studied the evidence intelligently could possibly have believed that only one murderer was involved in both crimes, or could have found the case against John Williams either convincing or conclusive."

The authors do not suggest any widespread conspiracy, but simply state that the authorities were under a tremendous amount of pressure to clear up this case. With Williams dead, this seemed a convenient out, so they stifled their doubts and questions and simply declared the case closed.

Who, then, committed the murders? James and Critchley point to a seaman named William Ablass, also known as "Long Billy." Ablass, who knew Williams, was actually arrested as part of the investigation, but later released. Ablass, who was quite tall and heavy, more nearly fit the description of the man seen at the King's Arms. Moreover, he was known to have a history of extreme violence. He had led a mutiny aboard the ship *Roxburgh Castle*, though he had managed to escape punishment. One of Ablass's shipmates on the *Roxburgh Castle* was John Williams, but Williams had declined to join the mutiny, and thus may have earned the hatred of Ablass. James and Critchley suggest the key to the Ratcliffe Highway mystery might have been found in the log of the *Roxburgh Castle*, which unfortunately has been lost or destroyed. Ablass had no good alibi for the time of the murders, and like many others he, too, had easy access to John Peterson's tools. The authors also name as a possible associate of Ablass in the crimes a carpenter named Cornelius Hart, one of Pugh's men who had been at work in Marr's shop on the day of the murder.

It is, of course, impossible to conclusively establish, over 175 years after the crimes were committed, what really happened. But James and Critchley have raised compelling doubts that the solution to the case is as simple or straightforward as writers like De Quincy and others have made it out to be.

1817

MARY ASHFORD   Aficionados of historical crime may still debate whether Mary Ashford accidentally drowned on May 27, 1817, or was murdered—and if murdered, by whom? But what makes this case truly memorable is that it was probably the last time in English history when the accused publicly appealed to the ancient rite of "trial by combat."

Mary Ashford was a lively and attractive twenty-year-old from the town of Erdington, near Birmingham. On the night of May 26, she attended a dance with her friend, Hannah Cox. She caught the attention of one of the young men, Abraham Thornton, who boasted to a friend that he "would have her" before the night was over.

Mary and Abraham left the dance at about midnight. At 4:00 A.M., Mary appeared at Hannah Cox's house. She changed from her dancing dress to her ordinary clothes, and left for home. According to later testimony, she was quite cheerful. An hour and a half later, her clothes were found neatly folded at the edge of a pond. The pond was dragged and Mary Ashford's body was discovered.

Murder was suspected, and Abraham Thornton was the prime, indeed the only, suspect. He freely admitted to having been with the girl until 4:00 A.M., and that he had seduced her. But he insisted that he had not raped or murdered her.

It was estimated that Mary had died somewhere around 5:00 A.M., and at that time a witness reported seeing Thornton walking home, miles from the pond where Mary died. There was no direct evidence linking Thornton with the girl's death. The jury deliberated for a few minutes and declared Abraham Thornton innocent.

However, Mary's brother was not at all satisfied with the verdict. He began a campaign to have Thornton tried again. At that time, there was no strict rule of double jeopardy. So Thornton

Abraham Thornton claims "wager of battle."

was brought once more to trial. When the judge asked him whether he would plead guilty or not guilty, the enraged Thornton shouted, "Not guilty, and I am ready to defend the same with my body."

He took out a pair of buckskin gloves, holding one over his head, and threw the other at the feet of Mary's brother, his accuser, thus challenging him to a duel. A century earlier, a duel might have settled this matter, but by the early nineteenth century, the era of dueling was over in England. Mary's brother was restrained from picking up the glove. The case was tried in the usual way, and for the second time Thornton was acquitted.

1821

THE DEATH OF NAPOLEON   The emperor Napoleon was
a particularly worrisome prisoner. After conquering much of Europe and terrorizing all of it, he was finally defeated and sent into
exile on the island of Elba. But he escaped, gathered another army,
and threw another massive scare into the ruling families of Europe
until he was finally defeated at the battle of Waterloo and sent into
exile on the remote island of St. Helena, from which it was assumed, and hoped, that he would never escape.

Even in his distant exile, Napoleon continued to worry the
European governments. There were constant rumors that some
plot or the other was being hatched to help the former emperor
escape. So long as Napoleon was alive, he remained a threat. It
would be so much more convenient for the rulers of Europe if he
were dead. But to execute Napoleon would be to create a martyr.
Besides, rulers do not like to kill other rulers, even their enemies.
It sets a bad precedent. However, there undoubtedly were many
powerful people who longed for the former emperor to die quietly
and swiftly.

Napoleon was aware that he was in the hands of his
enemies—his exile was under control of the British—and that many
wished him dead. So he feared, and probably expected, that he
would be poisoned.

Napoleon had been depressed and intermittently unwell since
his arrival on St. Helena in 1815. The island was not the most
cheerful or healthful of places, and while Napoleon was not exactly
a prisoner, he certainly wasn't a free man. By 1818, he began
suffering from fairly alarming symptoms—sharp pains in the side
and chronically cold feet. By January of 1821, Napoleon was feeling very ill, and he told people that he did not think he had long
to live. In addition to worrying about poison, Napoleon also worried about cancer. His own father had died of cancer at the age of

thirty-five, and Napoleon asked his doctor if the disease could be hereditary.

His symptoms multiplied: a dry cough, constant thirst, weak pulse, nausea, chills, shivering. Until the very end, Napoleon refused to take any medicines, which, in any case, probably wouldn't have done him any good. By mid-April, he made out his will and he expressed the wish that after his death an autopsy should be performed on his body. But he didn't want any English physicians to be involved. On May 5, 1821, after much suffering, Napoleon died.

An autopsy was performed by seven doctors, but contrary to Napoleon's wish, six of the seven were English. The doctors were in sharp disagreement as to what they had found. There was what appeared to be a growth in the stomach, but the doctors could not agree on whether it was cancerous or not, and whether it had been the cause of the emperor's death.

Napoleon was buried in an unmarked grave on St. Helena.

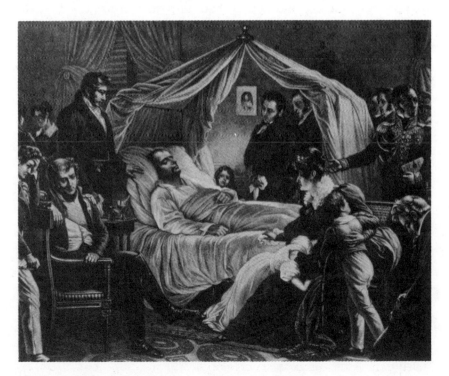

The death of Napoleon.

Nineteen years later, the political climate had shifted. Napoleon was once again revered as a hero in France, and his body was removed from St. Helena to be reinterred in the massive crypt of L'Eglise Royale, in the Hotel des Invalides in Paris. Those who witnessed the opening of Napoleon's grave in St. Helena were astonished that the corpse was in a remarkable state of preservation, though no special efforts had been made to preserve it.

From the moment of his death, rumors that Napoleon had been poisoned circulated widely, but there was no solid evidence to support them. There have been rumors of poison around the unexplained death of every prominent person in history.

Among those attracted by the controversy surrounding Napoleon's death was, improbably, a Swedish dentist and Napoleon buff named Sten Forshufvud. After reading and rereading the accounts of the emperor's final years, he became convinced that Napoleon showed all the signs of arsenic poisoning before his death. The doctors who performed the autopsy on Napoleon had no tests for arsenic, and if they had any suspicions, the English doctors would not have wished to make them public. More than a century later, how could Forshufvud test his theory?

In 1960, Forshufvud learned that a Dr. Hamilton Smith of the University of Glasgow had developed a test that could detect the presence of arsenic in a single strand of hair. It was well known that hair retained arsenic, but previous tests required a considerable quantity of hair. It would be hard enough to get a single strand of the emperor's hair.

It was known that several locks of Napoleon's hair had been cut as souvenirs on the day after his death. Forshufvud finally located one in the possession of Commandant Henri Lachouque, a leading Napoleon expert in Paris. Lachouque was intrigued by the project and was quite happy to part with a strand.

When the hair was tested by Dr. Smith, it showed that Napoleon had been exposed to relatively large amounts of arsenic. More sensitive tests on other strands of hair indicated that Napoleon had received large but not necessarily fatal doses of arsenic at times that corresponded roughly to the times when the emperor fell ill.

When news of Forshufvud's theory was published, he was

contacted by a descendant of Betsy Balcombe, a girl who had lived
on St. Helena and had become a great friend of the emperor during
his years of exile. He learned that it had long been a suspicion in
the Balcombe family that Napoleon had been poisoned. He also
learned more about the daily life of Napoleon in exile, and of the
individuals who had surrounded him in his final years. Forshufvud
was not content merely to prove that Napoleon had been poisoned;
he wanted to discover exactly who had done the poisoning.

Count Charles-Tristan de Montholon

Traces of arsenic began showing up in Napoleon in 1818; thus, everyone who arrived at St. Helena after that year was eliminated. The English, Forshufvud reasoned, would not have risked international scandal by doing the job directly. Some of Napoleon's servants had been with the emperor too long and had proved their loyalty so often they were considered above suspicion. Finally, Forshufvud was left with only one credible suspect—Count Charles-Tristan de Montholon. Montholon was a curious figure. He had been an aristocrat, but had served Napoleon. He switched back to the Bourbons when Napoleon was defeated, but after Waterloo he rejoined the defeated emperor and chose to follow him into lonely exile. His motives were unclear, for he had never been a particularly enthusiastic supporter of Napoleon. On St. Helena, Montholon largely took charge of Napoleon's household, including the food supply.

Forshufvud reasoned that Montholon had been sent to St. Helena for the specific purpose of killing Napoleon. The murder plot, Forshufvud believed, had been instigated by the Count d'Artois, known as Monsieur, the younger brother of the newly restored Bourbon king, Louis XVIII, and of Louis XVI, who had been beheaded during the French Revolution. Monsieur was fanatical in his hatred of anything remotely connected with the Revolution, which had deprived him of his power, and he was particularly passionate in his hatred of the usurper Napoleon. While in exile during Napoleon's reign, d'Artois had hatched a long string of unsuccessful plots against Napoleon. He had his own network of spies, and was convinced that even in distant St. Helena, Napoleon represented a grave threat. It would not have been difficult for him to enlist a man like Montholon, who was always in need of money, to slowly poison the menace.

D'Artois was to briefly rule France as Charles X, but he was again driven from power and into exile.

At the end of his long quest, Sten Forshufvud finally went to St. Helena, the scene of the murder that he believed he had effectively been able to reconstruct. He stood at the gravesite where Napoleon's body had first been buried and thought about the moment, in October 1840, when Napoleon's remains were dug up to be returned in glory to France. Most of those who had shared the emperor's exile and were still alive had returned to the gravesite. Montholon had not.

In their book *The Murder of Napoleon*, authors Ben Weider and David Hapgood write:

"It was just as well for Montholon, Forshufvud reflected, that he was not at this spot on that rainy, foggy day when the companions of the exile watched workmen open the Emperor's grave. The assassin might have feared that the witnesses would understand the meaning of the startling sight they saw in that grave. Napoleon's body had not been embalmed, but merely buried as it was after the autopsy. It was enclosed in four coffins, two of them of metal, but none of these were airtight. The witnesses expected, given the normal decay of nineteen years, that when the innermost coffin was opened they would see a skeleton.

"Napoleon's body was perfectly preserved. He looked as if he were asleep. His face had changed less in those nineteen years than the faces of those who were now gazing down into the grave. Napoleon's clothing, the uniform in which he was buried, was decayed, but not the body itself. Forshufvud knew the explanation for this seeming miracle—arsenic. Arsenic the destroyer is also a preservative of living tissue: museums often use it to preserve specimens, and a human corpse will decay much more slowly if the person is exposed to chronic arsenic poisoning. And so Napoleon's body was mutely testifying to the fact of his assassination. It could still testify today if the French would only agree to open the great tomb at Les Invalides and the coffins within which the Emperor's remains were sealed."

Forshufvud's findings about the arsenic in Napoleon's hair got a tremendous amount of international publicity, and many people have come to accept poisoning as the last word on the death of Napoleon. But it isn't. Sensational, and, yes, logical as this solution may seem, it is far from proved. First, there is not a single scrap of new documentary evidence supporting the conclusion. There is no deathbed confession from Montholon; no incriminating papers have turned up in the archives of Charles X.

There are also the results of the autopsy. The fact that no evidence of poisoning was found by the doctors is not significant, but they did find that Napoleon had a tumor in his stomach. It is more than probable that the tumor was cancerous, and that Napoleon died of stomach cancer, just as his father had. Even before the alleged poisoning began, Napoleon had complained of stomach pains. Forshufvud, however, believes that the condition of Napoleon's stomach was the result of the corrosive effect of the poison.

What about the arsenic in the emperor's hair? There are many ways that arsenic can get into the human body without assuming that an unknown poisoner is secretly sprinkling it on the food. A form of arsenic was once very popular as a pigment for coloring everything from fabric to wallpaper. In 1982, Dr. David Jones found that Napoleon's wallpaper at St. Helena contained arsenic.

Proponents of the murder theory respond that it is highly unlikely that Napoleon could have absorbed enough arsenic from the wallpaper to account for the quantity found in his body. Forshufvud had considered the possibility of arsenic in the environment, but decided that it was not a possible explanation because others who lived in the house had not come down with the same symptoms. But what if Napoleon had been in the habit of leaning on the wall or tracing the designs with his finger and then putting his finger in his mouth? This might have dramatically increased his risk of exposure. But we really don't know.

Opening the emperor's tomb and examining his remains with the sensitive tools of modern science might enable researchers to answer many of the questions, though probably not to everyone's satisfaction. But no one seriously believes this will be done—so the questions will always remain.

1841

MARY ROGERS   The mysterious death of the "Beautiful Cigar Girl" Mary Cecilia Rogers in July 1841 is significant for two reasons. The case came at a time when the popular press in America was growing in power and influence, and this was one of the first crimes to receive sensational (and sensationalized) attention. Even more significantly, the case became the basis for one of the first mystery stories ever written, "The Mystery of Marie Roget," by Edgar Allan Poe.

Mary Rogers was born about 1820, the child of Daniel and Phoebe Rogers. Her father was killed in a steamboat explosion on the Mississippi, and she and her mother lived in a boardinghouse in lower Manhattan. In 1837, Mary took a job in John Anderson's tobacco shop, on upper Broadway. The appearance of a very attractive young lady behind the counter of this most masculine of establishments was cause for considerable comment.

One reason that Mary's mysterious death was to attract so much attention in the press was that Anderson's tobacco shop was a favorite hangout for New York's reporters and editors. Poe himself might have frequented the shop. He and John Anderson certainly knew each other—Anderson was one of the advertisers in a magazine Poe started. So, while there is no evidence that Poe ever actually met the unfortunate Mary Rogers, he might have and that may have been why the case attracted him.

Mary Rogers must have led a troubled life. In October 1838, two and a half years before her death, she disappeared from her home leaving behind a message that she was going to kill herself. "The cause of this wayward freak of the young lady is supposed by her friends to be disappointed love . . ." wrote the New York *Sun*, which gave considerable coverage to the incident in its October 5, 1838, edition.

The next day, the *Times and Commercial Intelligencer* said

the whole thing had never happened. Mary had only gone off to visit friends in Brooklyn, and now was back home with her mother. The New York *Weekly Herald* was outraged. "Something should be done instantly to remedy the great evil consequent upon very beautiful young girls being placed in cigar and confectionery stores." Later, the *Herald* said that Mary had been seduced by a Navy man and kept in Hoboken, New Jersey, for two weeks.

So even before her mysterious death, Mary Rogers was something of a media star. On July 25, 1841, Mary told her fiancé, Daniel Payne, that she was going off to visit an aunt in Hoboken. She was not seen again until her body was found floating in the Hudson River three days later. The exact condition of the body is not clear from the records. It was bound, so obviously Mary was not a suicide or the victim of accidental drowning. As later events were to prove, some of her clothes were missing. An autopsy was performed, and the mayor of New York met personally with the doctor. What they discussed is unknown. Some said that Mary had been beaten to death. Others that she was strangled. The exact cause of death does not seem to have been determined. The verdict of the coroner's inquest was that Mary had died as the result of "violence committed by some person or persons unknown."

The first reaction, as usual, was to look for the outsider. There was a gang of "toughs" reputed to be causing much trouble in the Hoboken area, and they were the first suspects. Mary's employer, John Anderson, and a former boyfriend, Alfred Crommelin, were questioned. A prime suspect was her fiancé, Daniel Payne. Six weeks later, Payne committed suicide. His body was found about a mile from the spot where Mary's corpse had been pulled from the river. His suicide note said ambiguously, "God forgive me for my misfortune, or for my misspent time." There were hordes of rumors about Mary's having had a socially prominent "secret lover" who killed her when he found out she was pregnant.

In June of the following year, an entirely new light was thrown on the case by a Mrs. Frederica Loss. Mrs. Loss ran sort of a tavern near the river in New Jersey, and she had been accidentally wounded by her son's gun. On her deathbed, Mrs. Loss confessed to Justice Merritt of New Jersey that she knew the facts behind the death of Mary Rogers. Mary, she said, had come to her place on July 25,

1841, to have an abortion performed by an unknown physician. However, Mary died during the operation. Mrs. Loss's son took the girl's body and threw it in the river. Some of Mary's clothes were then scattered in the woods nearby.

Actually, Mrs. Loss had already come to the attention of the police. About a month after Mary's death, Mrs. Loss said that one of her sons had found some articles of women's clothing in a thicket near her place of business. She said further that the clothing had belonged to a young woman (presumably Mary Rogers) who had been at her inn on the twenty-fifth in the company of a "dark-complexioned young man." Later she heard the screaming "as of a young girl in great distress, partly choked and calling for assistance" nearby. She ran out in the road, but saw nothing. That's what she told the police in 1841. On her deathbed, she told a very different tale.

Poe picked up the story and transferred it to Paris—turning Mary Rogers into Marie Roget. He said the resemblance between the two cases was the result of "the Calculus of Probabilities." The case was solved by the remarkable mental powers of Poe's detective Chevalier C. Auguste Dupin. Poe sold his story to *Ladies Companion*, where it was serialized starting in June 1842. In his original version, Poe had the killer of Marie a secret lover. But then came the bombshell of Mrs. Loss's confession. Poe reworked the ending of his story in midpublication in order to take the new evidence into account.

"The Mystery of Marie Roget" is the weakest of Poe's three Dupin tales, but it is the first fictional attempt to solve an actual crime. And Dupin is the first real detective in the history of fiction. Weak or not, it's an important story.

There are persistent rumors that Poe was paid to write the story by his friend, cigar-store owner John Anderson, in order to draw suspicion away from himself. If Anderson did pay Poe, he didn't pay much, for at the time the writer was, as usual, very hard up.

Many years later, Mary Rogers's name was again brought up in connection with John Anderson. The cigar-store owner had done very well financially, particularly during the Civil War, and by the time of his death he was a millionaire. In 1891, his will was

EDGAR ALLAN POE

*From an engraving by Wilcox after a daguerreo-
type which gives probably the most
faithful likeness of Poe*

being disputed in court. During the proceedings, his business partner, Felix McClosky, testified that Anderson had told him that Mary had had an abortion "the year before the murder took place—or a year and a half—something of that kind—and he got into some trouble about it—and outside of that there were no grounds on earth for anyone to suppose he had anything to do with the murder."

The writer Irving Wallace suggested (perhaps not seriously) that Poe himself committed the murder. Poe was a strange and unhappy man who might possibly have known Mary Rogers. But there is nothing to indicate that he killed Mary Rogers or anyone else.

So who did kill Mary Rogers? Was she a murder victim or the victim of a botched abortion? The investigation of the case was poor, even by the standards of the times. The record is incomplete and the events can no longer be effectively reconstructed. It seems probable that she did indeed die as the result of an abortion, though there was nothing in the autopsy to indicate this. The "dark-complexioned young man" may have been an abortionist, not a "secret lover." Who arranged the abortion, Anderson or someone else? This historic case remains unsolved.

1857

DR. HARVEY BURDELL   The murder of Dr. Harvey Burdell is not a well-known case today. It is either omitted or barely mentioned in most histories of crime. Yet at the time, 1857, it was considered "The Crime of the Century," at least in New York City where it took place. The coverage of the Burdell murder case in publications like *The New York Times* and the *New York Tribune* was exhaustive (and exhausting). Author Jack Finney, who revived the case in his book *Forgotten News: The Crime of the Century and Other Lost Stories*, estimates that it must have been one of the longer-running stories in the history of the *Times*. He speaks of "numbly turning past endless columns of fine newsprint on this story running day after day . . ."

It's not hard to see why the story captivated the nineteenth-century newspaper readers, for it is a strange and fascinating one. Burdell was a dentist and physician who lived at 31 Bond Street. He was forty-five years old, fairly well-to-do, and had the reputation of being something of a ladies' man, and something of a miser. He was quoted by a relative as saying that "no man who owned real estate ought to marry."

Burdell made occasional trips to the fashionable summer resort of Saratoga Springs in upstate New York. There, in 1854, he apparently met a woman with five children named Emma Augusta Cunningham, the thirty-six-year-old widow of a Brooklyn distiller.

She was a woman with a formidable personality, and early on she must have decided that she was going to marry Burdell and inherit his money. Her own financial condition was precarious.

Mrs. Cunningham, who also lived in New York City, began to visit the doctor. First she took one of her daughters to have her teeth attended to. Burdell rented rooms in his house, and soon Mrs. Cunningham and her children moved in. Within a few months she had rented the entire house. Burdell retained a couple of rooms for his own living quarters and office, Mrs. Cunningham and her family lived in others, and still others she rented out. That seems an unusual arrangement today, but apparently such arrangements were not uncommon in the mid-nineteenth century.

The relationship between Burdell and Mrs. Cunningham is difficult to establish. At times they seemed close, at other times Burdell openly discussed his dislike and even fear of her, and he announced his intention to put her out as soon as her lease ran out. Occasionally they were seen together in a restaurant, but they also quarreled a lot. The relationship had certainly deteriorated by the end of 1856.

A third party entered the scene in October of 1856. His name was John J. Eckel, a former butcher and dealer in animal hides. Eckel appeared at 31 Bond Street looking for a room, and Mrs. Cunningham rented him one. There was some suspicion that Eckel and Mrs. Cunningham already knew each other, but this was never supported by solid evidence. However, the two did seem to get along well.

After Eckel had been living in the house for about two weeks, something very curious happened: Emma Cunningham married Dr. Harvey Burdell, or at least that is what Mrs. Cunningham claimed. Mrs. Cunningham and a bearded man who said that he was Harvey Burdell were married in the house of Reverend Uriah Marvine. One of the Cunningham daughters served as a witness. The reverend and his wife thought that the groom looked a bit strange, rather like he was in disguise. He didn't talk much, and he even misspelled his name on his marriage certificate.

The "marriage" was kept a secret. Mrs. Cunningham didn't tell anyone, and Burdell continued to live as before, and even wrote to a relative saying of his supposed wife, "I would sooner marry an old toad than to marry such a thing as she is." The couple still lived in separate rooms in the house, and the doctor persisted in his efforts to get Mrs. Cunningham out. In short, the "marriage" appears to have changed nothing.

By the end of January 1857, things at 31 Bond Street had become so strained that the doctor was spending as much time away as possible. He took all his meals out, and even asked a friend

The murder of Dr. Harvey Burdell as imagined by an artist for *Leslie's Weekly*.

to live with him until May, when Mrs. Cunningham's lease expired and he could evict her. The friend was unable or unwilling to do so. Later, people wondered why Burdell didn't simply take a room in a hotel until May. But he was a miserly man, and apparently didn't want the extra expense, no matter what the inconvenience or danger.

On the night of January 30, 1857, the doctor returned home late. As he sat at his desk in his study, someone crept up behind him and stabbed him. The first thrust was not fatal. He jumped up and tried to defend himself, but the intruder stabbed repeatedly, and one blow struck through the heart. Burdell was also apparently strangled.

It was a warm night, and several people were on Bond Street. At least two of them thought they heard someone in the house cry "Murd—," but the last syllables were choked off. The witnesses assumed the cry might be coming from a poor soul being garrotted in the street—today we would call it being mugged—and didn't want to get involved. Street crime in New York City was as much feared in the 1850s as it is in the 1980s, and the general reaction to it was about the same. People didn't want to get involved.

Oddly, though there were quite a number of people supposedly asleep on 31 Bond Street, not one of them reported hearing the struggle—which surely must have been a violent one. Dr. Burdell's corpse was not discovered until the following morning.

Mrs. Cunningham seemed to be greatly affected by the news of the doctor's death, and she revealed to neighbors for the first time her "secret marriage."

There was no sign of robbery or forced entry, nothing at all to indicate that some outsider had gotten into the house. The murder had all the earmarks of an inside job, and suspicion immediately fell on Mrs. Cunningham (or Mrs. Burdell, as she now wished to be called) and Eckel. The coroner Edward Connery opened an inquest. It was a long and very lively affair that was covered in the minutest detail by the newspapers.

Coroner Connery seems to have been convinced from the outset that Mrs. Cunningham and Eckel were guilty, and set out to convict them, though a coroner's inquest is not a trial. In addition to his ignorance or indifference to legal details, the coroner was quite a character, very fond of the limelight. He delivered long and fulsome speeches filled with classical references, and enjoyed telling odd and inappropriate jokes. He made sure everyone spoke slowly enough so that the reporters could write it all down. Ultimately, his courting of the press got him into some trouble, because the press soon began to complain about his behavior.

Yet despite its many irregularities, the inquest did bring forth a great deal of fascinating testimony, including a witness's who claimed that he had seen Eckel enter the house shortly before the murder and look out of the front door shortly after.

Mrs. Cunningham and Eckel were sent to the prison known as the Tombs to await trial. Reporters visited them there. Mrs.

Cunningham behaved with great dignity, but generally avoided interviews. Eckel was calm, relaxed, and convinced that the charges against him were absurd and that he would easily be acquitted.

Eckel's confidence was not misplaced. The trial was very different from the free-wheeling inquest. Most of the incriminating information that made such a splash at the inquest wasn't even introduced at the trial. Subsequent events were to prove that District Attorney A. Oakey Hall was convinced of Mrs. Cunningham's guilt, but he may have felt that the witness who told such interesting stories in the liberal atmosphere of Coroner Connery's procedure would not stand up well against Mrs. Cunningham's formidable defense team. Whatever the reason, the prosecution case was so weak that the not guilty verdict was practically a foregone conclusion. Without a conviction of Mrs. Cunningham, the case against Eckel was simply dropped.

It should have all ended there, but it didn't, for Emma Cunningham was a remarkably determined and bold woman. Her disputed marriage to Burdell was not going to give her possession of the doctor's estate. But if she had the doctor's child, an heir, then her case would be much stronger. So, after her acquittal, she announced that she was pregnant. The fact that she had spent weeks in jail under close observation and no one had noticed did not seem to bother Mrs. Cunningham at all. It had been nearly seven months from the time of the murder to the conclusion of the trial, and so the period in which she could credibly claim to have become pregnant by Burdell was rapidly running out.

Mrs. Cunningham began asking around for a baby. She slipped a note to a nurse at Bellevue that she wanted a newborn child and that money would be no object. The nurse threw the note away. Mrs. Cunningham then confided in her own physician, Dr. David Uhl, that she was not pregnant but that if he could get a newborn baby for her, she would give him a thousand dollars after she inherited Dr. Burdell's estate. Dr. Uhl was deeply troubled by the request, and on the advice of his lawyer went to see the district attorney, A. Oakey Hall. Hall, apparently chagrined that Mrs. Cunningham had defeated him once, worked out an elaborate scheme whereby she would be presented with an infant and then trapped in the act of trying to pass the child off as her own. It says a good deal about the conditions of the poor at that time that Hall found it quite easy to "borrow" a newborn infant from one of the indigent women at Bellevue.

Dr. Uhl helped to bring the infant to Mrs. Cunningham, and a short time later the police arrived, snatched the infant from her, and placed her under arrest.

The infant, by the way, was returned to its mother. When she left Bellevue, she and her daughter went directly to Barnum's Museum, where they were on display "on a raised platform, ready to answer (if able) all the curious questions that may be asked . . ." This attraction, which Barnum called "The Bogus Burdell Baby," attracted quite a crowd, and one hopes mother and child were paid well for their services.

After the exposure, Mrs. Cunningham was once again thrown in jail, but she was released quickly because no charges could be brought against her. It was no crime to say a baby is yours when it wasn't. She had not yet formally tried to claim Burdell's estate —so technically no fraud had been committed. It was later reported that she moved to California, and nothing more was ever heard of her.

She was unbelievably audacious, and lucky, up to a point. Emma Cunningham seems to have gotten away with murder, but was never able to profit from it as she had hoped.

1888

JACK THE RIPPER   Without any question, Jack the Ripper is the best-known unknown murderer in history. Not only are the details of his crimes recounted frequently in volumes like this one, but, though the case is a century old, new "solutions" are popping up all the time. There is a small coterie of "Ripperologists" devoted to study of the case. The Ripper murders have inspired countless books and films—and even a musical comedy! The centenary of the Ripper murders has inspired a flock of new books and a TV miniseries.

Yet, in a very real sense, the fame is undeserved. Certainly, the murderer was never identified. But as this volume amply demonstrates, there are many murderers who have never been identified. Only five murders can definitely be attributed to the Ripper—a paltry number compared to some of the really prolific mass murders. The killings were gruesome, but most killings are gruesome. The victims were obscure. They were all pathetic alcoholic prostitutes whose violent deaths would otherwise barely have been noticed.

The fame of this unknown murderer rests primarily on factors that lie outside of the murders themselves. First there is the name or label "Jack the Ripper." The name was signed to some of the grisly yet jocular letters sent to authorities during the murderer's reign of terror. Many students of the Ripper murders believe that some of these letters actually came from the murderer himself and thus Jack the Ripper is a self-conferred title, but this is far from certain. The one letter deemed most likely to be genuine, because it may have contained part of a victim's kidney, was not signed Jack the Ripper. In any event the name stuck, and is now part of our common cultural heritage.

Another reason for the Ripper's fame is the time and place of the murders. It was late-Victorian London—the London of

Sherlock Holmes. It was a time of gaslights and horse-drawn cabs, of high hats and opera capes, of cobblestone streets and foggy nights. It was also a time of prosperity and order, morality and stability. There was, of course, another side of Victorian London that was typified by Whitechapel, the district in which the Ripper's crimes took place. Whitechapel was a rabbit warren of narrow streets, alleys, courtyards, and terraces. It was a district of warehouses, gin shops, opium dens, and brothels. Living, or rather existing, in this cesspool were the poorest of the London poor, Cockney, Jewish, and Irish. Whitechapel was a place of disease, starvation, and utter desperation. London had a sort of Jekyll and

Hyde character, and not surprisingly, Robert Louis Stevenson's famous story was set in Jack the Ripper's London.

Whitechapel was also a district of "unimaginable vice." Of course, it is perfectly easy to imagine what the vices were, vices being pretty much the same throughout history, but the comfortable middle class of Victorian London did not care to speculate on such matters, at least in public. The Ripper crimes were quite clearly sex crimes of the most vicious sort, yet because of the Victorian reticence about sex, such crimes seemed tinged with an air of almost supernatural evil. There are sex murders aplenty in the modern world; they strike us as violent, squalid, terrible, but the same sort of crime committed in gaslit London (at least the gaslit London of the imagination) seems so out of place that it is even more terrible, more unearthly.

This is not to deny that there were certain elements peculiar to the Ripper crimes themselves that made them seize and hold a grip on public interest. There had been other killings and mutilations of prostitutes in London at that time. Indeed, the authorities had some difficulty deciding exactly which of the many similar murders should absolutely be attributed to the Ripper. But the Ripper was unusually vicious, and he was bold. Or perhaps he was just insanely driven and very lucky. A delay of a few moments, a little more curiosity on the part of a watchman, and the career of Jack the Ripper might easily have ended in discovery and hanging, not mystery.

The Ripper's first known crime took place on the night of August 31, 1888. The victim was a forty-two-year-old prostitute named Mary Ann Nicholls. Not only had her throat been cut, but her abdomen had been slit open.

One week later, the Ripper struck again. This time the victim was forty-seven-year old Annie Chapman, a pathetic prostitute dying of consumption. Her throat, too, had been cut, and as in Mary Ann Nicholls's murder, she had been horribly mutilated.

This second murder made the public and the police sit up and take notice. The two murders were linked with yet a third that had taken place early in August, before the murder of Mary Ann Nicholls. The victim had been another Whitechapel prostitute, but the woman had been stabbed rather than slashed, and the police doubted if she was a Ripper victim at all. (Most current Ripper-ologists think she was not.) The public, however, had no doubt that a mass murderer was loose in London. The Whitechapel district was now swarming with uniformed police looking for the killer. In addition, a group of businessmen formed the Whitechapel Vigilance Committee, and they hired private detectives and recruited civilian volunteers to patrol the streets and alleys.

The Central News Agency in Fleet Street received a letter written in red ink, boasting of the crimes. It was signed "Jack the Ripper." That was the first known use of the name. A second communication, a postcard, arrived a short time later. The reason many students of crime believe that these two communications were genuine is that they refer to things that would not have been known by the general public at the time they were written. In reality, however, the letters could have been posted shortly after the crimes became public. Thus, the "Jack the Ripper" letters may have been another ghastly and demented hoax. There were to be many.

On the night of September 29, the Ripper displayed not only his ferocity but his audacity. On that night, a man named Diemschutz discovered the body of a woman whose throat had just been cut. The blood was still pouring from the wound, so the murder could only have been committed moments before the discovery. Diemschutz heard footsteps in the darkness, almost certainly those of the murderer, but he never saw the figure. Jack the Ripper had very nearly been caught in the act. The murderer had been interrupted and was not able to perform his usual mutilations; this apparently left some compulsion unsatisfied, for within an hour he struck again.

This "second event" was perhaps the most astonishing Ripper crime of all. It was performed in a place called Mitre Square, which was flanked by tea warehouses guarded by a permanent watchman. In addition, the square was visited every fifteen minutes by a constable. The constable had been in the square at 1:30 A.M. and found it deserted. Fifteen minutes later, he discovered the hideously mutilated body of Catherine Eddowes. From the moment he had been interrupted, it had taken the Ripper a mere forty-five minutes to meet, kill, and butcher his second victim. He had done so with such skill, or luck, that a watchman sitting just a few yards away never heard a sound.

How had the murderer gotten away? It was an extremely bloody crime, and though there was some evidence that the Ripper wiped his knife on his victim's dress and washed his hands at the public fountain, he must have been covered with blood. Yet he made his escape through streets swarming with constables and members of the Vigilance Committee, as well as the usual late Saturday-night crowds, apparently without being noticed.

The following Tuesday morning, George Lusk, chairman of the Whitechapel Vigilance Committee, received a package. It contained a letter, "from hell, Mr. Lusk," boasting of the crimes. The letter ended, "Catch me when you can Mishter Lusk." It was not signed Jack the Ripper, but of all the communications attributed to the killer, this was the least likely to have been a hoax, because it contained half a human kidney, presumably, though not certainly, Catherine Eddowes's kidney.

This "double event" spread genuine panic in the Whitechapel area, and aroused interest throughout London. The queen herself was said to have discussed the case. Whitechapel was now so flooded with police and private investigators that they began arresting one another. Yet no authentic clue to the Ripper turned up. The commissioner of police admitted defeat and resigned. All in all, the Ripper investigation seems to have been poorly handled.

It was six weeks before the Ripper committed his final, and in many respects, most ghastly, crime. The victim was Mary Jeanette Kelly. Unlike the other Ripper murders, this one was not committed in the street but in Kelly's room in Miller's Court. In comparative privacy, the Ripper had several hours in which to completely butcher his victim. The scene that the police found on the morning of November 10, 1888, was literally indescribable.

The Ripper's reign of terror was over, but it was only the beginning of the mystery. Within a month after the murder of Mary Kelly, the extra police were withdrawn from Whitechapel and the vigilance committee was told by the police to disband because their services were no longer required. Privately, members were informed that Jack the Ripper was dead; he had committed suicide by drowning himself in the Thames. Unfortunately, the police never publicly identified the murderer, and their evidence for the identification, if any, has not survived. Indeed, despite many rumors of hidden Scotland Yard files on the case, it is fairly certain that everything Scotland Yard had on Jack the Ripper has now been made public. Those who suggest that there was a cover-up to protect a high-born killer believe evidence was destroyed.

The man the police apparently suspected was Montague John Druitt, a failed lawyer and probable psychopath who drowned himself on December 3, 1888. Druitt left behind a suicide note, but the note never became part of the Ripper file, and we don't know what it said. Later investigators have built an impressive though far from conclusive case against Druitt.

A new twist to the case against Druitt was made by authors Martin Howells and Keith Skinner in their book *The Ripper Legacy: The Life and Death of Jack the Ripper*, published in 1987. They named Druitt, and claimed the police knew he had done it and covered up the evidence.

Why would the police have done such a thing? In an interview, Howells said: "But the authorities kept quiet because Druitt was friendly with a lot of important people who were homosexuals." Among those associates, Howells names Queen Victoria's grandson the Duke of Clarence, who was in line for the throne.

Howells and Skinner say that Druitt's friends suspected that he was the Ripper and feared that an investigation would drag the Royal Family through the mud, so they killed him. The probable assassin, say the authors, was Henry Francis Williams, who they allege was a lover of the Duke of Clarence from their student days at Cambridge. Wilson had a house at Chiswick adjacent to the wharf where Druitt's body was recovered from the river.

Druitt's mother had gone insane and was committed to an institution in July 1888, shortly before the murders began. The authors speculate that Druitt blamed his mother's madness on syphilis—a disease he associated with prostitutes.

There has been no lack of other Ripper suspects. Because the Ripper's mutilations were carried out with what appeared to be surgical precision, many have speculated that the killer was an insane physician. Mad doctors always make good suspects. A prime candidate in this category was a Russian immigrant named Michael

Ostrog, a qualified physician and a raving maniac. He had been jailed several times for assault and was finally locked up for good late in November 1888. Some Scotland Yard investigators were sure that he was the Ripper, but direct evidence is lacking, and modern investigators feel the case against him is weak.

Another medical suspect was the monstrous Dr. Neill Cream. Cream hated prostitutes, and in 1891 was convicted of poisoning several. Dr. Cream was hanged on November 15, 1892. Cream's last words on the gallows, shouted just before the trap was sprung, were "I am Jack . . ."

Unfortunately for this theory, Dr. Cream was in prison in Joliet, Illinois, during the time the Ripper murders were being carried out. He had poisoned one of his patients but was declared "rehabilitated" and was released and moved to London, where he started killing again. Some supporters of the mad doctor declare that there were really two Thomas Neill Creams, and one of them was Jack the Ripper.

Recently one of the most popular theories as to the identity of Jack the Ripper is also one of the most bizarre. This scenario suggests that the Ripper was not one man but a group of high-ranking and fanatic Freemasons who killed women who knew about the secret marriage of Queen Victoria's grandson, the Duke of Clarence, to Annie Elizabeth Crook (or Cook), a Roman Catholic shop girl. In this theory, the Duke was not a homosexual.

This oddball idea began with the claim of an artist, named Joseph Sickert, that his mother Alice Margaret Crook was really the daughter of this shop girl and the duke. Now, claiming that one is related to royalty is a common British pursuit, but in this case Joseph Sickert's father, Walter Sickert, was a prominent artist in late-Victorian times and moved in aristocratic circles. The younger Sickert (not so young when he began relating his tale) said he heard the story of the murders, or at least some of it, from his father.

The whole case is reconstructed in *Jack the Ripper: The Final Solution*, by Stephen Knight. The reconstruction is complex, ingenious, intriguing, and shows a good deal of thought and hard work. Unfortunately, it is based on a number of unproved and quite unlikely premises: First, that ritual murder was part of the practice of English Freemasons in late-Victorian times, and second, that the Duke of Clarence actually married a low-born commoner, and a Catholic one to boot. Knight speculates mightily, but offers no solid proof of either of these astounding propositions. Then we must wonder why the presumed murderers went about killing the prostitutes who knew about this secret marriage while allowing the woman herself, Alice Margaret Crook, to live (albeit in a series of institutions). After all the trouble they went through to kill the witnesses and cover up the crime, it would have been easy to get rid of Crook. This theory was the basis for the play and later film *The Crucifer of Blood*, in which Sherlock Holmes uncovers the plot.

Others have named the Duke of Clarence himself as the murderer, again without any proof.

Yet another theory is that Jack the Ripper was a woman. (The suggestion that the murderer was actually Queen Victoria was not, one assumes, advanced seriously.) What makes the Ripper as a woman theory so intriguing, says the British writer John Godwin, is that it would help to explain one of the most puzzling features of the case, how the Ripper was able to escape so easily: "A female, even when stained with blood, wouldn't have rated a second glance during the East End panic. She could have walked anywhere at any time with the assurance that witnesses wouldn't register because all their observation faculties would be focused on men! The woman concerned might have been a midwife, which would account for her knowledge of anatomy. She would be familiar—probably friendly—with half the street girls in the district, nearly all of whom had children. She could carry surgical knives as belonging to the tools of her trade. And she could approach any woman without putting her on guard." That makes a lot more sense than a Masonic cabal, but it is equally unprovable.

See also: *Old Shakespeare.*

1889

MAYERLING   On January 29, 1889, Crown Prince Rudolf, of the House of Hapsburg, and heir apparent to the throne of the Austro-Hungarian Empire, was found dead in his bedroom at the Mayerling hunting lodge in the Vienna woods. The first public announcement said that the crown prince had died of a "heart attack." This story was believed by no one, and was soon followed by the account that Rudolf had died by his own hand, "while of unsound mind." This allowed Catholic Rudolf to be buried within the church though he was a suicide. Still, rumors about "The Mayerling Tragedy," as the incident became known, continued to fly. It was said that Rudolf's was not the only body found at Mayerling that day. Soon it was generally known that Rudolf's young mistress, seventeen-year-old Mary Vecsera, had also been found dead in Rudolf's bedroom at the hunting lodge.

The Imperial government launched an immediate investigation, and an immediate cover-up of the events. Witnesses who had been present at Mayerling, or who knew of incidents leading to the tragedy, were sworn or bribed to silence. The results of the full investigation were not made public; indeed, they have never been made public. Many who have investigated the subject believe that there was, and possibly still is, a package of "Mayerling papers" or a "Mayerling dossier" that contains much missing information. Thus the Mayerling tragedy has been surrounded with an air of mystery and of romance for nearly a century. The Emperor Franz Josef himself said "the truth is far worse than any of the versions." Count Joseph Hylos, who actually was at Mayerling that fateful evening, wrote to a friend: "His Highness is dead. That is all I can say. Do not ask for details. It is too frightful. I have given the Emperor my word that I shall not say a word about what I have seen."

The key to the tragedy lies in the character of Crown Prince

Rudolf himself. He was born in 1858, the only son (after three daughters) of the Emperor Franz Josef and the Empress Elizabeth. The Austro-Hungarian Empire was no longer the power that it had been in the heyday of the Hapsburgs, but it was still a major force to be reckoned with, and the crown prince, who it was assumed would one day rule the Empire, was an important person, not only in his own land but throughout Europe.

Rudolf appears to have been an intelligent, though rather high-strung, boy. The family, bound by rigid court etiquette, was not a close one. Rudolf's education was put into the hands of a variety of guardians, some rather bizarre. There was, for example, Count Gondrecourt, who believed in "hardening" his charge by doing such things as firing pistols in the child's bedroom in the middle of the night.

But by the time he reached his early teens, Rudolf fell under the influence of better teachers. He grew into a cultured and thoughtful young man, whose modern and liberal ideas contrasted sharply with the narrow conservatism of his father, and his father's government. This is not to imply that Rudolf was in any sense a democrat—far from it. It was his idea to reform the Empire, perhaps more along the lines of the British monarchy, so that it could continue to survive and prosper into the twentieth century. As soon as he came of age, Rudolf was given a post in the army, and he took to military life enthusiastically. But his ideas about reforming the army conflicted with those of the emperor and the emperor's principal advisers and ministers.

After Mayerling, many of those who wrote of Rudolf tended to dismiss him as a mere playboy. The charge is unfair. When Rudolf was given either military or diplomatic duties to carry out, he did so diligently. His letters and other writings show that he was well informed about politics. But it is true that Rudolf didn't spend all his time working. He was an enthusiastic, almost a compulsive, hunter. He loved parties, and he loved women. Of European royalty, Rudolf got along best with the Prince of Wales, himself a notorious womanizer.

Since the heir to the throne was himself expected to produce an heir, Rudolf was under some pressure to marry, and a search was launched for a suitable Catholic princess. There weren't too

Rudolf in 1888

many available. In 1880, he finally settled on Princess Stephanie, the daughter of King Leopold II of Belgium. She was a rather gauche and poorly educated girl, yet Rudolf seemed to genuinely like her—at first. Proper lineage, rather than romantic love, was then the basis for royal marriages.

From the time of his marriage until about 1886, Crown Prince Rudolf seemed to have everything in the world going for him. But there were serious problems just beneath the surface, and they were to become increasingly apparent in the years that preceded his death. The most obvious problem was that his father neither liked nor trusted him. It is doubtful that the stiff and formal Franz Josef could really have liked or trusted any potential rival—and an heir is always a potential rival—but he was certainly put off by many of his son's ideas. The crown prince was given a fair number of empty titles and ceremonial duties, but very little real work, and real power. His ideas about politics were dismissed almost contemptuously.

His marriage, which had started out promisingly, soon fell

apart, and Rudolf and Stephanie came to genuinely dislike each
other. They had one daughter, Elizabeth, but Stephanie could
never have another child. The reason: she had contracted the venereal disease gonorrhea from her husband. Many women had
recovered from the disease, but in Stephanie's case it had spread,
and made her sterile.

Illness was probably the chief reason for Rudolf's decline.
Not only did he have a virulent case of gonorrhea, he also had
syphilis. By 1886, Rudolf was in almost constant pain, and to ease
it, he took ever-increasing quantities of morphine. He was probably addicted to the drug. In addition, Rudolf had become a heavy
drinker.

Though Rudolf was the heir apparent to the throne of the
Austro-Hungarian Empire, in reality his prospects were very poor.
He would almost certainly not inherit the throne, for his father
was in far better health than he was. He could never have a son
who would inherit the throne, for even if he could somehow re-
marry, the disease had made him sterile as well. He had no influence
on the conduct of the affairs of state. His married life was a disaster,
and pain and disease prevented him from enjoying a life of idle
pleasure. Rudolf may also have brooded upon the strain of madness
in his mother's family. His mother's cousin, for example, was
known as Mad Ludwig of Bavaria. Ludwig had drowned himself
after being declared insane.

There is no doubt that by 1888 Rudolf was thinking seriously
of suicide. He read every newspaper account of suicide that he
could find. He talked of it often, and kept a loaded pistol and
human skull on his desk. Yet he seems to have felt that he lacked
the courage to commit the act on his own. He tried to talk a couple
of his army friends into joining him in a suicide pact, but they
refused. In December 1888, he proposed to his longtime mistress,
Mizzi Caspar, that they go to the park together and kill themselves.
She declined the honor. Mizzi was alarmed and warned the police,
but she was told not to say a word about Rudolf's intentions to
anyone. The emperor and empress seemed to have known nothing
of their son's state of mind.

On November 5, 1888, Rudolf met the perfect partner for
his suicide scheme, a pretty but rather flighty and hopelessly ro-

Mary Vecsera

mantic seventeen-year-old girl named Mary Vecsera, who came from a well-to-do and socially ambitious family.

Mary apparently had little difficulty slipping away from her chaperones to join the crown prince on numerous occasions over the next two months. But when the affair became public knowledge, there was a stormy scene between Mary and her mother, the Countess Vecsera. On January twenty-sixth or -seventh, the emperor summoned his son and ordered him to stop seeing Mary. After a heated interview, Rudolf said he would agree, if he could see Mary one more time. The emperor, who had no idea of what was being planned, gave his consent.

For seventeen-year-old Mary, suicide alongside her royal lover must have seemed a grand and romantic notion. She was much interested in the popular Wagner opera *Tristan and Isolde*, with its theme of love and death. Mary had made out her will, and was dropping broad hints of what was to come.

On January 28, 1889, Mary once again sneaked away from

her family to meet Rudolf, and they both drove together to the Mayerling hunting lodge. There were several other guests, who were apparently unaware of Mary's presence. Rudolf excused himself from going out hunting that day, saying he had a "heavy cold." The couple spent a good part of the day writing farewell letters. The one Mary wrote to her mother read:

"Forgive me for what I have done; I could not resist love. In agreement with him I wish to be buried by his side at Alland churchyard. I am happier in death than in life."

At 6:15 on the morning of January 29, Rudolf appeared at the door of his bedroom in his dressing gown. He told his valet to fetch breakfast and wake him at 7:30. When the time came, the valet found the door locked, and there was no answer to his knocking. At 8 A.M., Rudolf's companions, Prince Philip of Coberg and Count Hoyos, broke into the bedroom. They found Mary dead in the bed, and the body of Rudolf slumped nearby in a chair.

Almost immediately an attempt was made to deny that Mary had been at Mayerling at all. Her body was spirited away, and it was rumored that two of her uncles actually propped up the corpse between them and drove around with it to give the false impression that Mary was still alive. But her death at Mayerling soon became public knowledge. She was buried, not with her lover but in an obscure grave.

A number of disturbing unanswered questions remain about the Mayerling tragedy.

While it is clear that Rudolf involved a rather foolish and very young girl in his suicidal plot (and thus was a murderer in spirit if not in fact), it is not at all clear that Mary actually committed suicide. We do know that Mary died from four to six hours before Rudolf. But did she kill herself, or did Rudolf shoot her? Some who have read her final letters believe that Mary was not convinced she was really going to die. In his letter to his mother, Rudolf wrote, "I have committed murder," though he does not say whom he murdered. An autopsy report on Mary would clarify this question, but the report, like so much else, is missing. If Rudolf shot Mary, that would make the tragedy even more shocking for the House of Hapsburg.

Was Rudolf involved in a treasonous plot against his father, and did its exposure trigger his suicide? This has long been rumored, but once again the documentary evidence (if any) is missing.

Why didn't the government do something about Rudolf's suicidal intentions? While the emperor and empress may not have known of their son's state of mind, other government officials certainly did. The court was riddled with police spies and informers, and the conservative government kept a close and unfriendly eye on the liberal crown prince. Besides, Rudolf made no secret of his intentions.

Which leads to another question: Did Rudolf actually shoot himself? Rudolf certainly wanted to shoot himself, but in the past he seemed to lack the courage. In the hours after Mary's death, did he lose his nerve again? In her biography of Crown Prince Rudolf, Judith Listowel concluded from a study of the existing evidence, and from those who may have had access to the missing Mayerling Papers, that the government had dispatched a group of specially trained sharpshooters to Mayerling. "They were given explicit orders that if the Crown Prince had not taken his own life by 6:30 A.M. they were to shoot him. Rudolf was unable to carry out his desperate intention and accordingly at about 7 A.M. the two Roll Commando sharpshooters entered his room through the window and shot him."

And, finally, where are the "Mayerling Papers" that might have cleared up these questions? They were not found in the Imperial Archives when the archives were opened at the end of the First World War. Some papers had been given to the prime minister, Count Eduard Taaffe, and, according to some stories, they were destroyed by a fire. Other accounts say that the Mayerling Papers were sent for safekeeping to the Vatican, where they are still kept in utmost secrecy.

At present there is no way to prove or disprove any of these rumors.

1892

LIZZIE BORDEN

Lizzie Borden took an axe
And gave her mother forty whacks.
When she saw what she had done
She gave her father forty-one.

This is the most celebrated bit of doggerel about an American, or probably any other, murder case anywhere. Yet Lizzie Borden was never convicted of giving her mother or anyone else any "whacks." (The actual number was twenty-nine.) Not only was she unconvicted, Lizzie Borden had, and still has, staunch defenders who believe that she never committed any crime, and the grisly murder of the Bordens on a stifling hot day in August 1892 remains unsolved.

The scene of the tragedy was 92 Second Street, in Fall River, Massachusetts, a small industrial city. The principal actors were Andrew Jackson Borden, a man in his seventies, successful in business, highly respectable, but reputed to be very tight with his money, unimaginative, joyless, and stern. His wife Abby was an extremely stout woman of about sixty-four. Though the couple had been married for some twenty-eight years, Abby was Borden's second wife. He had remarried after the death of his first wife. The Borden children, two girls, were from his first marriage. Lizzie herself was the youngest; she was thirty-two at the time of the murders. Her older sister Emma was forty-one. They all lived in the two-story house on Second Street. Supporting characters in this drama were an Irish servant, Bridget Sullivan, and John Vinnicum Morse, a brother of the first Mrs. Borden, who happened to be visiting at the time of the killings.

The Borden household was not a particularly cheerful one. Lizzie and Emma were known to harbor long-standing resentments against their stepmother. They had also, from time to time, complained about their father's tight-fisted ways. But there were no violent arguments or threats. Nothing that would lead one to expect any sort of domestic violence.

Just two days before the murders, there was a curious incident at the Borden home. After eating dinner, both Mr. and Mrs. Borden became violently ill. Lizzie also claimed that she had been sick, though not as severely. The day of the murders, maid Bridget Sullivan had also been very sick to her stomach. Later, it was said that Lizzie had tried to purchase prussic acid, a deadly poison, from a local druggist. The druggist would not sell her the poison, and no trace of the substance was found in the stomach of the elder Borden. Lizzie herself denied ever having tried to buy the acid. The day before the murders, John Morse arrived. He ate at the house without any ill effects.

The day of the murder, sister Emma was away visiting friends in nearby Fairhaven. Morse had left the house about about 8:30 A.M. on business. Mr. Borden went out at about 9:00 A.M. Three women—Lizzie, her mother, and the maid Bridget—were then presumably alone. They busied themselves with a variety of chores in and around the house. Lizzie claimed that part of the time she had been in the barn. Bridget also went briefly to the barn to fetch a pail and brushes for window washing. The last undisputed act of Mrs. Borden was to go upstairs to change pillowcases in the guest room. When Mr. Borden returned home shortly before eleven, he had some trouble getting in, for the door was triple-locked. Bridget let him in, and as she did, Lizzie, who was at the top of the stairs, laughed. Lizzie told her father that Mrs. Borden had gone out because she had received a note from someone who was sick. It has never been established who the note came from, or indeed if there ever was a note. Bridget then went upstairs to her room, because she was still feeling ill. At 11:15, she was awakened by Lizzie, who was shouting, "Come down quick; Father's dead; someone came in and killed him!"

Bridget was sent across the street to fetch the family's physician and friend Dr. Bowen. He was not immediately available. And then Bridget asked the question that was to be asked by practically everybody over the next few months: "Miss Lizzie, where were you when this thing happened?"

The reply was: "I was out in the yard, and heard a groan, and came in and the screen door was wide open."

A neighbor, attracted by the excitement, asked Lizzie where her mother was.

"I don't know; she had a note to go see someone who was sick, but I don't know but that she is killed too, for I thought I heard her come in . . . Father must have an enemy, for we have all been sick, and we think the milk has been poisoned."

The police arrived, followed almost immediately by Dr. Bowen. Then, for the first time, witnesses entered the sitting room, where Lizzie said the body lay. It had been Andrew Jackson Borden's habit to nap on the horsehair sofa in the sitting room. That is apparently what he was doing when the murderer struck and hacked him viciously around the head and face with some sort of sharp instrument. There were no signs of a struggle, no indication that Borden even knew what hit him. He was probably killed by the first blow, and the rest were administered in a rage, or simply to make sure the old man was really dead.

Dr. Bowen was shocked.

"Physician that I am, and accustomed to all kinds of horrible sights, it sickened me to look upon the dead man's face."

He estimated that Mr. Borden had not been dead for more than about twenty minutes. That means that Lizzie must have summoned Bridget within five minutes of the actual murder.

Lizzie, who remained remarkably self-possessed despite the horrifying discovery, then suggested that Mrs. Borden should be located. She had already hinted her stepmother "is killed too." Bridget, accompanied by one of the neighbor women, went upstairs, and there they found Mrs. Borden. She was in the guest room, and may have been kneeling down to tuck in the sheets at the edge of the bed when the assailant struck. Once again the victim had been viciously hacked about the head. The wounds on Mrs. Borden were not as fresh as those of her husband, and the killing might have taken place anywhere from an hour to two hours before the body was discovered.

The Fall River police were so shocked by the brutal murders that they were rather slow to react and investigate thoroughly. It is possible that in the hours after the crimes were discovered, vital evidence was lost or destroyed.

One of the first reactions of many people in Fall River was to attribute the crimes to an outsider, a "tramp." There were unconfirmed reports of a "wild-eyed" stranger having been seen in the vicinity. But none of these rumors produced any solid evidence.

The Borden house was not an isolated one. There were plenty of neighbors around who would almost certainly have noticed any stranger. Then there was Bridget, and Lizzie herself. They saw no strangers, wild-eyed or otherwise.

The scenario for the murder of Mr. and Mrs. Borden by an outsider was highly improbable. The stranger would have had to have crept unseen into the house in the middle of the morning, killed Mrs. Borden almost noiselessly, then either sneaked out or hidden somewhere in the not very large house for an hour or more until Mr. Borden returned, come downstairs, and killed him without a struggle. Then the stranger would have had to escape immediately, almost certainly wearing clothes covered with blood, for the crime had been an exceptionally bloody one. In crime fiction, such things happen regularly. In reality, they happen rarely, if at all.

From the very start, investigators suspected that Lizzie herself knew more than she was saying, and indeed might be an accomplice in the crime. Rapidly the idea grew that Lizzie was the sole perpetrator of the crime.

Suspicion of Lizzie grew partly from her reactions immediately after the bodies were discovered. She seemed too calm; she was too quick to hint that her stepmother had been murdered, even before the body was found. Lizzie's account of her own movements during the morning of the murder was not entirely credible. For example, she said she had gone to the barn to find some lead for sinkers with which to go fishing. Yet she had no fishing line or hooks. She claimed to have spent something like twenty minutes—the critical period just before her father was killed—in the barn loft. But the barn loft was the hottest place on the Borden property, and the day itself was exceptionally hot. Lizzie never denied that she disliked her stepmother. Both she and her sister would profit handsomely from the deaths of their parents. Lizzie may even have feared that she would be cut out of her father's will. But what weighed most heavily against Lizzie in the minds of the investigators was the sheer improbability that anyone else could have committed the crime. Only the maid, Bridget Sul-

A drawing made during the trial of Lizzie Borden. She has her hand on her chin. Sister Emma has a hand over her eyes.

livan, who was also in the house at the time of the murders, would have had as good an opportunity. Yet at the time she was not suspected at all. Bridget had an excellent reputation, and absolutely no known motive for killing the Bordens. Besides, if Lizzie had been where she said she was during the period of the murders, it would have been almost impossible for Bridget to have done the deeds without being observed.

Though there was no eyewitness account, no "smoking gun," the weight of the circumstantial evidence against Lizzie Borden was compelling. She was indicted, and in June 1893 brought to trial. The case attracted an enormous amount of attention, and all of New England, and particularly all of Fall River, was divided into pro- and anti-Lizzie factions.

Lizzie Borden's greatest assets were her sex and her respectability. An awful lot of people simply could not believe that this thirty-two-year-old woman, without a hint of scandal attached to her life, could possibly have hacked her parents to death. Fall River's leading ministers were firmly in Lizzie's corner. They often accompanied her to court. Her cause was also aided by groups such as the women's auxiliary of the YMCA and the Women's Christian Temperance Union. Lizzie had always been active in church affairs. It is also possible that there were those in Fall River who thought tight-fisted old man Borden "got what he deserved."

There were two major shortcomings to the prosecution case. First, the lack of a weapon. A small axe that could have been used as the murder weapon was found in the cellar of the Borden home. But if it was the murder weapon, it had been washed clean of blood. A more serious problem was the lack of bloodstains on Lizzie's clothes. She had plenty of time to change her dress after the murder of her mother, but there was almost certainly not enough time to change clothes after the murder of her father. However, there was a large roll of paper in the house, some of which might have been used for protection. She might also have worn the murdered man's coat. It was found blood-soaked and folded at the head of the couch, rather than hanging up, as it normally would have been. There was a good deal of confusion as to what dress Lizzie actually was wearing on the fatal day, indicating that she may have worn more than one. She was observed burning a dress in the stove the day after the murder. The dress had been splattered with paint, she said, and it was a family custom to burn old dresses.

It would seem that the evidence against Lizzie Borden was compelling, even overwhelming; yet the jury deliberated less than an hour before bringing in a verdict of "not guilty." Later, jury members reported that they stayed out that long only so that they would not give the appearance of having made a hasty judgment.

Most of the press of New England applauded the verdict. But in Fall River itself, there was a feeling of outrage in some quarters. For years, on the anniversary of the murders, the *Fall River Globe* printed a series of long articles that revived the case and virtually accused Lizzie of being the killer. Libel laws were less strict in the nineteenth century.

However, Lizzie did not leave Fall River, though she moved from the rather plain family home to a more elegant and spacious house about a half-mile from the murder site. For a time, Lizzie shared the home with her older sister, Emma, but they quarreled over money, and Emma moved elsewhere. Lizzie, who now preferred to be called Lizbeth, lived quietly though not reclusively until her death in 1927. At that time, she had an estate of more than two hundred thousand dollars, some thirty thousand of which she bequeathed to a society for the prevention of cruelty to animals.

Though the jury at Fall River exonerated Lizzie Borden, in the years since 1893 the general presumption has grown that she was indeed guilty. No solid evidence linking anyone else to the crime has been found. But even today, Lizzie has her defenders. Some crime writers who have reexamined the case have suggested that sister Emma could have returned from Fairhaven in time to commit the crime. Others have accused Bridget Sullivan. If either of these two was involved, however, it is more likely they were passive accomplices.

Yet, there are undeniably some unanswered, and probably unanswerable, questions about this celebrated case. The core question is still the same as it was in August 1892. Could this otherwise respectable woman coldly commit a brutal double murder? It is probably easier to answer yes to that question today than it was in the late nineteenth century. Yet there remains a nagging doubt.

3

Was It A Crime?

????

SWEENEY TODD   The most celebrated murderer who never was is Sweeney Todd, called the "Demon Barber of Fleet Street." Accounts of Sweeney Todd first began to appear in print in the cheap sensationalistic publications called "penny dreadfuls" that became extremely popular in England during the early Victorian era. Though these publications were enormously popular and probably highly influential on the Victorian public's imagination, their history is not well documented.

E. F. Bleiler, an expert on popular literature of the era, has written about one of the most prolific of the "dreadful" writers:

"Thomas Peckett Prest's work has an unbelievable reputation in certain circles, but his books are seldom read (even if they can be found), being nearly unreadable. He is now best remembered for his connection with the legendary history of Sweeney Todd. *The String of Pearls*, begun (according to tradition) by George McFarren and finished by Prest, first gave to the world the great story of the Demon Barber of Fleet Street. Sweeney had a tilting barber's chair, a trapdoor, and a basement where he made veal pies out of his customers. The pies were sold next door. Stage versions of Sweeney Todd are still given in Great Britain, and not many years ago one of these plays was still in print. Removed some distance from the original novel, it has become sort of a pseudo-folkplay, given in the same tongue-in-cheek way as the story of Maria Marten and the Red Barn."

The highly melodramatic play inspired America's leading writer and composer of musical theater, Stephen Sondheim, to create a show based on the story. It was called, naturally enough, *Sweeney Todd*, and it ensures that the tale of the murderous barber will continue to be retold in the modern era.

The story of Maria Marten was based on a very real murder of the Regency era, and it has always been generally assumed that the Sweeney Todd story, too, had some basis in an actual crime or series of crimes. However, scholars who have checked the police records of the era in which Sweeney Todd was reputed to have lived (and these records are surprisingly good) can find no trace of anyone by that name, any murderous barber by any name, or any case at all that seems to have served as an inspiration to the writers of the original penny dreadful tale. There may be a link to a fourteenth-century French ballad or series or early nineteenth-century Parisian murders. But this is sheer speculation. Sweeney Todd, therefore, may be entirely a creature of the imagination.

If there is any historical figure who inspired the character of Sweeney Todd, it must have been Sawney Bean, a reputed mass murderer and cannibal of fifteenth-century Scotland. But Sawney Bean himself has acquired semilegendary status. Bean was the brutal and illiterate son of a sheepherder. He was supposed to have run off with a woman nearly as bestial as himself, and according to one chronicle, "These two took up their habitation in a cave by the seaside on the shore of the county of Galloway; where they lived upward of twenty-five years without going into any city, town or village."

During these years, Bean and his wife and their many offspring, some through incest, lived by robbing, murdering, and eating travelers coming from Edinburgh. During their long reign of terror, they are reputed to have killed some fifteen hundred people—though the figure sounds absurdly high.

One day, so the story goes, the Bean family slipped up and allowed a potential victim to escape. The man fled to Glasgow, telling his story to the king, who responded by sending an army to route out the cannibals. Dogs led the soldiers to the huge cave that was the Bean family lair, and there they found parts of human bodies "hung up in rows, like dried beef." The family members were captured, after quite a struggle, and taken to Leith, where they were immediately burned at the stake. "They all in general died without the least sign of repentance."

Though there may be more basis in reality for Sawney Bean than Sweeney Todd, that story, too, was turned into at least one penny dreadful, with the title of *Sawney Bean: The Maneater of Midlothian.*

1857

MADELEINE SMITH   There is in Scottish law the verdict "not proven," which is somewhere halfway between guilty and not guilty. With that verdict the jury is saying to the defendant, "We think you did it, but we don't have the evidence to hang you" or, more charitably, "We think you did it, but we don't want to hang you." The defendant is freed, but a cloud of suspicion remains. When, on July 9, 1857, the verdict "not proven" was announced in the trial of Madeleine Smith for the poisoning of her lover Pierre Emile L'Angelier, there was cheering in the courtroom. One suspects that an awful lot of people who cheered figured that Madeleine had dosed Emile with arsenic, but that since he was a seducer, a fortune hunter, and a foreigner he probably deserved what he got. A closer examination of the case indicates that the verdict "not proven" was quite a proper one on the basis of the evidence that had been introduced in court. But that is not the same as saying Madeleine didn't do it.

Madeleine Smith was the eldest child of a well-to-do and highly respectable family in Glasgow. She was, as events were to show, intelligent, proud, passionate, adventurous, and determined. She was also supposed to have been beautiful, though the one surviving drawing of her in court shows her looking rather hawk-like. Still, in 1855, Madeleine Smith caught the eye of Emile L'Angelier, and he went through great trouble to be introduced to her.

Emile was from the Isle of Jersey, though, as his name implies, he was of French extraction and he had spent some years in Paris. He claimed to have served briefly in the French National Guard, which helped to crush the revolution of 1848. However, Emile was something of a braggart, and this part of his life is impossible to confirm. He also boasted of his experience with women. He was employed in Glasgow as a poorly paid shipping clerk. Though he had the reputation of being hardworking and a regular churchgoer, his friends also described him as being very restless and dissatisfied. When he first saw Madeleine, he was twenty-six, she nineteen.

There was a vast social gap between the clerk and the daughter of a prosperous family, who was expected to make a "good marriage." His prospects were poor, yet Madeleine seemed receptive to Emile's good looks and charm. He had lived in France, and had once been engaged to be married; her experience outside of the tight circle of her family was a strict boarding school in London. It was obvious to Madeleine that her family, particularly her autocratic Victorian father, would never approve of any sort of relationship between her and the clerk, so the pair established a secret correspondence using the Smiths' servants and a sympathetic elderly woman friend of Emile's named Mary Perry as confidential go-betweens. Emile carefully saved Madeleine's letters, and they were all made public at the trial.

The letters chronicle the growing intimacy between Madeleine and Emile, their professed plans for marriage, and their sexual experiences. Madeleine, though she was raised in the most Victorian of Victorian surroundings, was quite frank about her enjoyment of sex, and there is nothing in the letters to indicate that she believed there was anything unusually depraved about her feelings. Historian Mary S. Hartmann observes about the letters that they raise doubts "concerning some received opinions about Victorian beliefs and behavior." The couple did not seem to have had any great trouble finding places to meet, either. Madeleine often was able to sneak Emile into her family home at night, the Smiths apparently being remarkably sound sleepers. Mr. Smith did finally figure out what was going on and forbade Madeleine to see Emile anymore, but after some hesitation she ignored her father's wishes and their clandestine affair continued. At the height of the affair, Madeleine expressed her willingness to marry her lover, even without her family's approval; but Emile did not wish to marry a girl who might be cast off without a penny. He was determined to marry Madeleine and be accepted into the Smith family, no matter how long it took.

By the autumn of 1856, Madeleine had become disenchanted and bored with her lover. Unknown to Emile, she became engaged

Madeleine Smith

to an older man, William Minnoch, who was a friend of the Smith family. She tried to break off her affair with Emile by saying that it was clear he no longer loved her, and that "you deserve a better wife than I." What she meant was she no longer loved him and wanted a better husband.

All of Emile's correspondence was destroyed by Madeleine, but it is clear that he was not to be easily dismissed. His trump card was that he threatened to show all her letters to her father, thus ruining her reputation and chance for marriage. It was going to be him or no one.

At first Madeleine seems to have been panic-stricken by the threat and begged Emile to return the letters. "No one can know the intense agony of mind I have suffered last night and today. Emile, my father's wrath would kill me. You little know his temper. Emile, for the love you once had for me do not denounce me to my P [papa]." Emile would not back down, and quickly Madeleine changed her tactics.

A few days later, Madeleine wrote, "I hope to see you very soon. Write me for next Thursday, and then I can tell you when I can see you." February 19, 1857, five days after that letter was posted, Emile was taken violently ill with stomach pains in the middle of the night. He went to the doctor and was given some medicine, which eased the symptoms.

On February 21, Madeleine bought and signed for a quantity of arsenic at the shop of a Mr. Murdoch. She said it was "for rats." On February 22, Emile suffered another and even more serious attack of stomach pains and vomiting. He was so ill he had to stay away from work for over a week.

On March 6, Madeleine bought arsenic from the shop of a Mr. Currie. Once again there was nothing secretive about the purchase, and she signed for the poison, as the law required. She even had a friend with her. Emile took a brief holiday, but on the twenty-first was summoned back to Glasgow by an urgent letter from Madeleine: "Why, my beloved, did you not come to me? Oh, beloved, are you well? Come to me, sweet one. I waited and waited for you, but you came not."

Emile returned to Glasgow on the twenty-second, looking and feeling much better. He went out that evening at nine o'clock. At about half past two in the morning, his landlady was awakened by a violent ringing of the bell; Emile L'Angelier was so doubled up with pain that he was unable to use his pass key.

A doctor was sent for immediately. Emile lingered for hours, and apparently felt he was getting better—but then he died. A postmortem examination indicated that his stomach contained massive doses of arsenic.

Over the next week there were two curious and unexplained incidents. Emile's friend Mrs. Perry, who had played an important role in the affair, went to see Madeleine's mother. What they talked about is unknown. A few days later, Madeleine tried to flee from Glasgow, but she was brought back by her family.

Once the death by poisoning had been established, and the cache of letters had been discovered, Madeleine was arrested and swiftly brought to trial. She did not testify in her own behalf, but she issued a statement that she had not seen Emile for three weeks prior to his death, and that she had purchased the arsenic for her complexion—not an uncommon practice.

Madeleine's trial at the High Court of Justiciary in Edinburgh created a sensation. Her very frank letters were read out in court to an audience that probably was not nearly as shocked as it was supposed to be. No other members of the Smith family appeared in court; in true Victorian fashion, the elder Smiths pleaded illness and took to their beds. Madeleine, however, remained remarkably cool and self-possessed throughout the trial. The weight of evidence was strongly against her, but her defense, which was brilliantly conducted, hammered away at weak points in the prosecution's case. The weakest point was that the prosecution could present no evidence that Emile had been with Madeleine in the hours before any of his three attacks. Actually, a pocket notebook had been found among his effects that had many incriminating notations. "Saw Mimi [his nickname for Madeleine] for few moments. Was very ill during the night." The date was February 19. A few days later, "Saw Mimi in drawing room. Promised me French Bible. Taken very ill." The notations were devastating, but they were not allowed as evidence. The theory was that a person might put any sort of accusation in a diary, and without a chance to cross-examine the individual who had made the notations (in this case the dead man), such evidence was inadmissible. Said the judge, "A man might have threatened another, he might have hatred against him and be determined to revenge himself, and what entries might he not make in a diary for this purpose."

Another point that the defense fastened upon was that Emile could not possibly have ingested a large quantity of the sort of arsenic Madeleine had purchased without knowing that he was being poisoned. This arsenic was mixed either with charcoal or indigo, specifically so that it could not be taken by accident. This "over-the-counter arsenic" had a characteristic taste and gritty texture that would have been nearly impossible to disguise, no matter what it had been mixed with. The defense hinted that Emile took medicines with arsenic or was a confirmed arsenic-eater. Arsenic was believed to be an aphrodisiac. Emile had also boasted of taking arsenic, but there was no evidence that he ever purchased any. The defense hinted more strongly that Emile might have committed suicide. He had also, on occasion, threatened suicide, but, as noted, he was an extravagant talker. F. Tennyson Jesse, who reviewed this case for *Famous Trials*, calls Emile the real mystery. "Madeleine herself, innocent or guilty, is a comparatively straightforward proposition; it is L'Angelier, that little scheming, sensual, iron-willed, lady-killer who is the insoluble riddle."

Jesse observes that if Emile had decided to commit suicide, he certainly chose a slow and extremely painful way of doing so. "This, however, is not by any means a conclusive argument. Human nature holds so much that is strange, and L'Angelier in particular was a man of such devious ways that it is just possible he might have planned to revenge himself on Madeleine by suicide. He may have meant the moral blame for his self-killing to be laid at her door, or he may even—for nothing is too fantastic to happen in real life—have killed himself, meaning her to be accused of his murder; but if either of these suppositions be true, it is strange that he failed to ensure that they should occur. He had only to let fall, when lying in his death agony, some remark . . . for the onus of the deed to be firmly fixed on Madeleine, but through all those hours of agonized consciousness he said no word of her."

But, on the other hand, if Madeleine had poisoned him, he surely would not have been unaware of this, or at least deeply suspicious. Three times she had given him something to eat or drink, and three times he had fallen violently ill. Did he, in the end, try to protect his love?

"He had shown himself entirely relentless to Madeleine up to that time, he was prepared to ruin her life, and yet when, as he must have believed, she had committed the last betrayal of him, he closes his lips. There is nothing in the whole of the case so strange as the problem of L'Angelier's mind and soul during those last hours of his life. No possible solution to the riddle of his death provides any possible solution to the riddle of his life," writes Jesse.

Whether such considerations weighed upon the mind of the jury is unknown. It was reported that the majority believed she was guilty, but shrank from the inevitable punishment, death or a long jail sentence, and so returned "not proven."

The spectators in the court broke into cheers when the verdict was announced. Madeleine was calmly led out of a side door and went home to her family in Glasgow. Later, she wrote to the matron of the Edinburgh prison where she had been kept during the trial: "You shall be glad to hear that I am well—in fact, I am quite well, and my spirits are not in the least down . . . The feeling in the west is not so good towards me as you kind Edinburgh people showed me. I rather think it shall be necessary for me to leave Scotland for a few months . . ."

Madeleine Smith had not been crushed by her ordeal, nor was she weighed down with guilt, if indeed she was guilty. The entire Smith family left Glasgow, and Madeleine eventually moved to London, where she drifted into a circle of artists who were less concerned about respectability. In 1861, she married an artist named George Wardle, who became a close associate of William Morris. The couple settled in Bloomsbury, had two children, and joined the Socialist League with Morris. After her husband's death around the turn of the century, Madeleine moved to the United States and remarried. She outlived her second husband and continued to live in Brooklyn, where she died in 1928 at the age of ninety-three.

See also: *Florence Maybrick.*

1865

THE TICHBORNE CLAIMANT

The missing heir who suddenly turns up alive after being presumed dead for many years is a staple of melodrama. Yet in the mid-nineteenth century, just this sort of melodrama played out for years in the courts and in the press of Victorian England. The central figure was a man who claimed to be Roger Charles Doughty Tichborne, heir to one of Britain's oldest fortunes.

Roger Tichborne was born in 1829. His father, James Francis Tichborne, owned a title and a huge estate, which Roger was to inherit. In 1853, Roger set out on an extended tour of South America, going first to Chile, then to Argentina and Brazil. In 1854, he boarded the ship *Bella* in Rio; the ship, with Roger on it, disappeared without a trace. The assumption was that the *Bella* sank and all on board were lost, so in 1855 Roger Tichborne was officially declared dead.

But Roger's mother refused to accept the fact of her son's death, and when her husband Sir James Tichborne died in 1862, she began a campaign to locate the missing Roger. She put ads in newspapers all over the world asking about information about the fate of her son. In November 1865, Lady Tichborne got a letter from Australia that said there was a man named Thomas Castro who was working as a butcher in a remote town called Wagga Wagga in the Australian outback, and that this man was, in reality, Roger Tichborne.

Lady Tichborne was overjoyed and immediately sent for the man, who afterward became known as the Tichborne claimant. The claimant was not an attractive fellow. He was grossly fat and seemed both ignorant and coarse. Yet Lady Tichborne accepted him immediately, as did some others who had known Roger. After all, no one had seen Roger in over fourteen years, and people can change a lot. The claimant said he had been seriously ill, and both his memory and his appearance had been affected.

The Tichborne claimant

Most members of the family did not accept the claimant, however. And those most strongly opposed were those who stood to lose a great deal by the sudden reappearance of the real Roger Tichborne. After Roger had been declared dead, his younger brother Alfred had inherited the estates and the title. But Alfred, too, had died at about the time the claimant arrived in England, and the inheritance passed to Alfred's son and his family. They all said the claimant was lying and set out to prove it.

The claimant's enemies hired investigators who found evidence to indicate that the claimant was really one Arthur Orton, son of an English butcher. Orton had become a sailor, and in 1849 had deserted his ship while in Chile. For a while he had lived with a family named Castro and had taken their name. Later, he went to Australia. Then, in 1862, when he heard of Lady Tichborne's search, Orton fabricated the story about being the missing heir. He was, in short, a con man.

The claimant admitted that he had stayed with the Castro family while in Chile, but hadn't Roger Tichborne been in Chile, too? He insisted he was the rightful heir and sued to get his part of the Tichborne fortune.

After a long delay, in which charges by one side against the other filled the air, the case was finally brought to court in 1871. More than a hundred people who had known Roger Tichborne trooped to the witness stand to swear that the claimant was the missing heir. But when the claimant himself took the stand, he was a terrible witness and fatally damaged his own case. He didn't know his mother's maiden name, he knew little of the Tichborne estates, and he knew nothing at all about the school Roger had attended. In fact, he didn't seem to know much about Roger Tichborne at all. He sounded just like what his enemies claimed he was—the poorly educated son of a poor family. The jury threw the claimant's case out of court.

But that wasn't the end. The claimant was then arrested for perjury, and all the evidence was run through the courts a second time, in a trial that lasted 188 days. By all accounts, the claimant's lawyer wasn't particularly competent, and he was found guilty. The claimant's enemies had won the final battle, but the long, costly legal fight had put a severe strain on the Tichborne fortune, and the passions unleashed ripped the family apart.

The Victorian public had watched the whole drawn-out affair with fascination, and ultimately public opinion had come down firmly against the claimant. People even applauded when he was given a long prison sentence for fraud. But the claimant still had his defenders, who tried to keep his case alive.

During the fourteen years he spent in prison, the claimant stuck to his story that he was indeed the missing Roger. However, prison did not leave him unchanged. The claimant lost a great deal of weight, dropping from over three hundred and fifty pounds to about one hundred and fifty. As he shed the weight, his personality seemed to alter for the better. His letters became quite remarkably literate. In one, he quoted from the Psalms in Latin. The letters were completely out of character for the uneducated butcher's son, Arthur Orton. In short, the claimant began, for the first time, to sound like the man he had always claimed to be.

The claimant was released from prison in 1884 and died in poverty and near obscurity in 1898, still claiming to be Roger Tichborne.

The evidence for this famous case was gone over exhaustively in court, and reexamined several times since. It is unlikely that new evidence will ever turn up. The strong probability is that the Tichborne claimant was an impostor. But we do know that illness and great changes in weight can also cause personality changes, and so Douglas Woodruff, who wrote the definitive account of the case, concludes, "The great doubt still hangs suspended."

1889

FLORENCE MAYBRICK   This is a case that is suffused with arsenic. Florence Maybrick was convicted of poisoning her husband with arsenic. Yet evidence brought out during the trial indicated that James Maybrick had been a habitual "arsenic-eater." Even if Florence had fed her husband arsenic as alleged, that probably didn't kill him, for there wasn't enough arsenic found in his body at the time of his death to be fatal, particularly to a person who had built up a tolerance to the poison. It was Victorian morality more than murder that nearly got Florence Maybrick hanged.

Florence Chandler, of Mobile, Alabama, was only eighteen when she met Liverpool cotton broker James Maybrick on a transatlantic voyage in 1880. Her extravagant and social-climbing mother physically pushed Florie into marriage with the much older Maybrick, who she assumed was a very wealthy man. For the cotton broker she painted an exaggerated picture of her daughter's prospective inheritance. Maybrick was also a liar; his business was already in serious difficulty. It was a bad way to start a marriage. Still, the couple, after spending time in America, moved to Liverpool in 1882. Despite financial difficulties, they lived well, and more or less happily, for about six years.

Inevitably, problems arose. Florence, who had expected a wealthy husband, found living on a budget almost impossible. James was frantically engaged in keeping up appearances, and so the couple was living well beyond its means. The strain was telling.

Florence wrote: "I am utterly worn out, and in such a state of overstrained nervousness I am hardly fit for anything. Whenever the doorbell rings I feel ready to faint for fear it is someone coming to have an account paid . . . I would gladly give up the house tomorrow and move somewhere else but Jim says it would ruin him outright. For one must keep up appearances . . ."

There were other problems. Before he had married, James

had kept a mistress. After a few years of marriage, he apparently
went back to her; indeed he seems to have been something of a
womanizer in general. Florence was not a passive Victorian wife
who would either suffer in silence or look the other way. She was
very lively and a great favorite among the men she met socially.
Perhaps it was her American background that gave her a freedom
that more tradition-bound English women of the time would not

Florence Maybrick

have felt. Whether she had many affairs or was primarily a flirt is uncertain, but she certainly had one rather public affair with a cotton broker named Alfred Brierley, a bachelor about fifteen years younger than her husband.

In March 1889, Florence reserved rooms for Brierley and herself under the name of Mr. and Mrs. Thomas Maybrick, her brother and sister-in-law, at a London hotel that was known to be used by cotton brokers. Brierley was immediately recognized by some business associates and was mortified. He left after one night. Why Florence had acted so openly and rashly is unknown. She could have chosen a different hotel or a different name. Perhaps this was a deliberate provocation to get her husband to sue for divorce; perhaps it was an act of anger, or simple blunder. Whatever the reason, this act was to weigh heavily on her future. Over the next few weeks, there were violent arguments between the Maybricks. He blackened her eye and tore her clothes, and threatened that if she left she would never be allowed to see her children again.

James Maybrick fell ill on April 19. The primary symptoms were pains in the head and numbness. Then came stomach pains and almost constant vomiting. The illness grew worse; the doctors diagnosed gastritis and gave James a variety of medicines, but nothing seemed to help.

James's family already knew about the strained relations between him and his wife, and they were suspicious. They started listening to the servants' gossip. The children's nurse saw Mrs. Maybrick mixing a white powder into her husband's beef tea. A maid, appropriately named Alice Yapp, intercepted a letter from Florence to her lover Brierley and brought it to one of James's brothers. There was nothing in the letter to indicate that Florence was trying to poison her husband, but she indicated very clearly that she wished the affair with Brierley to continue. Florence was forbidden to bring any more food to her husband. A few days later, he was dead.

At first the doctors did not find anything suspicious about James Maybrick's death, but the family refused to allow a death certificate to be signed without further investigation. An autopsy turned up arsenic in James's body, and Florence was arrested for

his murder. She went on trial in July 1889. (This was shortly after
Britain had been alternately fascinated and horrified by the Jack
the Ripper murders.)

Arsenic figured heavily in the trial. Florence had been seen
soaking flypapers that contained arsenic—a common way of sep-
arating the poison. Florence had a perfectly natural explanation.
"The flypapers were bought with the intention of using them as a
cosmetic. Before my marriage, and since for many years I have
been in the habit of using a face-wash prescribed by Dr. Greggs
of Brooklyn. It consisted principally of arsenic, tincture of ben-
zoin, elderflower water and some other ingredients. This prescription I lost last April, and as at that time I was suffering from slight
eruption of the face, I thought I should like to try a substitute
myself. I was anxious to get rid of this eruption before I went to
a ball on the thirtieth of the month." She did go to the ball, while
her husband was near death, a fact that was not lost on the jury.
However, she had purchased the flypaper after James had been
taken ill. As for the white powder that she mixed with the beef
tea—Florence insisted her husband had asked for the powder.

Probably the most sensational new evidence brought out at
the trial was the information that James Maybrick had regularly
dosed himself with arsenic for years. He was not unique in this,
for arsenic was a common ingredient of many patent medicines,
and Maybrick was a notorious hypochondriac who constantly
downed all sorts of medicines and who had complained for years
of symptoms characteristic of the arsenic-eater. A druggist also
testified that Maybrick and other men from the cotton exchange
regarded arsenic-laced tonics as aphrodisiacs. He said that they
lined up regularly at his shop every morning for their dose. Maybrick was one of his best customers.

Maybrick's habit would explain the rather sinister fact that a
day after his death, bags containing several hundred grains of arsenic were found in the Maybrick home. Four years after the trial,
a friend of Maybrick said that he had supplied the arsenic, left over
from an industrial experiment, to Maybrick, who was very happy
to get it. Why Florence had to soak flypaper to get arsenic, which
seemed to have been in such abundant supply in her home, is not
known.

Doctors could not agree on the cause of Maybrick's death. Traces of arsenic were found in his body, but these did not seem large enough to cause death, particularly in somebody who had built up an immunity to the poison. One expert suggested that Maybrick had really died of severe gastroenteritis, and that the small doses of arsenic had been an irritant, nothing more. The possibility that Maybrick was an "arsenic addict" and that his death resulted from withdrawal of the poison was also raised.

So the medical evidence that a crime had been committed at all was at best ambiguous. Yet when the jury retired, it took a mere thirty-eight minutes to decide that Florence Maybrick was guilty. It is quite clear that she was condemned more for her adultery than on the strength of the evidence that she had committed murder.

In his charge to the jury, the judge told them: ". . . you must remember the intrigue which she carried on with this man Brierley and the feelings—it seems horrible to comparatively ordinary innocent people—a horrible and incredible thought that a woman should be plotting the death of her husband in order that she might be left at liberty to follow her own degrading vices."

Florence was sentenced to hang. The public had been rather evenly divided between supporters and opponents of Florence—but the speed of the judgment and the severity of the sentence shocked nearly everyone. There was an enormous public outcry, and the Home Office was forced to commute the sentence to life imprisonment. The reason given was that there was not enough evidence to conclude that James had actually been poisoned. The decision was conveyed to Florence only after she had spent days in solitary confinement listening to the sound of her gallows being constructed in the courtyard outside her cell.

But if there was no evidence a crime had been committed, there seemed no justification for keeping Florence in jail.

Agitation to free her continued for years, and she had particularly strong supporters in the United States, though by marrying an Englishman she had given up her United States citizenship. All efforts failed, and there was a rumor that the Home Office possessed secret information not revealed at the trial that proved Florence to be guilty. There was no secret information, though some authorities may have believed that she tried unsuccessfully to poison James. What was really keeping Florence Maybrick in jail was the attitude of Queen Victoria. The queen had very strong views on adultery, and was disappointed that Florence had not been hanged. She said she regretted that "so wicked a woman should escape by a mere legal quibble . . . but her sentence must never be further commuted." It wasn't, as long as the queen lived. Six months after Victoria's death, under the reign of the more tolerant Edward VII, Florence Maybrick was released. She had spent fifteen years in jail. After leaving prison in 1904 at the age of forty-one, Florence Maybrick wrote a book entitled *My Fifteen Lost Years*. She moved to the United States, where on October 23, 1941, she died in Kent, Connecticut.

One writer on the case states: "To some legal observers it appeared that Mrs. Maybrick had been cleared of the charge of murder; yet she was to serve a life sentence on a charge of attempted murder, for which she had never been tried."

See also: *Madeleine Smith*

1893

MURDER BY MAGIC   Can a magic spell cause a person to sicken and die? Most medical authorities would probably agree that if an individual believed strongly enough in the power of magic, and if those beliefs were supported by the society at large, a spell could have a devastating effect. The authorities would doubtless hasten to add that it is the belief and not the spell itself that would be the key element in the death. In the absence of belief, magic has no power.

Most stories of "murder by magic" come from relatively undeveloped or primitive societies—but this is not always the case. One of the best-known incidents of alleged murder by magic took place in France in the late nineteenth century. It came about because of an angry rivalry that had developed among occultists.

On one side was a defrocked priest called Abbé Boullan, who led a sect called the Work of Mercy. Despite the rather bland title, the group was said to be engaged primarily in sex orgies and black-magic rituals.

In 1886, the Boullan group was visited by a young occultist, Marquis Stanislas de Guaita. Guaita claimed he was disgusted by what he discovered, and the following year joined forces with another of Boullan's former followers, Oswald Wirth. So far, all is common enough, for schisms and personal rivalries are inevitable in groups, occult or otherwise. But Guaita and Wirth announced that they had judged Boullan and had condemned him. Later they insisted that they merely meant to expose the former priest as a scoundrel. But Boullan believed that the pair was out to destroy him through the use of black magic.

Though it is tempting to regard Boullan as a cynical faker, there is no doubt that in the face of what he regarded to be a magical attack, he was genuinely frightened. He believed in much of what he preached. Boullan was assisted by the clairvoyant Julie Thibault, who said that she "saw" Boullan's enemies putting his

Joseph-Antoine Boullan

portrait in a coffin—trying to kill him by imitative magic. Next she "saw" them saying a black mass against him. The black mass is an obscene parody of the catholic mass, and is used for summoning demons. Boullan retaliated with a series of frantic anathemas, conjurations, and incantations, but these seemed to have no effect upon his enemies. The novelist J. B. Huysmans, a friend of Boullan wrote, "Boullan jumps about like a tiger cat, clutching one of his hosts [communion wafers marked with blood and commonly used by black magicians] and invoking the aid of St. Michael and the eternal justicares of eternal justice. Then standing at his altar he cries, 'Strike down Peldan' [one of the Guaita group] . . ."

The climax of this bizarre magical warfare, which in occult literature is often referred to as the Battle of Bewitchment, was reached in 1893. On January 3, Boullan wrote to Huysmans saying that the new year was one of ill omen. "The figures $8 + 9 + 3 = 20$ form a combination which foreshadows bad news." Boullan did not explain what he meant, but it is possible that the explanation is that $8 + 9 + 3$ and $2 + 0 = 2$, the number of the devil. This sort of calculation was and still is common in numerology, and if you think that it is possible to come up with practically any conclusion you wish by using such calculations, you are right. Huysmans said, "During the previous night Julie Thibault dreamed of Guaita and in the early hours of the morning a black bird of death cried out. It was the herald of the attack." By the next day, January 4, Abbé Boullan was dead.

Now, it is quite impossible to confirm that magic had anything whatever to do with Boullan's death. People die suddenly all the time without the aid of black magic. Boullan was not a young man. But it is also not unreasonable to suspect that the strain of nearly six years of believing himself to be under some sort of powerful magical attack may have taken its toll on Boullan and contributed to his death. We do not know how the mind can affect the workings of the body, but we do know that it does.

Whatever the doctors might have said, Boullan's friends were convinced that he had been killed by Guaita's sorcery, and they said so in print. As a result, a real duel, one fought with pistols and not spells, was arranged between Guaita and Jules Bois, one of Boullan's supporters. Before the duel, each side did its best to disconcert the other by magic. On his way to the duel, one of Bois's carriage horses had a fit, and Bois was sure that magic had been responsible. In the duel itself, each man fired once, but no one was hit. Three days later, Bois fought another duel with a member of the Guaita group. This time his carriage overturned on the way to the dueling ground. He arrived battered and bleeding, but in the duel, which was fought with swords, no one was hurt. This ending to the celebrated magical battle was peaceful and almost comical.

See also: *The Black Dog Murder.*

1910

NATHANIEL MOORE   Young Nathaniel Ford Moore, heir
to the Rock Island railroad fortune, was one of the richest playboys
in Chicago around the turn of the century, and if gossip was to
be believed, and there was plenty of gossip, he was one of the most
dissolute.

Moore's favorite haunt was the celebrated Everleigh Club, an
expensive, exclusive, and, considering the nature of its business,
respectable bordello. Everyone knew about the club run by the
Everleigh sisters, Ada and Minna (nicknamed "the Scarlet Sisters"),
and it was protected by some of Chicago's most powerful and most
crooked politicians, such as John J. "Bathhouse" Coughlin and
Michael "Hinky Dink" Kenna. The Everleigh Club was the sort
of place a rich man could go without fear of being robbed or
assaulted, though there was the occasional beating or killing.

The club, located on Chicago's Dearborn Street, was beautifully furnished, and the Everleighs demanded that their girls appear stylish and charming. They also required a measure of good
behavior from their customers.

On January 8, 1910, Nathaniel Moore showed up at the Everleigh Club very drunk. Normally, the sisters refused admittance
to any customer who was obviously drunk, but in the case of a
regular customer like the very wealthy young Moore, this rule was
relaxed. However, Minna refused to allow the young man to be
served any more to drink. This enraged Moore, who was used to
having his own way.

Moore staggered out of the club and over to another bordello
in Chicago's red-light district, this one run by "Vic" (for Victoria)
Shaw. There, Moore proceeded to die. The Everleighs got a tip
that Shaw and some of the other local madams were going to try
to frame the Everleighs by sneaking the young man's body back
to the club, planting it in the furnace, and then calling the police.

A belief that Moore had not only died at the club, but that the Everleighs then tried to burn his body, would certainly hurt their playboy business and might even scare off some of their political support. That would open up the market for the competition.

Minna Everleigh was a forceful woman. As soon as she heard of the plot, she gathered some strong-arm supporters and marched over to Vic Shaw's. The corpse was discovered, the police informed, and the young man's body was shipped back to his family's Lake Shore Drive home rather than to the furnace of a whorehouse.

The official report of Moore's death stated that he died of a heart attack. Minna Everleigh insisted that it was an accidental but lethal mixture of morphine and champagne that did him in.

However, there were whispers that Moore had actually been murdered, though no one was sure how or why, and the wealthy family used their influence to cover up the even more shocking nature of his death and limit the scandal. No one has ever been fully satisfied that the full story of playboy Nathaniel Moore's death has ever been made public. But the alleged furnace plot became part of Chicago's rich folklore of the underworld.

1915

THE *LUSITANIA*   On Friday, May 7, 1915, the Cunard line's luxury passenger liner the *Lusitania*, sailing from New York to Liverpool, England, was destroyed off the Irish coast by a single torpedo fired by a German U-boat. The supposedly "unsinkable" ship went down in less than twenty minutes with an appalling loss of life—1,201 perished, nearly two-thirds of those who had boarded the vessel in New York.

Of those who died, 128 were American citizens, and while the sinking of the *Lusitania* did not lead directly to America's entry into World War I, it certainly helped to harden U.S. attitudes against Germany and ultimately influence President Woodrow Wilson's decision to join the Allies.

On the surface, it appeared as though the sinking was an act of sheer German barbarism, an unprovoked attack on an unarmed, civilian passenger liner. In February 1915, the Germans had declared the waters around Great Britain a war zone in which all vessels were liable to be attacked. Warnings published in American newspapers by the German Embassy appeared to indicate that the *Lusitania* was in special danger. But as one of the *Lusitania* passengers, American millionaire Alfred Vanderbilt, said, "Why should we be afraid of German submarines? We can outdistance any submarine afloat."

Off the Irish coast, the great ocean liner encountered the U-20, a small, slow, and not particularly well-armed German submarine. Vanderbilt was right: the *Lusitania* could easily have outrun the U-boat and remained well beyond the limited range of its torpedos. But, unaware of the danger, the *Lusitania* sailed directly toward the German ship. The captain of the U-20 could hardly believe his good fortune. The sub fired one small G-type torpedo, fitted with 290 tons of TNT. The torpedo slammed into the *Lusitania*'s starboard side and exploded. The damage from this one

The sinking of the *Lusitania* drawn from eyewitness accounts.

hit was substantial but should not have been severe enough to sink the ship. Less than a minute later, there was a second and even louder blast that tore a huge hole in the port side, allowing thousands of tons of water to rush in. It was this second explosion that really doomed the *Lusitania* and most of those aboard. Within moments, the great ship was listing badly. The lifeboats on the port side were swinging well away from the hull, while those on the starboard were hanging uselessly over the deck. Sometimes loaded boats crashed down on people standing under them. The water poured in so quickly that many people were trapped below deck. Those who actually managed to get away in the lifeboats reached shore rather easily. Other survivors were picked up hours later clinging to pieces of floating wreckage. It was weeks before the awful death toll was known.

The outrage in America was enormous, and the anger was deftly exploited by a British government eager to publicize yet another German atrocity. The Germans countered that, far from being a harmless civilian target, the *Lusitania* was carrying a large cargo of munitions, and in addition was heavily armed. These countercharges got very little notice in the United States press, but as it turned out they were probably true.

The British Admiralty has never admitted that the *Lusitania* was carrying war materiel, but in 1972, British journalist Colin Simpson revealed in his book *Lusitania* that the ship's manifest declared that among the cargo were 4,200 cases of cartridges and 1,259 cases of steel shrapnel. In addition, there were many suspicious items, like "3,863 boxes of cheese" destined for the Naval Experimental Establishment at Shoeburyness.

Explosives carried aboard the ship may have been the real cause of the disaster. As noted, after the German torpedo exploded, there was a second and more powerful blast. Underwater photos of the wreck taken in 1982 show two holes in the hull, one created by the torpedo and a second, far larger, one in the port side, probably created by the explosion of ammunition stored in that area.

From the time construction of the *Lusitania* began in 1905, it was assumed that she could be quickly and easily converted from civilian liner to warship. The Admiralty itself underwrote the cost of construction. There was plenty of space provided for mounting guns, for ammunition hoists and magazines.

The armaments were not actually installed until 1913 and 1914. The British government tried to keep this a secret, but accounts of the refitting of the *Lusitania* as a warship appeared in the American press. Guns were loaded on board, but not permanently mounted. They were hidden below deck and could be brought to their mounts if needed. By the end of 1914, the *Lusitania* seemed destined to become a warship patrolling the South Atlantic. Then the Admiralty returned her to Cunard, apparently feeling that she would be more useful as a passenger liner, and for the transport of American-made armaments to Britain. It is still unknown whether the guns were taken off the ship, but it seems unlikely.

The most controversial part of this case centers around the charge that the British government deliberately set up the *Lusitania* for U-boat attack so that the resulting outcry against Germany would hasten America's entry into the war. What makes this charge particularly sensitive is that the person most involved with a decision of that sort would have been Winston Churchill, then First Lord of the Admiralty. Churchill was known to be very interested in prodding President Wilson into a pro-Allied anti-German policy. Just a few weeks before the sinking of the *Lusitania*, Churchill had written to a fellow cabinet minister about the importance of attracting neutral shipping to Britain "in the hope especially of embroiling the U.S. with Germany."

"For our part," Churchill continued, "we want the traffic— the more the better and if some of it gets into trouble, better still."

On her passage through the war zone, the *Lusitania* was to be accompanied by the Royal Navy warship *Juno*, an aging cruiser that probably would not have provided a great deal of real protection, though it was known that U-boats rarely attacked shipping when there was a patrol boat in the vicinity. However, on May 5, the *Juno* was withdrawn, and the *Lusitania* was allowed to enter the war zone without any additional protection, even though U-boats were operating in the vicinity. Churchill was at the Admiralty on May 5, the day the protection of the *Juno* was withdrawn. It is unknown whether Churchill had anything to do with changing the *Juno*'s orders.

Years later, Churchill wrote of the sinking of the *Lusitania*: "The poor babies who perished in the ocean struck a blow at the German power more deadly than could be achieved by the sacrifice of a hundred thousand fighting men."

Using the *Lusitania* as bait was the sort of thing Churchill might have done, for he could be ruthless. But none of this proves that Churchill or anyone else in the British government actually did use the *Lusitania* and her passengers as pawns in the war. All the relevant papers have not yet been released, and may never be made public. It's probable that if a definite decision to put the *Lusitania* at risk was made on May 5, 1915, nothing was written down. But even if there had been no specific plan about the fate of the *Lusitania*, it is clear that the safety of the ship and its passengers was not the highest priority at that moment.

1921

THE "FATTY" ARBUCKLE CASE   Three-hundred-and-twenty-five-pound Roscoe "Fatty" Arbuckle was, next to Charlie Chaplin, the most popular and highest-paid film comedian of his day. His career and popularity all came to an end on the night of September 5, 1921, when, after working on three films in a row, Fatty threw a wild party—some described it as an orgy—at the St. Francis Hotel in San Francisco.

Among those at the party was a twenty-five-year-old small-time actress named Virginia Rapp. She was the wife of one of Fatty's directors. Exactly what happened has never been made clear, because the accounts of witnesses varied so widely and changed so frequently. According to one version, Fatty took a more or less willing Virginia into the bedroom. About twenty minutes later, she began screaming, "I'm dying, he's killing me. I'm dying."

It was said that Fatty then walked out of the bedroom wearing Virginia's hat and giggling. "Go in and get her dressed and take her back to her hotel. She makes too much noise."

Other versions of the story held that Virginia Rapp collapsed during the party. Whatever happened, she was taken to another room in the hotel. Three days later, she died from the results of a ruptured bladder.

Fatty Arbuckle was arrested and tried for felony rape and murder. This was to become the greatest Hollywood scandal ever. The revelations of the Fatty Arbuckle case confirmed public suspicion that Hollywood was the sin capital of the United States. They also helped to inaugurate an era of film censorship and made the studios insist that their stars at least appear to be leading highly moral private lives. Even during the Arbuckle case, the studios worked hard to whitewash everything. The press worked equally hard to make the case seem as sensational as possible. The result was a muddle, with accusations of bribed witnesses, altered testimony, and flagrant jury tampering.

"Fatty" Arbuckle

Arbuckle was actually tried three times. At first, some of the descriptions of what Arbuckle was supposed to have done were considered so shocking that they were written down rather than spoken. But the result of the first two trials was a hung jury. In the first trial, the jury voted 10 to 2 for acquittal. In the second, the vote was 10 to 2 for conviction. In the third trial, the jury returned a not guilty verdict in six minutes. Not only that, the jury added that an injustice had been done Fatty Arbuckle and "there was not the slightest proof to connect him in any way with the commission of any crime." The jury then gathered around to have their pictures taken with the comic.

That was the verdict of a California jury; it was not the verdict of the American public. In addition to regarding Hollywood as a modern Babylon, connecting a three-hundred-twenty-five-pound man with a sex crime seemed doubly obscene to the general public.

Virginia Rapp had been a rather delicate-looking woman. To the public, Fatty Arbuckle became a gross and animalistic monster.

After the acquittal, there seemed some chance of relaunching the comedian's career. But theater owners throughout the nation said they would refuse to show his films. No new Fatty Arbuckle films were made. His old ones were junked. Fatty made an attempt to go into vaudeville, but it didn't work.

Many of Fatty Arbuckle's Hollywood friends stuck by him. Though he was later divorced from his wife, she always maintained that he was not guilty. He directed a few films for friends like Marion Davies and Eddie Cantor under the pseudonym William B. Goodrich. The not-too-subtle double meaning of the name was "Will Be Good." In 1933, he did a rather dismal music-hall tour in England, and when he returned to the United States, Warner Brothers signed him for some two-reelers. Briefly, it seemed possible the worst was over for Fatty. On June 30, he was found dead in his New York hotel room of a heart attack.

See also: *William Desmond Taylor*.

1935

THELMA TODD   Aficionados of Hollywood scandal point to an eerie moment in the otherwise hilarious Marx brothers classic *Monkey Business*. Groucho takes the arm of the beautiful blond actress Thelma Todd and says, "Now be a good girlie, or I'll lock you up in the garage." A few years later, Thelma Todd died locked in a garage, but whether her death was murder, suicide, or an accident is still a matter of dispute.

Todd had been one of a flock of good-looking starlets hired by Paramount Studios. In her first film, *Fascinating Youth* (1926), she displayed a real talent for comedy, and after that her career took off. She starred in a series of short comedies with ZaSu Pitts and Patsy Kelly, did two films with the Marx Brothers, and one each with Buster Keaton and Laurel and Hardy. There were serious roles as well, but she was best-known for comedy. Unlike many who had started in the silent era, Todd made an easy and successful transition to talkies because she had a beautiful speaking voice.

Thelma Todd was a highly successful movie actress. By 1935, she had completed some seventy films, an enormous number over a period of only nine years. She was beautiful—one critic called her "the loveliest blonde ever seen on the screen." She was also rich. Not only did she command a star's salary, she had begun to invest her earnings. Todd was not one of those stars who could be easily cheated out of her money or who would throw everything away on high living. One of her investments was a popular restaurant called Thelma Todd's Roadside Rest, located on the Pacific Highway between Santa Monica and Malibu, beneath the Palisades. Her partner in the venture was director Roland West, a former lover. Todd often stayed in a large apartment above the restaurant. West had a bungalow out back.

Todd's private life was not nearly as successful as her professional life. She had a brief and stormy marriage to talent agent

Thelma Todd

Pasquale "Pat" DiCicco and she continued to see her ex-husband from time to time, but they were not exactly on the best of terms. Todd was rumored to have had affairs with many, many men. It was also rumored that she was often deeply depressed and was addicted to drugs. These rumors, which surfaced only after her death, were never proven.

On December 14, 1935, Thelma Todd attended a party given by Ida Lupino at the celebrated Hollywood nightclub the Trocadero. Pat DiCicco showed up accompanied by two starlets, and Todd got into a loud argument with him. A few hours later, she left the nightclub, waved to the fans clustered outside the nightspot, and stepped into a limousine driven by her chauffeur, Ernest O. Peters.

Peters was told to drive to the apartment at the Roadside Rest, and he recalled that the star was acting very strangely. She wanted him to drive faster because "gangsters are following us."

They arrived at the Roadside Rest at about 2 A.M. on the morning of Sunday, December 15. Todd got out of the limousine and told the chauffeur to go home. She declined his offer to walk her up to her apartment. That may have been the last time anyone saw Thelma Todd alive.

On Monday morning, Todd's maid came to work but could not find her employer anywhere. At about 10:30 A.M., the maid climbed up the 270 steps leading to the top of the hill and to the garage where the actress kept her car. Thelma Todd was there, slumped over the wheel of her open Packard convertible. She was wearing the same evening gown and fur coat she had worn when she left the Trocadero party, and she was quite dead.

Very rapidly a coroner's jury concluded that the death had been an accident. It was reconstructed this way: The actress had come home drunk, and after parting from the chauffeur had decided to drive somewhere. She went up to the garage, started the car, passed out, and died from asphyxiation. Her key was in the ignition and the gas tank was empty. An alternate theory was that she had lost her keys to the apartment and went up to the garage and turned on the car in order to keep warm. Apparently she did not keep her house and car keys together.

This verdict of accidental death didn't satisfy very many people, who insisted the actress's death wasn't an accident at all, and the official conclusions were nothing more than a classic Hollywood cover-up. In 1935, the major studios were extremely powerful, and extremely sensitive to any hint of scandal. Studio executives were often able to keep the seamier side of Hollywood life hidden from the public. A drunken accident was bad enough, suicide or murder would have been much worse.

Skeptics pointed out that there was blood on the actress's face, and some unexplained bruises on her body. Investigators said that she hurt herself when she fell forward on the steering wheel. Her delicate evening shoes were unscuffed though she was supposed to have climbed 270 steps in a drunken state. There were inconsistencies in the coroner's report. But the most intriguing evidence came from several witnesses who said that they had either spoken to Thelma Todd or actually seen her on Sunday afternoon and evening, many hours after she was supposed to have died. Roland West's estranged wife said that she had seen Todd in a car driven by a handsome, well-dressed, but unknown man on Sunday evening. A druggist also reported seeing her with the mystery man. The man was never identified, and authorities believe that these accounts are either mistaken or fabricated.

A deputy district attorney openly ridiculed the finding that Thelma Todd had died accidentally. It was clearly a case of suicide, he said. But Todd's friends insisted that she had absolutely no reason to kill herself. There was a more sinister and more thrilling possible explanation—murder. But who could the murderer be?

There was ex-husband Pat DiCicco, who had argued publicly with Todd shortly before her death. There were the unknown gangsters. Todd had expressed a fear of gangsters on the ride home on Saturday night. It was suggested the mob tried to move in on Todd's restaurant, and when she resisted, they killed her as a warning to others in Hollywood.

But most rumors centered around business partner and ex-lover Roland West. West was said to be furious because Todd dumped him. Her body was found in a garage that West actually owned. Some neighbors said that they heard a violent argument between Todd and West late that fatal Sunday morning. According to the coroner, Todd was really dead by that time, so one variation of the theory was that West had killed Todd early on Sunday and then staged the argument using another actress as a stand-in. What made West such an intriguing suspect was that he had directed a number of complex murder mysteries, and was supposed to be fascinated by the possibility of the perfect crime. The police, however, never seriously considered West as a suspect, and he died in obscurity in 1952.

The uncertainties and ambiguities surrounding the death of Thelma Todd have never been resolved, and probably never will be. It is more than likely that the official verdict of accidental death is correct. But given the power of the Hollywood studios to squash any hint of scandal, doubts will always remain.

See also: *The Black Dahlia, The "Fatty" Arbuckle Case, William Desmond Taylor.*

1965

DR. CARL COPPOLINO   Was it a nearly perfect murder or a "crime that never was"? In two of the most sensational murder trials of the 1960s, New Jersey anesthesiologist Dr. Carl Coppolino was accused first of murdering the husband of his lover, and later of murdering his own wife. He was acquitted of the first charge, but found guilty on the second, by a jury that didn't seem completely convinced that he was.

Coppolino was a student at Long Island Medical School when he married fellow student Carmela Musetto, the daughter of a well-to-do New Jersey doctor who helped pay Coppolino's way through medical school. He became the staff anesthesiologist at a New Jersey hospital, but in 1961 he resigned under suspicious circumstances. After that, at the age of only thirty, Dr. Carl Coppolino retired from practice, claiming he had heart trouble. The insurance company that paid him twenty thousand dollars a year in disability benefits was suspicious but could do nothing. With his insurance money, and his wife's income as a research physician, Coppolino was able to live quite comfortably in New Jersey.

Near neighbors of the Coppolinos were Colonel William Farber and his wife, Marjorie. Later, Marjorie Farber was to claim that she and Coppolino became lovers, moreover that Coppolino exercised a hypnotic power over her. Coppolino had first started using hypnosis on her to help her break her smoking habit.

When Carl Coppolino wanted to take a vacation in Florida but his wife couldn't get away, Marjorie went along "to take care of him." They took several more trips together. Finally, William Farber began to get uneasy, and that's when Coppolino decided to get rid of him. He tried to get the hypnotized Marjorie to inject him with a deadly drug when he was asleep, but she couldn't do it. She sent for Coppolino, who did the job himself, ultimately smothering Farber with a pillow. Coppolino's wife signed the death certificate, certifying that he had died of heart failure, and that seemed to end that.

Two years later, the Coppolinos moved to Florida, and Marjorie Farber followed, buying the house next door. But by this time, Carl Coppolino had found himself a new love interest, a woman named Mary Gibson whom he had met at a bridge club.

Coppolino was not going to be satisfied with an affair this time. He wanted to marry Mary Gibson, and he asked his wife for a divorce. She refused, and on August 28, 1965, Carl Coppolino called a local doctor to report that his wife had just died of a heart attack. He said that she had suffered from chest pains the night before. The local doctor assumed that Coppolino, who was also a doctor, knew what he was talking about, and quickly certified a heart attack as the cause of death—though fatal heart attacks are quite rare for women in their thirties with no previous history of heart problems.

There the matter might have ended if Coppolino had not gone ahead and actually married Mary Gibson, thus enraging Marjorie Farber. She went around telling people that Carmela Coppolino had been murdered, and eventually she told the story of the murder of her husband. The authorities believed her. Both bodies were exhumed, and Coppolino was indicted for one murder in New Jersey and another in Florida.

He was tried first in New Jersey for the murder of William Farber. It was a difficult case to prosecute, for there was no physical evidence that Farber had indeed been murdered. The only testimony against Coppolino came from his former lover, whom defense attorney F. Lee Bailey successfully portrayed as "a woman scorned." Coppolino was acquitted.

Florida authorities decided to press on with their own case anyway, though on the surface, at least, the evidence seemed even weaker than in the New Jersey case. There were no witnesses to the crime. But an autopsy had been conducted on Carmela's body by the celebrated New York City medical examiner Dr. Milton Helpern. Helpern found that Carmela had not died from a heart attack. Indeed, at the time of her death, she was apparently in good health. He did, however, discover a small puncture mark in her left buttock indicating that she had been given some sort of injection shortly before her death. The prosecution then called toxicologist Dr. Joseph Umberger, who testified that the poison in Carmela Coppolino's body was succinylcholine chloride, a commonly used muscle-relaxing drug. If given in large doses, the drug could paralyze the lungs and cause death. If succinylcholine was the instrument of death, it was an uncommon and extremely sophisticated one, but the sort a trained medical man would have been familiar with. The drug was not easy to identify in the corpse, and Dr. Umberger's testimony was long, complex, and confusing. He spent two and a half days on the stand, mostly under Bailey's close and tough cross-examination.

Ultimately, the jury brought in the curious verdict of second-degree murder. Clearly this was a case where it was either first-degree, that is, premeditated murder, or no murder at all. Second-degree murder seems to have been a compromise. Coppolino was sentenced to life imprisonment, still protesting his innocence. Coppolino's own book, *The Crime That Never Was*, which sets forth his defense, was published in 1980.

1980

LINDY CHAMBERLAIN   In the 1975 Australian film *Picnic at Hanging Rock*, director Peter Weir tells the eerie and atmospheric story of a group of three nineteenth-century schoolgirls and their teacher who go for a picnic at a large landmark rock in Australia and mysteriously disappear. The viewer is left unsure as to what really happened.

In what has come to be known as the Dingo Baby Murder Case, life has imitated art in the most horrible way. In August 1980, Lindy and Michael Chamberlain and their three young children went for a camping trip at Ayers Rock, a beauty spot in the rugged Northern Territory of Australia. The family spent a carefree day scrambling around the rock, but on the second night, after their nine-and-one-half-week-old baby had been put to bed in the tent and the family was preparing dinner, Lindy thought she heard the baby crying. Then she saw a dingo, one of Australia's wild dogs, rush from the tent with "something" in its mouth. She ran to the tent, and found the blankets scattered and the baby gone. She then rushed out of the tent crying, "My God, the dingo's got my baby." Michael ran through the campsite and was quickly able to gather several hundred men and women, who clambered all over the Ayers Rock looking for the missing baby. They found nothing.

An official search continued for several days, and while no body was found, the baby's bloodstained and torn clothing was located about a week later near what was said to be a dingo's den. Ironically, according to aborigine lore, Ayers Rock was the lair of a giant dingo.

At first it all seemed a tragic and ghastly accident. But Northern Territory Chief Minister Paul Everingham was not satisfied and ordered the investigation reopened. Some scientists who examined the torn clothing were not convinced that the tears had been made by an animal's teeth. It looked to them more like the clothing had been deliberately cut with a scissors. There was no animal saliva on the clothing. What appeared to be blood was also found in the Chamberlains' car.

There were two other emotional factors that are difficult to weigh, but certainly played a part in what was to happen. First, the dingo is generally a popular animal in Australia. Most people believe it to be benign and don't think it would, or could, carry off a human baby, particularly from a campsite where there were so many people around. T-shirts with the slogan "The Dingo is Innocent" were being sold. Second, the Chamberlains were devout Seventh-day Adventists; Michael was a minister. The Adventists are a small sect that is often met with hostility. There were bigots who claimed that Seventh-day Adventists performed human sacrifices.

Ultimately, Lindy and Michael were put on trial for the murder of their baby daughter. Expert witnesses clashed over the evidence. The prosecution was unable to present any convincing theory as to why Lindy Chamberlain, who had the reputation of being a good mother, would have killed her own child. The "Dingo Baby Murder" trial generated an enormous amount of interest in Australia and throughout much of the English-speaking world. It lasted seven weeks, but it took the jury only six hours to declare a confused and pathetic Lindy Chamberlain, who was about to give birth to her fourth child, guilty of murdering her baby daughter. She was given a life-with-hard-labor sentence. Michael was convicted of being an accessory and was given an eighteen-month suspended sentence and fined about five hundred dollars. The lawyer's argument was that "the children need their father."

The sensational case was over, but there was a growing feeling that justice had not been done. The case was appealed, and Lindy was freed on bail. But in 1983, the appeal was turned down and she was sent back to prison. Still, the case would not die, and as of this writing Lindy Chamberlain is once again out of jail, pending yet another judicial review.

Australian lawyer and journalist John Bryson wrote an influential and authoritative account of the case, *Evil Angels*. Bryson contends that Lindy was railroaded by ambitious police officials and tripped up by incompetent "experts." He also says that new evidence has surfaced that will conclusively prove that Lindy Chamberlain did not kill her child, and that the whole affair has been one long hideous miscarriage of justice.

1980

CLAUS VON BÜLOW   This is a case that sounds like it was dreamed up at a soap-opera story conference. A fabulously wealthy heiress is thrown into an irreversible coma under mysterious circumstances. Her children by her first marriage (a prince and princess, no less) suspect her second husband, an arrogant, womanizing European aristocrat with a shady past. The loyal lady's maid tells of seeing a mysterious black bag with hypodermic needles. It all begins in a huge mansion, and moves from courtroom to courtroom, picking up a supporting cast of ambitious prosecutors, pricey lawyers, goofy drug dealers, world-renowned experts who contradict one another, vengeful socialites, a couple of big-name celebrities, and hundreds of reporters. There are plot twists, dramatic courtroom confrontations, and a surprise ending. It's all played out on television, of course. There's even a real soap-opera actress.

But the story wasn't dreamed up; it is quite real—the Claus von Bülow case is one of the glitziest and oddest of recent times. And it all turns on the question, not of whodunit, but was anything done at all?

The apparent victim was Martha "Sunny" von Bülow. She was heiress to an enormous fortune. Despite her wealth, good looks, and cheerful nickname, Sunny was apparently not a very happy woman. She was shy, and often extremely depressed and withdrawn. At times she was barely able to get out of bed. She suffered from a variety of puzzling, and possibly psychosomatic, ailments. Later, some people who knew her were to say that she was a heavy drinker, and habitual user of a wide variety of legal and illegal drugs.

Her second husband was Claus von Bülow, a Danish aristocrat who, while not destitute when he married Sunny, certainly stood to gain millions from her death. Once the case broke, the public perception of Claus was of a stolid, cold, and rather arrogant

man. His friends, on the other hand, found him warm and charming, if somewhat pompous. His enemies found him sinister and
circulated dark rumors about his past.

Sunny's two children by her first marriage (also to a European
aristocrat), Prince Alexander (Alex) von Auersperg and Princess
Annie Laurie (Ala) von Auersperg, were suspicious of their stepfather. So was Sunny's loyal German maid, Maria Schrallhammer.

The scene of the crime, or perhaps we should say events, for
it is far from certain that any crime was committed, was Clarendon
Court, a fabulous twenty-room mansion at Newport, Rhode Island, home for some of America's super-rich. Clarendon Court,
by the way, was once used as the set for the film *High Society*.

Claus had married Sunny in 1966, and they had one child,
Cosima, born in 1967. After Cosima's birth, the couple apparently
gradually abstained from sexual relations. Claus took up with a
variety of women, including a long-term mistress, and Sunny seemed
to sink into apathy. But there was no overt talk of divorce, and
the couple stayed together, shuttling between their huge Fifth Avenue apartment in Manhattan and Clarendon Court.

Over the Christmas holidays in 1979, which were spent at
Newport, Sunny became ill, but Claus seemed curiously uncon-
cerned. When the maid said that Sunny was unconscious, Claus
insisted that she had just had too much to drink and would "sleep
it off." After hours of delay and repeated pleas and finally threats
from the maid, Claus called a doctor. By that time, Sunny was in
a coma and was rushed to the hospital near death. She recovered,
but it had been a close call. The whole incident left Sunny's family
bitter and more suspicious of Claus von Bülow than ever; Claus
himself acknowledged that he might have been a little slow in
calling for medical help.

In the months that followed, Sunny continued to have bouts
of illness and weakness. At one point, she was hospitalized with
an aspirin overdose. One day, while cleaning a closet in the couple's
Fifth Avenue apartment, Martha Schrallhammer found a suspi-
cious-looking small black case containing a variety of pills and
powders—obviously drugs. She alerted Sunny's children Ala and
Alex, who took samples of the drugs and had them analyzed. They
were Valium, a mild tranquilizer, and the barbiturate secobarbital.

Sunny had been known to take these drugs, but not in the form found in the bag. Claus was never asked about the bag, but the maid continued to keep an eye out for it, and Ala and Alex looked with greater suspicion and hostility than ever upon the man they called "Uncle Claus." But no one appears to have tried to warn Sunny or taken any other steps to protect her.

Shortly after Thanksgiving 1980, Maria looked in the black bag again. She was later to testify that this time she found a small bottle marked "insulin," along with several needles and a syringe. Insulin is, of course, used often by injection to treat diabetes. But Sunny wasn't a diabetic; she suffered from a condition called hypoglycemia, which is, in many ways, the opposite of diabetes. For hypoglycemia, insulin is not a treatment, and it could be deadly. Still, no one confronted Claus; no one warned Sunny.

The family went off to Newport for the Christmas holidays. On December 21, Sunny was once again taken ill. This time a doctor was called quickly, but she slipped into a deep and irreversible coma. She remains in a coma as of this writing, and doctors hold out absolutely no hope that she will ever recover. Sunny von Bülow is as good as dead.

Sunny's children hired a private investigator. The investigator, along with Alex, searched Claus's locked closet at Clarendon Court and found the little black bag. Exactly what that bag contained became the matter of considerable dispute later, but what they said they found in the bag were vials of pills, some liquid in a bottle, and three hypodermic needles, two sealed in the original containers, but one loose and apparently used. They also found a vial of Dalmane sleeping pills with a prescription label in the name of Claus von Bülow. The needle was sent to a laboratory, and after testing was found to have a high concentration of insulin, plus traces of Valium and amobrabital. By this time, medical tests on the comatose Sunny had come back showing her blood had unusually high levels of insulin.

The family also discovered that Leslie Baxter, whose name had been found on one of the vials spotted earlier in the black bag, was a prostitute whom Claus had frequented.

The family took their evidence to the Rhode Island authorities, and on July 6, 1981, Claus von Bülow was indicted by a

Claus von Bülow (*Wide World*)

Newport County grand jury on two counts of assault with intent to murder. The charge was that he had twice tried to kill his wife by injecting her with insulin.

The trial, which began in February of the following year, was an absolute sensation. Claus hired some good lawyers and seemed quite confident that he would win. But the case that the state (with

the help of Sunny's children and their money) had put together
was both dramatically strong and compelling. First, there was the
loyal maid Maria Schrallhammer describing how strangely Claus
had behaved at the time of Sunny's first coma, and how he had
delayed in calling a doctor. Then there was the surprising finding
of the black bag with its suspicious contents. There was expert
testimony that Sunny's coma had been caused by insulin, and that
the needle found in the black bag had insulin on it. Sunny's banker
testified that upon her death Claus would receive approximately
fourteen million dollars, plus Clarendon Court, the New York
apartment, and all both residences contained. If he and Sunny had
divorced, he would still get plenty, but he would have to cut back
on the lavish life-style to which he had become very accustomed.

A high point was the appearance of the "other woman" in
Claus's life, Alexandria Isles. She was invariably referred to as a
"soap-opera actress," and she had a major role in the afternoon
series *Dark Shadows. Dark Shadows* was more of a supernatural
Gothic show than simple soap opera. The central character was a
vampire. It ran for about four years and has become something of
a cult favorite. Alexandra played Victoria Winters. Alexandra herself came from the sort of European background in which Claus
had lived. Her father was a Danish count who knew Claus's parents. Alexandra and Claus often discussed marriage, and in 1981,
before Sunny's second and final coma, she had handed Claus an
ultimatum—leave Sunny or lose me. After Sunny's coma, they
remained together. She testified that when Claus was first charged
with attempted murder, she thought it was nonsense. But on the
witness stand, she admitted that she was no longer sure of his
innocence.

The defense's star witness was a woman named Joy O'Neill,
who claimed she knew Sunny well and testified that Sunny regularly injected herself with insulin in order to lose weight. But the
defense strategy backfired when the prosecutor was able to prove
that Joy O'Neill had seen Sunny only a handful of times. Claus
himself never took the stand. He insisted he wanted to testify, but
his lawyers wouldn't let him. At least part of the problem was
Claus's personality. He came across as stiff and arrogant, the sort
of man who felt superior to the comparatively humble folk who

made up the jury. He would not have made a sympathetic impression. And then, his lawyers may genuinely have been afraid of the questions he would have been asked.

On March 16, 1982, after thirty-one days of testimony and thirty-seven hours of deliberation, the jury found Claus von Bülow guilty of two counts of assault with intent to murder. He was sentenced to thirty years in prison, but was allowed to remain free on a one million dollar bail pending appeal.

Oddly, despite his stiff demeanor and the unsympathetic picture of him that emerged in the Newport courtroom, Claus became something of a hero to those who flocked to the court. Outside the courtroom, Claus was cheered and the prosecution booed. In Rhode Island, trials can be televised, and this one was given live coverage for hours every day. It was better than the soap operas.

Claus, facing a long jail term, hired top lawyer and Harvard law professor Alan Dershowitz to handle his appeal. Appeals are supposed to be granted only if errors were made in the original trial, but Dershowitz notes that what the appeals judges think about the guilt or innocence of the defendant also plays a large part in the decision. At the end of April 1984, the Rhode Island Supreme Court reversed von Bülow's convictions. The grounds for the reversal were fairly narrow—one was that certain notes of the private investigator had not been turned over to the defense. But narrow or not, Claus von Bülow was, for the moment, a free man.

The state now had to decide whether to retry him or drop the case, and in January 1985, the newly elected district attorney said she would go for a new trial. Both sides began preparing their cases in an atmosphere that became increasingly frantic. A book, *The Von Bülow Affair*, which was written with the cooperation of Alex and Ala and was intensely hostile to Claus, was published. In it there were suggestions that Claus had been engaged in every imaginable form of vice. The various principals of the case were busy giving interviews to TV, newspapers, magazines, almost everyone who would listen. Claus, who did not testify at his first trial and would not testify at his second, had no hesitation about talking to Barbara Walters. Author Truman Capote, a friend of Sunny's, said she had used drugs for a long time. Johnny Carson's ex-wife backed up the claim. Neither actually testified under oath.

The defense found a man named David Mariott, who claimed that he had delivered drugs to the von Bülow house, presumably drugs meant for Sunny. He was paid by the defense (a perfectly legal procedure), but proved to be so wildly unreliable that he was dismissed. Mariott then began giving his own press conferences and threatening everyone with tapes of conversations with Claus he had secretly recorded. (The tapes actually contained nothing of importance.) Alex and Ala also went on TV, and they hired a public relations firm. It was indeed a media circus, but one created by the people involved in the trial more than by the media itself.

The second trial of Claus von Bülow was even better theater than the first, and it was dramatically different. Claus's trial lawyer was Thomas Puccio, an aggressive ex-government prosecutor who had become famous during the Abscam trials. He was able to show that there were contradictions between what the maid told the jury and what she had originally told the private investigator. The contradictions were not enormous, but they were enough to plant doubts in the mind of the jury. The heart of the defense, however, was an array of expert witnesses who testified that Sunny von Bülow's coma had not been caused by insulin shock, and that the needle found in the mysterious black bag could not have been used to inject her with insulin. The underlying argument was that no crime had ever been committed. On June 10, the second jury acquitted Claus on both counts of assault with intent to kill.

No trial answers all the questions that might be asked, and the trials of Claus von Bülow leave an extraordinarily large number of loose ends. Even lawyer Dershowitz, who insists that he is convinced of Claus's innocence, admits there is much that he doesn't know and he awaits Claus's full account.

"I will pay close attention to Claus's account if and when he tells it, because although I believe he is innocent, I also suspect that we never have been told the whole story. Under our system, the legal story is almost never the whole story. Some of the juiciest parts end up on the cutting room floor."

Dershowitz also speculates on the possibility that someone tried to frame Claus.

We can be assured that even if we do not get the full story we will continue to get parts of it in various forms. The case has already spawned two books, and will doubtless produce more, some by the main actors in the drama. And the case, which looked like a TV soap opera and was played out on TV, will doubtless return to the screen in a variety of dramatic guises. Fittingly, Claus von Bülow's latest companion, Andrea Reynolds, was once involved in producing television shows.

See also: *Joan Hill.*

4

Motive Unknown

1853

HENRIETTA ROBINSON   There is no doubt that Henrietta Robinson poisoned two of her neighbors. Her reasons for this are obscure, though she was probably insane. The real mystery concerns the true identity of the murderess, for although she spent more time in prison than any other woman in United States history, virtually nothing was ever known about her.

The young woman calling herself Henrietta Robinson (Mrs. Robinson) appeared in Troy, New York, around 1852. She lived

Henrietta Robinson, "The Veiled Murderess."

in a small cottage across from Lanagan's grocery store. She had no relatives, and no close friends. According to local gossips, she was the mistress of some powerful New York State official, who arrived occasionally in an expensive private carriage with the shades drawn. Some contemporary accounts call her "beautiful," but a drawing made after her trial shows her to be rather ordinary-looking.

Sometime in March 1853, Henrietta's mysterious visitor arrived for the last time. Some said there was a loud argument concerning a wife and children. Some days later, the generally reclusive young woman showed up at a local dance. A young man named Smith went up to her and whispered what was apparently an indecent proposition. Henrietta turned scarlet and stormed out.

Several days later, Henrietta confronted Smith in Lanagan's store. She put a pistol to his head and said that if he ever insulted her again, she would kill him. The threat appeared to be a serious one. Mr. and Mrs. Lanagan, who witnessed the scene, were horrified, and told Henrietta never to threaten anyone in their store again.

Over the next few weeks, Henrietta became more reclusive than ever, and it was said she was drinking heavily. She continued to shop at Lanagan's grocery store, but she was clearly furious at the owners. By May, however, her behavior underwent a change. She tried to be friendly to the Lanagans, but they still distrusted her and behaved coldly, even rudely.

On May 15, 1853, Henrietta Robinson purchased two ounces of arsenic from a local druggist, to get rid of rats, she said.

On May 25, she went to the Lanagans' store in an apparently cheerful and forgiving frame of mind. She said they should all be friends, and she offered to buy them some beer so they could drink a toast together. The Lanagans were suspicious, but figured that a beer could do no harm.

Henrietta then asked for some sugar to sweeten the beer. Nineteenth-century beer could be heavy and bitter, and adding sugar was not uncommon. For a brief period, Henrietta was left alone with the beer. She filled the glasses of Mr. and Mrs. Lanagan and another relative, Catherine Lubee, who worked in the store. Lanagan and Miss Lubee drank their beer. Mrs. Lanagan was interrupted by the arrival of a customer. By the time she got back,

Henrietta was on her way out: "I have some errands. Sorry, I cannot stay. Don't forget to drink your beer." But Mrs. Lanagan did not drink hers, because the others reported the beer had tasted funny.

By the next morning, Lanagan and Miss Lubee were dead, and Henrietta Robinson was under arrest for murder. Autopsies showed that the deaths had been caused by arsenic poisoning, and a small quantity of arsenic was found hidden under a rug in Henrietta's cottage.

Henrietta protested her innocence, but even more significantly, she seemed to ignore the fact that a crime had been committed and that she was under arrest. She chatted on about spring fashions, and often was quite incoherent. It was her behavior at the trial, however, that made her most famous.

One New York paper reported, "Mrs. Robinson attracted all eyes. She was richly and fashionably appareled, wearing an elegant black silk dress, white hat trimmed with artificial flowers, and spotless white kid gloves. Her face was shrouded with blue veils from the time she entered the courtroom until she left it."

Except for brief moments, Henrietta refused to show her face, and she became known as "The Veiled Murderess." At one point, the judge became angry and insisted that Henrietta remove the veil. She threw back her veil for a second, but grabbed a handkerchief to cover her face. This is the way she acted throughout the trial.

She would lift her veil so a witness could identify her. When the druggist who had sold her the arsenic leaned forward to look beneath the veil, he found Henrietta grinning maniacally at him. It was an unsettling experience.

Attempts to find out something about her background foundered, because she had told everyone a different story. Sometimes she said she was the daughter of a great Irish lord, and had been abandoned by her family because she had married a poor man. Other times she said she had been raised in England or France, and was related to European aristocracy. There were accounts of her bizarre behavior—she might break out laughing or dancing at almost any moment, as one example.

She was found guilty and sentenced to hang on August 3, 1853. When the judge pronounced "And may God have mercy on your soul," Henrietta responded, "You had better pray for your own soul."

Her case was reviewed, and on the very day that she was to be executed, the governor of New York commuted her death sentence to life imprisonment. She was sent to Sing Sing, where she continued to attract the interest of reporters for decades.

Henrietta seemed to adjust well to prison life, and she dropped much of the extremely strange behavior that had been evident at her trial. But a newsman wrote that she retained the "singular practice of concealing her face from visitors. In that respect she seems to be incurable. Whenever a visitor approaches her, she hastens to hide her countenance with whatever may be within her reach . . ." It is unknown whether the portrait of her was drawn from life or the artist's imagination.

Despite the digging of a generation of reporters, nothing more was discovered of her history.

Since she had become a model prisoner, some began to wonder if Henrietta had not been putting on an act in order to escape the gallows. Then, in 1890, she set her cell on fire, and the wardens came just in time to prevent her from throwing herself into the blaze. Henrietta Robinson was then sent to an institution for the criminally insane, where she died quietly in 1905. She was presumed to be eighty-nine years old, and had been behind bars for well over half a century. At her death, "The Veiled Murderess" was just as much of a mystery as she had been in life.

1889

GABRIELLE BOMPARD   The mental image of the hypnotic subject entirely under the control of the hypnotist has been passed down to us from the nineteenth century and such works of fiction as George du Maurier's *Trilby*. The idea that a subject could be hypnotized to kill has appeared frequently in fiction, most notably in the silent film classic *The Cabinet of Dr. Calagari*. But hypnotism has also been raised as a defense in a number of murder cases, most notably in L'Affaire Gouffe, which shocked and titillated Parisians in 1890.

The case began on August 13, 1889, in the small French town of Millery, with the discovery of a trunk containing the partially decomposed body of a Parisian bailiff named Toussaint-Augustin Gouffe. Gouffe was a widower who was known to regularly frequent prostitutes. Inquiries established a connection between Gouffe and an unsavory character named Michel Eyraud, who had disappeared from France with his mistress, Gabrielle Bompard, at about the time Gouffe had been killed. Eyraud and Bompard were traced to North America, but there the trail went cold.

Then, quite unexpectedly, on January 22, 1890, Gabrielle Bompard walked into a Paris police station accompanied by a man named Garanger and said she was going to help the police by telling them what had happened to Gouffe. She unhesitatingly blamed the crime entirely on Eyraud, first denying that she had even been present when the murder took place and then saying that she had been on the scene but had only watched in horror. She was rather surprised when she found herself under arrest for murder.

At the time of her arrest, Bompard was about twenty-two. She was the daughter of a hardworking and modestly successful metal merchant from the town of Lille. Her mother had died when she was thirteen, and after that she was shunted from one school to another, apparently learning very little in any of them. As she

Gabrielle Bompard

recounted her life, it sounded as if she had met an unbroken string of men who were interested in hypnotism—and they all had tried, with great success, to hypnotize her. The first was a Monsieur Risler, whom she met right after she returned home from her last school and who became her lover. Risler admitted that he had hypnotized the girl many times.

Gabrielle's father, who felt he was no longer able to control her, enlisted the aid of a doctor and practicing hypnotist named Sacreste, who was also his brother-in-law, to try to get Gabrielle to behave in a more seemly manner. Sacreste also found that the girl was extremely easy to hypnotize; she would fall into a trance if he just stared at her. While in a trance, she seemed impervious to pain. He appears to have performed a minor operation on her using hypnosis instead of conventional anesthesia. Yet she successfully resisted the doctor's efforts to improve her behavior.

After this hypnotic failure, Bompard went to Paris, where she said she met Michel Eyraud, a man who boasted he had never worked a day in his life. He was also, she said, a hypnotist. Actually, she did not at first claim that Eyraud had hypnotized her, but somehow the idea was introduced into her defense and she

seized upon it. It was even said that she did not specifically remember being hypnotized by Eyraud because her memory of the
incidents had been erased by hypnotic suggestion! That was a
difficult proposition to argue with, and a more difficult one to
believe.

Eyraud was arrested in Havana, Cuba, in May of 1890, and
brought back to France for trial. There was no love now between
the former lovers. Bompard tried to pin all the blame on Eyraud,
while Eyraud wanted her to share the guilt and the punishment.
He could have been under no illusion that he would not be found
guilty and sent to the guillotine.

Exactly what happened on the night of July 26, 1889, the
night of Gouffe's murder, is in dispute. Apparently, Eyraud and
Bompard had a murder plan from the start. She was to bring a
man back to the apartment they had just rented. She was to seat
him near a curtained alcove that concealed her bed and then play-
fully wind the cord from her dressing gown around his neck. She
was then to secretly tie the cord to a rope that was attached to a
pulley. (Exactly how this was to be done is not clear.) Eyraud,
who was on the other side of the curtain, was then to pull on the
rope and hang the victim, and he said that was what happened.
Bompard insisted that Eyraud had burst from behind the curtains
and strangled the bailiff with his bare hands. The medical evidence
was inconclusive on this point, though one doctor said it appeared
more as if Gouffe's death had been caused by manual strangulation.

After the murder, the pair took whatever money the bailiff
had on his body, and with the keys Gouffe had carried, Eyraud
went back to his office and searched it. But he overlooked a large
sum of money kept there. An incompetent robber, Eyraud was
nearly caught.

They then stuffed the body into a trunk they had apparently
bought specifically for that purpose, dumped it carelessly near
Millery, and took off for America. Though Bompard said she had
been hypnotized to kill, she wasn't thoroughly under Eyraud's
influence, for she left him and ran off to Canada with Garanger—
incredibly, another amateur hypnotist. Garanger denied, however,
that it was his hypnotic suggestion that Gabrielle return to Paris
to tell what she knew of the crime.

The trial was filled with conflicting medical testimony. A trio of doctors who had examined Bompard agreed that she was very susceptible to hypnosis, but they also agreed that she was very good at pretending to be hypnotized.

In France at that time, there were two conflicting schools of thought about the powers of hypnosis. One insisted that there had never been a single documented case of a crime's being committed under the influence of hypnosis. The other school believed that a susceptible subject under the control of a strong hypnotist was completely obedient and thus was quite capable of committing a crime that would be against his or her will when in a normal state.

Dr. Auguste Voisin had studied Bompard and hypnotically regressed her to the time of the murder. At the critical moment in the regression, when the girl was to put the cord around the bailiff's neck, she collapsed. According to her supporters, this was proof that on the night of the murder she had rebelled against the final deed, forcing Eyraud to finish the job without her help.

The jury, faced with conflicting medical testimony about the powers of hypnosis, may simply have ignored all of it—and voted the way one would have expected anyway. Eyraud was condemned to death, but there was never much doubt that would be the result. The prosecutor did not actively press for the death penalty for Gabrielle Bompard, hinting that her youth and poor upbringing contributed to her wayward life. She was sentenced to twenty years—an average sentence for women convicted of murder in France at that time. She actually served only thirteen years, and when she was released she was besieged by eager hypnotists. She also wrote a book about the crime, called *My Confession*. By this time, the hypnosis defense was entirely forgotten, and she said that the bailiff had been killed by a gang of counterfeiters whose activities he had uncovered. The hypnosis defense was more believable.

See also: *Adelaide Bartlett.*

1908

THE PILTDOWN MAN   In 1908, an English lawyer and amateur scientist named Charles Dawson located some fragments from an ancient human skull in a gravel pit near the village of Piltdown in Sussex. Over the next few years, Dawson said that he excavated other fragments of the skull, as well as the bones of other animals and what appeared to be flint tools.

In 1912, Dawson made a truly exciting and unexpected discovery—a lower jaw and a few teeth. It was assumed that both the jaw and the skull went together.

Though dating of fossils at that time was a fairly inexact procedure, Dawson said that the fossils were from the Tertiary period, some ten million years ago. That would have made the Piltdown skull far and away the oldest human remains ever found, and completely out of line with all other fossil finds. The dating seemed incredible, and when Arthur Smith Woodward of the British Museum examined the fossils, he delivered the opinion that the Piltdown man had flourished in the Lower Pleistocene period, perhaps five hundred thousand years ago. Still an astonishing age, particularly in the early twentieth century, when relatively few fossil human remains of any kind had been located and identified.

Though popularly known as the Piltdown man, the fossil was given the scientific name *Eoanthropus dawsoni*, "Dawson's Dawn Man." It was put on display in the British Museum and proudly hailed as the first example of fossil man ever found in Britain. Casts of the skull and reconstructions of Piltdown man began appearing in museums throughout the world, and information on the find and its place in evolutionary history made its way into textbooks, and remained there for over three decades.

Virtually all new fossil finds of early man are controversial at first, and Piltdown man was no exception. The main problem, in the view of many scientists, was a theoretical one. The creature had an essentially human cranium, but a thoroughly apelike jaw. This would imply that the brain had evolved first. Yet fossils found in other parts of the world indicated that evolution had taken a different course, and that the jaw became modern while the brain case remained primitive and apelike. Many experts insisted that the fossils of cranium and jaw came from two different individuals, and that they had been wrongly linked together just because they had been found in the same pit. But ultimately the backers of Piltdown man prevailed, though no one could account for Piltdown man's unusual appearance. When diagrams were made of the evolutionary tree of the human race, Piltdown man was placed on some side branch, a freakish evolutionary offshoot.

Publicly the dissenters argued that Piltdown man was a mistake, the mismatching of two disparate fossils. Privately some had darker suspicions. A group of scientists led by Kenneth P. Oakley, a geologist from the British Museum, set out to reexamine Piltdown man and all of the circumstances surrounding its discovery. Starting in 1949, they ran a series of chemical tests on the fossils, and these confirmed what Oakley and his associates had long suspected— Piltdown man was not only a mistake, it was a fraud.

The conclusion of their report, published in 1953, was uncompromising: "From the evidence which we have obtained, it is now clear that the distinguished paleontologists and archaeologists who took part in the excavations at Piltdown were victims of a most elaborate and carefully prepared hoax." They acknowledged that the faking had been skillfully done and that it probably would not have been completely detectable with the methods available in 1912.

The cranium was old, but fifty thousand rather than five hundred thousand years old. It might well have been found in the area, and the dating could have been an honest mistake. The jaw, however, was quite modern, probably the jawbone of an orangutan. It had been artificially stained, and the teeth had been filed down to give it the appearance of age and make it look more human. Many of the tools found in the area were also modern fakes. The evidence of faking presented by Oakley and his colleagues was so overwhelming that their conclusions have never been seriously questioned; indeed, they have been completely confirmed by further research.

Though that part of the Piltdown puzzle had been settled, a couple of truly intriguing questions remain. First, why was this fake so thoroughly accepted for so long, even though many serious questions were raised about it at the time of discovery?

That question can only be answered in a general way. As Oakley and his colleagues pointed out, the hoaxer did an excellent job, and the tools for detecting such a hoax conclusively did not exist in 1912.

But there were some psychological and social reasons for accepting Piltdown as genuine, too. As human beings, we are extremely proud of our brain, which we rightfully consider the key to our success. Therefore, it is logical as well as satisfying to believe that the brain evolved first. But real fossils tell a different story, that the human brain was a relatively late development. But when a fossil turned up that appeared to confirm what seemed to be the most reasonable premise, people were willing to accept it uncritically.

Then there was British nationalism. Most of the significant fossil discoveries were being made in far-off places like Java. The British public, and indeed many British scientists, were delighted with the idea that a significant step in human evolution might have taken place in the British Isles. This nationalistic desire may have blinded them to some of Piltdown man's more obvious faults.

The second, and more intriguing, question concerns the identity of the hoaxer. Who buried the phony fossils? The obvious candidate is Dawson himself. Dawson was long dead before the controversy broke wide open, and thus had no opportunity to confess or defend himself. He certainly never confessed to anything while he was alive, and nothing has ever been found in his private papers to indicate that he concocted a fraud. He seemed an unlikely sort of hoaxer, a rather stodgy country lawyer with a considerable reputation for honesty. He certainly never made a penny off Pilt-down man. Yet the find did make him famous, and people have done much worse for fame. The history of hoaxing also shows that some hoaxers are quite content to take their secret to the grave, and that even the most honest of people will sometimes behave entirely out of character.

So Dawson had both the best motive for the hoax and the greatest opportunity. But others insist that Dawson didn't have the knowledge or skill to construct such an elaborate fraud, and that he was also a victim. It has been suggested that after Dawson found the original, and genuine, skull someone else planted the phony jaw and tools. But who? There have been numerous suggestions. One is that the hoaxer was Pierre Teilhard de Chardin, a Jesuit priest, philosopher, and skilled hunter of human fossils. De Chardin was a frequent visitor to the gravel pit at Piltdown. He was more knowledgeable and subtle than Dawson. He could conceivably have constructed the hoax, and he might have wished to do so in order to support some of his own philosophical ideals, but there is no direct evidence that he did.

Recently, an even more interesting candidate for hoaxer has been advanced—Sir Arthur Conan Doyle, creator of Sherlock Holmes. Doyle, who was by that time an ardent spiritualist, lived in the region. Since he was a trained physician, he might well have possessed the skills to prepare the fakes. As his Holmes stories prove, he certainly knew about fooling people. As a spiritualist, as well as a nationalist, he might have had some motive for the hoax. But once again there is no credible evidence that he did anything of the sort.

Unless and until additional information turns up, Charles Dawson remains the prime suspect, though it would not be fair to mark the case of the Piltdown man closed quite yet.

1932

THE HORN PAPERS   In fraud, as in many crimes, the key to finding the guilty party is to find out who profits. Yet, in what turned out to be one of the most elaborate cases of literary/historical fraud ever uncovered in America, there seems to have been no intention to defraud anyone, and certainly no one ever stood to gain anything material. In the midst of so much violence and greed, the case of the Horn Papers has a gentle and soothing charm.

In some areas of the United States, local history is a source of great interest and pride. This is certainly true in the southwestern Pennsylvania area of Washington and Greene counties. Thus, when in 1932 local historians were told of the existence of notebooks, diaries, and other historical material dating from the days of early settlement of the region, they became very excited.

The historical material was supposed to be in the possession of one W. F. Horn of Topeka, Kansas. The original papers and other material were handed down to him from his own ancestors, who had lived in the Pennsylvania area in the mid to late eighteenth century. The written material was in poor shape, and Horn had to recopy it himself. The contents of what came to be called the Horn Papers would force a revision of local history.

Now, this may not seem like a great event, but historians Arthur Pierce Middleton and Douglass Adair, who investigated the matter, note:

"In many parts of the United States a threat to revise drastically long cherished local traditions or to rewrite local history would hardly cause a ripple of interest except among a tiny group. This was not the case in Green and Washington counties. The visitor to this region cannot but be impressed by the consciousness and deep-rooted pride of the local people in their own rich heritage from the past."

If Horn had been trying to sell the papers, suspicions might immediately have been raised. But he asked for no money. He offered the contents of the papers free of charge. Though he didn't live in the area, he often visited and donated his services to aid local historians, or simply local people who wanted to check out the histories of their own ancestors with the Horn Papers. The papers appeared to provide a wealth of detail, particularly about the everyday life of the common man in those pioneering days. Horn himself proved to be an engaging and popular figure, willing to talk to anyone with great skill and enthusiasm about his subject. He was described by a local historian as "a wonder," and Middleton and Adair comment:

"Few historians and few historical documents ever generate such intense and widespread enthusiasm as this."

For nearly ten years, the Horn Papers were regarded as a new gospel by local historians, and they were published in three massive volumes in December 1945. Local funds financed the publication, but once again Horn himself made nothing.

However, from the start there was at least a small undercurrent of criticism and disbelief. Some of the facts presented seemed too much at variance with known history. Many new facts were unsupported by other sources. Some of the words and phrases employed by the eighteenth century settlers were disturbingly modern. Horn himself was quite cavalier in discussing the criticisms. He said most of the original material on which these papers were based had disappeared, and the information existed only in copies that he had made. A map, a court docket, and a box full of artifacts were the only original pieces of eighteenth century material said to still exist. Horn made no serious attempt to defend himself, and at first more people believed him than believed the critics.

Persistent criticism finally led some professional historians to take a closer look at the Horn Papers. A report issued in 1947 concluded that, beyond the shadow of a doubt, the Horn Papers were fake. They were fairly clever fakes, but still the deception should have been discovered long before so much time, money, and effort had been expended on publishing them, before they had become so large a local embarrassment.

Since no one profited financially from the papers, suspicions about their authenticity were held in check, and this "crime," if it can be called that, went undiscovered for over a decade.

Horn himself refused to cooperate with the investigation, and simply withdrew, refusing all requests to talk about his ancestors' papers anymore.

1937

THE HINDENBERG   At 7:25 P.M. on May 6, 1937, the great
German airship the *Hindenberg* burst into flames during docking
at Lakehurst, New Jersey. On the ground was Herbert Morrison,
a radio news reporter for station WLS, "The Prairie Farmer Station," in Chicago. It was Morrison's job to record a description
of the landing for use on the station's "Dinner Bell" program the
next day.

Though always impressive, the arrival of the *Hindenberg* had
become a fairly routine affair. In the previous year, "The Great
Floating Palace," as the craft was sometimes called, had made ten
successful and uneventful trips to North America. Morrison was
doing his best to make his broadcast interesting: "Passengers are
looking out the windows waving. The ship is standing still now.
The vast motors are just holding it." He was reaching for visual
images that could make the listeners see what was going on.

"Here it comes, ladies and gentlemen, and what a sight it is,
a thrilling one, a marvelous sight. . . . The sun is striking the
windows of the observation deck on the westward side and spar-
kling like glittering jewels on the background of black velvet . . .
Oh, oh, oh . . . !"

What followed was to become one of the most famous, and
certainly the most anguished, on-the-scene accounts of a disaster
ever recorded. His voice breaking with near hysteria, Morrison
exclaimed:

"It's burst into flames . . . Get out of the way, please, oh
my, this is terrible, oh my, get out of the way, please! It is burning,
bursting into flames and is falling. . . . Oh! This is one of the
worst . . . Oh! It's a terrific sight. . . . Oh! . . . and all the hu-
manity! . . ."

A tongue of flame leaped from the rear of the ship, and within
seconds the whole length of the great airship was in flames, and it
came crashing to the ground.

The destruction of the *Hindenberg*. (*Wide World*)

The fire started when the *Hindenberg* was hovering about a hundred feet from the ground. A number of people saved themselves by jumping from the windows of the airship before it hit the ground. An acrobat and dancer named Joseph Spah landed skillfully on his feet, suffering only a fractured ankle. Most jumpers, however, were more seriously injured. Some aboard survived the crash and were able to get out of the wreck before it was totally consumed in the flames. The fire and crash were so sudden, so spectacular, that it looked as if no one could possibly have survived, yet a majority of those who had been aboard, sixty-two out of a total of ninety-seven passengers and crewmen, did survive, though many suffered severe burns or other injuries. Thirteen passengers and twenty-two crewmen perished, and one ground crewman was killed by the flaming debris.

As disasters go, the destruction of the *Hindenberg* is a fairly modest one, yet, though it happened half a century ago, its fame endures. There are a number of reasons why the *Hindenberg* sticks in the public memory: It was a spectacular and well-witnessed tragedy. There was Morrison's broadcast, and a whole series of astonishing photographs and newsreel films of the great airship in flames. It marked the end of an era. After the *Hindenberg* disaster, no lighter-than-air ship ever carried another paying passenger. Where they had once been promoted as a safe, smooth, and luxurious means of long-distance transport, rigid airships or dirigibles were thereafter seen as dangerous and obsolete. But a large part of the eternal fascination of the *Hindenberg* disaster is that there is a genuine mystery as to why and how the ship was destroyed. Was the explosion and fire the result of an accident, an "act of God," or was it sabotage?

In order to understand the controversy that has surrounded the *Hindenberg* disaster, it is necessary to recall the political situation of the time. In 1937, Hitler and the Nazi party were in the ascendancy in Germany. Everything German was treated as a symbol of Nazi power and superiority. The tail fins of the great airship sported huge swastikas. In 1936, the *Hindenberg* had played a prominent part in the Nazi-rigged elections in the Rhineland. It had been used to drop leaflets and blare propaganda from a large radio and loudspeaker installed in the belly of the ship. The great ship flew over the opening-day ceremonies of the Berlin Olympics in 1936. Some of those connected with the *Hindenberg*, like Dr. Hugo Eckener, director of the Zeppelin Company, which operated the great ship, were not at all happy about its use as an instrument of Nazi propaganda, but there was little they could do about it. The majority of the young officers and crewmen aboard the ship appear to have been either Nazi Party members or sympathizers. The ship itself was an unmistakable symbol of the superiority of the "New Germany."

Other nations had tried to construct dirigibles along the lines of the *Hindenberg*, but these invariably crashed or burned, often with lives being lost. Only the Germans seem to have mastered the technology of the lighter-than-air ship. The Germans had begun building airships under the direction of Count Ferdinand von Zeppelin before World War I. The *Graf Zeppelin*, launched in 1928, was taking paying passengers across the Atlantic only a year after Charles Lindberg had barely been able to reach Paris alone. The *Hindenberg*, successor to the *Graf Zeppelin*, was an even more magnificent creation. It was over 800 feet in length, and capable of flying nonstop up to 8,800 miles. It had seventy staterooms, a lavishly decorated staircase leading from one deck to another, a lounge with an aluminum piano, a dining room, and a bar. The *Hindenberg* provided passengers with a luxury and comfort unmatched, even by the great ocean liners.

The ship was powered by four 1,200-horsepower diesel engines, placed so far back that they could barely be heard by the passengers. Travel was not speedy by today's standards—the *Hindenberg* averaged just over eighty miles per hour in good weather, and the trip across the Atlantic took about three days, subject to weather delays. But this compared favorably to ocean-liner crossings, and on the *Hindenberg* the passengers didn't get seasick.

Everyone knew that the potential for explosion and fire on a craft like the *Hindenberg* was very real. The ship was held aloft by sixteen balloon-cloth gas cells containing 7,000,000 cubic feet of hydrogen, one of the most explosive and hottest-burning gasses known. The builders of the *Hindenberg* had wanted to use non-explosive helium, but the main supplier of helium in the world was the United States, and the gas had been reserved for the exclusive use of the United States Navy since 1927. The United States was certainly not about to supply helium to a potential adversary like Nazi Germany.

Precautions against fire aboard the *Hindenberg* were elaborate. To give just one example, all matches and lighters were confiscated from passengers on boarding. The craft had a specially insulated smoking room with a double-door entrance, located well below the hydrogen bags. This room was pressurized to keep stray hydrogen out, and a steward was on duty at all times to light the passengers' cigars and cigarettes, and to make sure that no fire left the room.

As a result of the builder's skills and experience, and the many precautions taken, the *Hindenberg* had built up an enviable safety record—it had already made ten trips across the Atlantic without a mishap. Lloyd's of London had insured the craft at a very modest premium, and most people considered the *Hindenberg* just about the safest means of transatlantic transportation available. Thus, the shock of the fire and crash was even greater because it was so unexpected.

Almost immediately after the disaster, a board of inquiry was convened in the United States to investigate the causes. The United States investigators got surprisingly little help from the Germans. In Berlin, a decision had been made that sabotage as a cause of the disaster should not be discussed publicly. The destruction of the *Hindenberg* had been a blow to the pride of Nazi Germany. To admit that the great symbol of Nazi power had been destroyed by the enemies of the Nazis would have been a humiliation, and the success of such an act (which today we would call terrorism) would doubtless have encouraged other enemies of Hitler to attempt more acts of sabotage. Time bombs had actually been planted on other zeppelins, but none had been successfully detonated.

However, it is now known that the German government was extremely concerned about the possibility of sabotage on this particular trip of the *Hindenberg*. The backgrounds of all the passengers had been checked carefully, and there were a couple of SS men infiltrated among the passengers, just to keep an eye on those considered suspicious. The careful check of the luggage for explosive devices or any sort of weapons would have been familiar to today's air travelers. But it was unprecedented in 1937. Clearly the Nazis were worried.

The wreckage of the *Hindenberg* had burned so completely that very little was left for investigators to look at. However, New York detectives did find pieces of material that could possibly have been the remains of a timing device for a bomb. This evidence, however, was ignored, and the inquiry concluded that the disaster was probably due to the electric atmospheric phenomenon known as Saint Elmo's fire igniting the hydrogen gas. In fact, it is almost certain that the U.S. investigators had decided to deliberately rule out the possibility of sabotage, because the implications would have created a very nasty international incident.

Privately, it seems that practically all of those who were experts on airships had concluded that the cause of the disaster was almost certainly sabotage.

Who could have been the saboteur? A number of passengers

had been suspects, but years later, members of the Gestapo quietly confided that their chief suspect was one of the crew, a tall, fair-haired young rigger named Erich Spehl. Shortly before the *Hindenberg's* departure, Spehl had been seen around a drinking place where Communists were known to congregrate. He had also frequently been seen in the company of a woman who was suspected of having Communist associations. This woman was also known to have visited the Frankfurt offices of the Zeppelin company three times during the final flight of the *Hindenberg*—she was either just curious or anxious about something. She must have known of Spehl's plan.

Unlike the passengers, Spehl had almost unlimited access to the cavernous interior of the great airship. He had been on duty alone, near the rear of the ship, until 6 P.M. on the fatal night. The fire had started in the rear of the ship. After being relieved of his watch, Spehl went to the forward portion of the ship, and was one of the crewmen farthest from the place where the explosion occurred. It did no good, for Erich Spehl was one of those killed in the crash.

A few other bits of circumstantial evidence had been gathered by the Gestapo: Spehl was an enthusiastic photographer, and an exploding flashbulb, if strategically placed, might have been enough to ignite the hydrogen.

Writer Michael M. Mooney, who sifted through all the evidence for his book *The Hindenberg*, believes that Spehl, a devout Catholic, may have been motivated more by private religious feelings than by politics. His connection with Communists appears to have been very slight. Mooney believes that Spehl had not intended to kill anyone, and certainly not himself, in the explosion. The explosive device, says Mooney, was probably timed to go off after the ship had docked and passengers and crew had left, but something must have gone wrong with the timer. The docking of the *Hindenberg* had also been delayed for nearly ten hours because of bad weather. This could easily have upset the timing of Spehl's plan and explain why he tried to flee to safety in the front of the ship.

The evidence against Erich Spehl is intriguing but entirely circumstantial. Since he is unable to tell his own story, uncertainty will remain. However, the evidence that someone exploded a bomb aboard the *Hindenberg* on May 6, 1937, is much stronger. Indeed, it's hard to imagine what else could have caused the disaster.

It has often been said that when the *Hindenberg* was destroyed, the potential of the rigid airship as a means of transportation was also destroyed. That's an exaggeration, for while the disaster may have hastened the end of the rigid airship, the vehicle was doomed anyway. Though luxurious, and probably safe enough, it simply was too slow to compete with the rapidly developing airplane.

5

Whatever Happened To...?

1593

CHRISTOPHER MARLOWE   On the night of May 30, 1593, the brilliant twenty-nine-year-old English poet and playwright Christopher Marlowe was killed in a drunken brawl in Eleanor Bulls's Tavern in Depford, near London. It was said that the poet and three companions—Nicholas Skeres, Robert Poley, and Ingram Frizer—had spent the day in the tavern drinking. When time came to pay up, so the story was told, Marlowe objected violently to his share of the bill. There was a fight, and he grabbed Frizer's dagger and cut him on the head. Frizer wrested the dagger back and killed Marlowe with one stab above the eye. Frizer claimed self-defense, and less than a month after the killing, he was granted a full pardon.

The case seems straightforward enough. Marlowe was known to be a drinker and a brawler as well as a poet, and such an end might have been expected. Yet from time to time, questions have been raised about the violent death of Christopher Marlowe.

A different version of Marlowe's death holds that the quarrel did not erupt over money, but over homosexual advances that Marlowe made to Frizer. A variation of that theory is that Frizer was ordered to kill Marlowe by his master, Sir Thomas Walsingham. It seems, according to this version of events, that Walsingham and Marlowe had been homosexual lovers, but Sir Thomas now wished to end the affair permanently.

But by far the most intriguing theory about the death of Christopher Marlowe suggests that he didn't die in that tavern brawl at all; that he lived on for many years successfully writing plays under the name of William Shakespeare!

Just a few days before the apparent fatal encounter in the Depford tavern, Marlowe had been arrested on the charge of atheism. It's difficult today to determine just exactly what such a charge really meant in Elizabethan times, and how serious a danger the playwright was really in. Many intellectuals of the day freely advocated highly unorthodox religious views without any censure at all, yet, theoretically at least, Marlowe could have been executed on such a charge.

This theory holds that Marlowe's sponsor and lover Walsingham contrived the "murder," that another body was substituted and Marlowe sailed to France, where he lived in comfort writing plays and having them presented under the attribution of an obscure Stratford actor named Shakespeare.

The dates work out fairly well. Shakespeare's first work appeared just a few months after Marlowe's supposed death. Shakespeare and Marlowe would have been roughly the same age. They both wrote poetry and plays, and at least one writer, Calvin Hoffman, has attempted to show that Marlowe was the author of the Shakespeare plays. The American title of Hoffman's 1955 book is *Murder of the Man Who Was Shakespeare*. This theory, however, has gained virtually no support among other scholars. A more popular pretender to Shakespeare's works is Sir Francis Bacon—but there isn't much scholarly support for that theory, either.

Since Shakespeare came from an obscure town and an undistinguished, indeed, uneducated family, and the details of his life are not well documented, it is inevitable that some people would try to prove that someone else wrote his plays. But the truth almost certainly is that William Shakespeare wrote Shakespeare's plays and Christopher Marlowe was really killed in a drunken tavern brawl.

1701

CAPTAIN KIDD'S TREASURE   Captain William Kidd was not a particularly lucky man. The name Captain Kidd is associated more closely than any other with the romantic image of the pirate—yet the real Captain Kidd was neither as notorious nor successful as legend would have it. The crimes for which he was tried and ultimately executed at Wapping on Friday May 23, 1701, would, under other conditions, not have been considered crimes at all. Kidd felt, with considerable justification, that he had been betrayed by powerful men who had once encouraged his activities. As he stood beside the hangman, he claimed his right to deliver the traditional "last speech" to the crowd. It was usual for the condemned to confess their sins and ask God's forgiveness. But drunk and angry Kidd would have none of that. He denounced his enemies and all those who had testified against him. The pastor of Newgate Prison did not consider this a satisfactory last speech.

But one need not shed too many tears over William Kidd, for in his career he had indeed been a pirate. He was a tough, arrogant, often violent man who had killed when he felt it was necessary to do so. The irony in Kidd's career is that his final voyage, the one for which he was condemned, had been conceived as an expedition to capture pirates. The voyage, which began in 1697, was supported politically and financially by a group of powerful Whig politicians in London.

Kidd was to capture ships that belonged to enemies of British interests, and his backers were to share in what they hoped would be the very substantial spoils of these captures. The venture had a quasi-legality in Britain. But Kidd's voyage went awry from the start, and he ended up attacking some vessels that he should not have touched. But the laws and customs were so fuzzy that his guilt was, at best, ambiguous. However, in the more than two years that Kidd was at sea, there had been political changes in

An eighteenth century drawing of a pirate hanging at Execution Dock. (National Maritime Museum, Greenwich, England)

London. The powerful Whig lords had lost some of their power, and their enemies were looking for ways to further discredit them. One way was to link them with Captain Kidd "the pirate." The issues surrounding the capture, trial, and ultimate execution of William Kidd are complex and often murky. But it is safe to say that had there not been a shift of political fortunes in London, William Kidd would not have ended his life at the end of a rope; indeed, he might have wound up a fairly wealthy and respectable retired sea captain.

But what has really intrigued most people about Captain Kidd over the years are the stories of his "lost treasure" that is supposed to be buried somewhere. Searches have been conducted from Nova Scotia to the South China Sea, but most have centered on the East Coast of North America, where Kidd's final voyage ended. Rumors as to the location of Captain Kidd's treasure continue to circulate even today.

Alas for romance, there almost certainly was no treasure buried by Captain Kidd; indeed, the whole idea of buried pirate treasure is more legend than reality. In his biography of Captain Kidd, historian Robert C. Ritchie has written:

"No image is more closely associated with pirates than the habit of burying treasure: on a moonlit beach buccaneers drag ashore a heavy chest, then stagger across the sand to find a convenient spot back from the water where they can safely bury their loot. Sometimes dead bodies accompany the chests, as only one or two men return to the ship in full possession of the secret. This familiar tale is a pleasant fable, but it does not jibe with the facts.

"The men who turned to piracy did so because they wanted money. As soon as possible after capturing a prize they insisted on dividing the loot, which they could then gamble with or carry home. The idea of burying booty on a tropical island would have struck them as insane, especially since all the men on board would demand to know the 'secret', which would then be no secret. . . ."

Rumors of Captain Kidd's "lost treasure" began in his own lifetime. He had returned from his final voyage with a considerable quantity of gold, silver, and jewels. He gave shares of the loot to his crew. A substantial portion was held to pay off his powerful backers, and what he considered his share he apparently gave to his wife when he reached New York. (Yes, there was a Mrs. Kidd and several children. One cannot resist calling them kiddies.) Much of this loot was traced down and confiscated after Kidd was arrested.

Writes Ritchie: "What remains behind cannot be known with any degree of certainty. With so many ships and men slipping about with shares of the booty, we will never know conclusively whether a 'treasure' remained behind. If there *was* a substantial amount, it was surely put into the hands of some individual and subsequently spent."

There was a story at the time that Kidd had hidden a forty-pound bag of gold somewhere between Boston and New York. The tale is an unlikely one. It's doubtful that Kidd's sharp-eyed crew would have allowed him to slip away unnoticed with such an amount. And if Kidd did have a hidden treasure somewhere, he would certainly have tried to get his hands on it in order to buy his way out of the troubles that would ultimately engulf him. With a large, well-placed bribe, William Kidd might well have escaped the gallows. But he didn't have the resources. However, this commonsense observation will do nothing to dim the luster of Captain Kidd's treasure in the eyes of those who wish to believe in it— and hope perhaps to find it someday.

1872

LORD GORDON-GORDON   His true identity remains a
mystery. He first turned up in Edinburgh, Scotland, in 1868. Then
he called himself Lord Glencairn. Elegantly attired and accompanied by a liveried servant, he walked into the establishment of
Marshall and Son, dealers in rare gems. He made a satisfyingly
large purchase and paid by check. He continued to make large
purchases over the next few months, but always on credit. By early
1869, the handsome young "lord" owed the jewelers £25,000, or
about $100,000, a lot of money today, a fortune in 1869. The
jewelers finally became suspicious and sent for the police, but Lord
Glencairn had disappeared. A thorough investigation revealed that
there was no Lord Glencairn. The man was a charming and per-
suasive impostor.

Two years later, the same man appeared in Minneapolis, Minnesota, now calling himself Lord Gordon-Gordon. He told the
people of Minneapolis that he was prepared to buy up vast tracts
of land owned by the Northern Pacific Railroad on which he would
relocate some of the impoverished tenants of his native Scotland.
Sensing a land boom, the Minnesotans were enthusiastic. And they
were flattered by the attention paid them by so obviously noble
and wealthy an aristocrat. Not many lords visited Minnesota in
the late nineteenth century.

After a few months of being wined and dined in the most
lavish style possible in Minnesota, Lord Gordon-Gordon moved
slowly eastward, allegedly to arrange for the transfer of funds from
England to America to pay for the huge land purchases. His reputation for wealth and pious intentions preceded him, and by the
time he arrived in New York in February 1872, he was well known.
Lord Gordon-Gordon immediately checked into the finest suite
in the best hotel in the city.

Once in New York, he moved with great care toward his real

intended victim, the financier Jay Gould. Lord Gordon-Gordon
had not chosen an easy mark, for Gould himself was little more
than a con man. He was notorious even among his robber baron
associates, for he had cheated some of them as well. There probably
wasn't a tighter man with the dollar in America than Jay Gould.

The center of Gould's power was the Erie Railroad, a company that he had looted and often used as a cover for his other
dubious financial dealings.

Lord Gordon-Gordon's first act was to establish his bona
fides with Horace Greeley, editor of the *New York Tribune* and
a powerful voice for reform. His lordship confided to Greeley that
he and his English associates had quietly bought up a huge block
of Erie Railroad shares, indeed, that they now had a controlling
interest in the line and wanted it cleaned up, which meant getting
rid of Jay Gould as president and manager. Greeley was delighted,
but Gould certainly was not. He did believe, as did Greeley and
others, that Gordon-Gordon could deliver on his promise to clean
up the railroad and that he was in serious trouble, so he finally
arranged a meeting with Gordon-Gordon to discuss the matter.

During the discussion, the usually crafty Gould seemed to
have been in awe of Gordon-Gordon's apparent wealth and mas-
tery of the situation. Reluctantly, the elegant Englishman appeared
to agree to allow Gould to continue in his position of power on
the promise that he would mend his ways and operate the Erie
honestly, for the benefit of the shareholders rather than for his
own personal benefit. But promises, said Gordon-Gordon, were
not enough. He also got from Jay Gould a signed letter of resig-
nation, which he could use at any time. More important, Gould
gave Gordon-Gordon stock worth about five hundred thousand
dollars as a pledge that he would carry out his agreement. As a
further pledge, Gould turned over some two hundred thousand
dollars in cash to be held in escrow. So great was the financier's
trust in the bogus lord that he did not even require a written receipt,
saying his lordship's word was "more than sufficient."

Gordon-Gordon immediately began selling the stock, and
only then did Gould realize that he had been stung. And he was
furious. He had Gordon-Gordon arrested for fraud. But there were
plenty of people who still believed in "his lordship," and even
more who hated Jay Gould and wished to see him brought down.

Commodore Cornelius Vanderbilt put up the cash for the lord's bail. Vanderbilt had lost a bundle on one of Gould's deals and was seeking revenge. A prominent lawyer whom Gould had once cheated offered to represent Gordon-Gordon free of charge.

When he first appeared in court, Lord Gordon-Gordon seemed confident, almost aloof from the proceedings, but he must have known that the game was nearly up. Gould had cabled England and learned, beyond a doubt, that the man calling himself Lord Gordon-Gordon was an impostor.

Shortly after being released from jail, Gordon-Gordon stuffed one hundred fifty thousand dollars, all the cash he could lay his hands on, in a suitcase and grabbed the first train to Canada. Gould offered twenty-five thousand dollars for his capture. The Edinburgh jewelers also discovered that Lord Gordon-Gordon and Lord Glencairn were one and the same and sent investigators to track him down. Even the embarrassed citizens of Minneapolis were on his trail.

Gordon-Gordon holed up in the remote outpost of Fort Garry, Manitoba. He once again used his considerable charm to win over the people of Fort Garry, and successfully staved off all attempts at extradition. The angry Minnesotans, having no legal claim, tried to kidnap Gordon-Gordon. The attempt was foiled by the Canadian police and five Americans, two of whom would later become governors of Minnesota, the others, three congressmen, were jailed because of the attempt.

In the end, it was the Scottish jewelers who had the most clout with Canadian authorities, for Canada was still part of the British Empire. A clerk for the jewelers got a warrant for "Lord Glencairn" and, surprisingly, the con man agreed to return to England to rebut these "foolish charges."

A going-away party was held by the citizens of Fort Garry for their distinguished visitor. The festivities went on until three in the morning, with Gordon-Gordon displaying the same easy charm he had always shown. Still smiling, he retired to his room and, a few moments later, shot himself through the head.

This unknown adventurer had played for high stakes, and when his luck finally ran out he decided to end the game quickly. He left behind the mystery of his identity.

1873

THE BENDERS   In the 1870s, immigrants were streaming to the West in hopes of making better lives for themselves. When the Bender family moved to Cherryvale in southeastern Kansas and built a log cabin out on the plains, they seemed like just another immigrant family. No one knew where they came from, though they spoke with a guttural accent everyone took to be German.

The family consisted of William John Bender, the father, about sixty years old, his wife "Ma" Bender (no one seems to have ever called her anything else), their moronic son John, and daughter

John Bender (*NYPL*)

Kate Bender (*NYPL*)

Kate. Kate was the most interesting of the lot. She apparently posed as a spirit medium and healer, and gave some public séances in small Kansas towns.

The Benders used their isolated cabin as a combination store and inn. They sold canned goods and coffee to travelers. Sometimes they would put travelers up for the night, not an uncommon practice in a place where houses were few and far between. If the traveler happened to be alone, and appeared to be carrying money, chances were good that he would never leave the Bender cabin alive.

The cabin was divided by a canvas curtain—visitors ate on one side and slept on the other. Though no one knows for sure, it was surmised the Benders carried out their killings by having Kate maneuver the victim against the canvas curtain. Then old man Bender or moronic John would smash his skull from behind with a sledgehammer. The victims were then taken to the cellar, stripped of all money and valuables, and buried somewhere near the cabin.

In March 1873, a man named Colonel A. M. York showed up in Cherryvale looking for his brother, Dr. William H. York, who had disappeared. The colonel had traced his brother as far as Cherryvale, but there the trail went cold. Colonel York stopped at the Bender place and asked a few questions, but the family insisted they had never seen the missing man. York rode on, but finding no evidence that his brother had ever gotten beyond Cherryvale, he headed back to the Benders. The cabin door was standing open, and the family wagon was gone. The Benders, obviously alarmed, had fled.

A group of men went out to the Bender place, and when they examined the cellar they found dried blood. It didn't take long to locate about a dozen shallow graves around the cabin. Little effort had been made to hide them. One of the graves contained the remains of Dr. William H. York.

A posse of seven men rode out in search of "the Bloody Benders," or the "Hell Benders," as they came to be known. The posse was gone for several weeks, and upon their return said they could find no trace of the murderous family. However, the members of the posse were remarkably uncommunicative about where they had been and what they had done. There was an immediate suspicion that the posse had actually found the Benders, lynched them, and didn't want to admit it. There was also the matter of any money or other valuables the Benders might have been carrying. That was never found, either.

In the meantime, the Benders had become famous. Souvenir hunters demolished the cabin, and boards from it were selling well, as far away as New York. Inevitably, the Benders themselves were being reported all over the country. In 1889, two women were arrested in Michigan and identified as Kate and Ma Bender. They were both sent to Cherryvale, Kansas, where many people positively identified them as Ma and Kate. However, positive proof was produced that the women had been in Wisconsin in 1872, and the "positive" identification was false.

In 1909, and again in 1910, two dying men confessed that they had been members of the Bender posse and had helped to butcher the Benders and bury them in a twenty-foot well. Rumor had it that Kate was supposed to have been burned alive. One of the men said that the posse had taken several thousand dollars from the bodies of the Benders. A search was made where the Benders' bodies were supposed to have been buried, but the area had long since been planted over with corn, and nothing was found.

There is no way of proving that the Benders actually were killed by the posse, and it's entirely possible that one or more survived. In 1884, some eleven years after they fled from Kansas, an old man with a German accent was seized in the Montana Territory for a murder in which the victim's skull had been crushed from behind—the old Bender murder technique. He was said to resemble old man Bender—at least he was about the right age. Local authorities were convinced that they had in their hands the patriarch of the notorious Hell Benders clan.

The old man was clamped in ankle irons and thrown in jail. The next morning he was found dead. He had tried to cut off his own foot in a desperate effort to escape, but as a result he had bled to death. The dead man's skull, invariably identified as Bender's skull, was kept on display in a local saloon for years, until, like the Benders themselves, it disappeared.

188?

"MYSTERIOUS DAVE" MATHER   A stock character of many western melodramas is the mysterious, silent gunslinger who rides into town, kills a few people, and rides away into the sunset. This character may have been modeled on David Mather (or Mathers), known by the nickname of "Mysterious Dave."

Mysterious Dave was just one of many rootless and violent men who roamed the West during the rough and lawless, but now legendary, 1880s. No one seemed to know where he came from, or even what his real name was. He had the reputation in Texas of being a horse thief and train robber. No one dared ask him about himself, because his temper was as notorious as his reticence.

At that period of Western history, the line between outlaw and lawman was often a hazy one, and anyone who could handle a gun might be a fugitive one day and sheriff the next. Mysterious Dave had been appointed a constable in Las Vegas, Nevada (a small, undistinguished town in the 1880s). On January 25, 1880, he came upon a drunken railroad worker named Joseph Costello. Dave ordered the drunk to move on, and when Costello appeared to fumble for his gun, Dave shot him dead. This wasn't a crime in the eyes of the citizens of Las Vegas, who in the 1880s had fairly tolerant views on such subjects as police brutality and the excessive use of force. Yet having a constable who was so quick to gun down a citizen who just had too much to drink may have made folks a bit nervous. In any event, Dave lost his job.

Dave next appeared in Dodge City, Kansas, a rip-roaring cattle town that has attained truly mythic status in the history of the American West. It was now whispered that Dave had helped three of his friends break out of a New Mexico jail and that he had been responsible for a number of killings throughout the Southwest. Despite this record, or possibly because of it, Mysterious Dave was appointed assistant marshal in Dodge City in

June 1883. But when a new marshal, William "Bill" Tilghman, was elected, Dave was replaced by Thomas Nixon, a famous buffalo hunter.

That may have given Dave a reason to resent Nixon. There were other, more substantial, reasons. Both men owned saloons, and they got into a price war. When Nixon started offering two beers for a quarter, Dave lowered that to two for twenty cents. Then Nixon allegedly began to play dirty by bribing a distributor to cut off Mysterious Dave's beer supply. Dave responded in his traditional way—he went gunning for Nixon.

The assistant city marshal believed that the best defense was a good offense. On the evening of July 18, 1844, he hid outside of Dave's saloon, and when Dave came out, Nixon took a shot at him. The shot grazed Dave's head, and Nixon, as he fled down the alley, thought he had killed his rival. But he was wrong.

There was never much of a secret about who had fired the shot, yet when Nixon was brought in for questioning, Mysterious Dave refused to press charges. He had plans of his own. Three days after the ambush, Mysterious Dave walked up behind Nixon, who was standing outside a saloon on Front Street, and said quietly, "Hello, Tom." He then fired four bullets into Nixon's back.

Another legendary Western character, gambler and gunfighter Bat Masterson, was in a nearby saloon when he heard the shots. He rushed up to the dead man, who had been his friend, and the thought of revenging himself on Mysterious Dave may have crossed Masterson's mind. But Dave was quickly arrested by Tilghman. He was brought to trial for murder in Kinsley, Kansas. Dave's lawyer insisted that his client could never get a fair trial in Dodge City, and he was probably right. Dave freely admitted to shooting Tom Nixon. His justification was that Nixon deserved it. The jury abided by the code of the Old West, and decided that since Nixon had fired the first shot in the feud three days earlier, Dave was merely acting in self-defense. He was acquitted.

After that, the tight-lipped killer vanished just as mysteriously as he had appeared.

1908

BELLE GUNNESS   A hefty farm widow from LaPorte, Indiana, was one of America's most notorious "lonely hearts" murderers at the turn of the century. She became a widow when, as she told a coroner's jury, a meat grinder toppled off a shelf and fell on her husband Peter's head, killing him. The LaPorte coroner thought it was a case of murder. One of Belle's three children told a schoolmate: "My mama killed my poppa. She hit him with a cleaver." But the coroner's jury couldn't bring itself to believe this simple, hardworking woman was a killer, and brought no finding against her.

Belle Gunness was now on her own, more or less, for she seemed to have taken up with a simple-minded handyman named Ray Lamphere. The small Gunness hog farm wasn't particularly profitable, and Belle started a new line of work. She began advertising in the lovelorn columns of various papers for a new husband. One of her ads read: "Rich, good-looking widow, young, owner of a large farm, wishes to get in touch with a gentleman of wealth with cultured tastes. Object, matrimony. No triflers need apply."

The ad was an exaggeration, for she was not rich, good-looking, or young, and her farm was not large. But ads like that did attract a number of potential suitors. From time to time, Belle was seen with one of these gentlemen in town, though they never seemed to hang around too long. What the people of LaPorte didn't know was that the suitors never really left. This they discovered after April 28, 1908, when Belle's farmhouse burned down. Remains of what were taken to be Belle and her three children were found in the ruins, but the feeling of tragedy turned to wonder, and then to horror, as the Gunness property was further explored.

The brother of one of Belle's suitors had arrived in LaPorte and insisted that, after visiting the Gunness farm, his brother had not been heard from again. Suspicions were further aroused when a cache of men's watches were found in the farmhouse rubble.

Cover of dime novel on Belle Gunness case. (*N.Y. Historical Society*)

Still, searchers were not prepared for what they discovered as they began digging around the house. Four bodies were found buried in the hog pen. The next day, another three bodies were unearthed. All in all, the remains of fourteen prospective husbands were located, and some might easily have been overlooked, so no one really knows how many people Belle Gunness killed.

Belle had thrown Ray Lamphere out of her house, and after the fire he began drinking heavily. The sheriff recalled that there had been quite a fight between Ray and Belle, and that she said she was afraid the handyman would try to burn the place down. She even had him arrested once. The sheriff arrested Ray for arson and murder.

The prosecution was never able to convince a jury that Ray had actually killed Belle, but they did think he set fire to the house, and he was sentenced to twenty-one years in jail. He contracted tuberculosis and died in prison, but before his death he allegedly told a cellmate that he had helped Belle dispose of many of the corpses. She would first drug her suitors, then kill them, just as she butchered the hogs on her farm.

According to Lamphere, Belle had not really died in the fire, but rather had found life as a farm woman and murderer too taxing and had decided to disappear. She lured a drunken woman derelict from Chicago to her farm, poisoned her, then burned the house down around her and around her own three children. From the start there had been uncertainty about the identification of Belle Gunness's badly burned corpse. She was then supposed to have taken the twenty or thirty thousand dollars she had gathered from her various occupations and headed for California, where she lived out the remainder of her life in comfort in San Francisco. This, however, is simply rumor, for Belle Gunness was never heard from again and, in fact, might really have died in that fire.

1910

DOROTHY ARNOLD   On the morning of December 12, 1910, a wealthy and socially prominent young woman named Dorothy Arnold left her parents' elegant Manhattan home and walked down Fifth Avenue on a shopping trip. Along the way, she was observed by several people who knew her, but somewhere around 2:00 P.M., she disappeared. As far as we know, Dorothy Arnold was never seen again.

We all know that disappearances are tragically common, but there are a number of features about this case that make it highly unusual. First, Dorothy just wasn't the sort of person who was supposed to disappear—not only was she rich, but her family was extremely respectable. She was the niece of a justice of the United States Supreme Court. Even odder was the way that many of those close to the case, particularly members of her family, acted; it was as if they knew a lot more than they were willing to admit.

The basic facts are simple enough. At 11:00 A.M., Dorothy left her family's home on East Seventy-ninth Street in Manhattan. She said that she was going to buy a dress for a party. Her mother offered to go with her. That was unusual, since her mother was supposed to be an invalid who rarely left the house. (The nature of Mrs. Arnold's presumed illness has never been made clear.) Dorothy said she needn't bother and walked over to Fifth Avenue alone.

Dorothy was dressed expensively in the fashion of the day. She was wearing a large blue hat, a blue coat and skirt, and she carried a large fur muff. On Fifth Avenue, she looked like many other rich young ladies. But in other parts of the city, her expensive clothes would have made her stand out at once. The difference in dress between the classes was even greater in 1910 than it is today.

Dorothy took a long walk. Her first stop was a candy store at Fifty-ninth Street and Fifth Avenue. The salesgirl recognized

Dorothy Arnold (*Culver*)

her, and she bought a half pound of chocolates that she charged
to the family account. She then walked another thirty-five
blocks—fifty-two in all—to a bookstore on Fifth Avenue and
Twenty-seventh Street. She looked through some books and bought
one, a collection of short stories. This, too, she charged to a family
account.

MRS. ARNOLD ARRIVING FROM ITALY; HER SON, HUSBAND AND DOROTHY'S SUITOR.

MRS. FRANCIS R. ARNOLD and JOHN ARNOLD LEAVING the STEAMER

GEORGE C GRISCOM JR.

(Culver)

The length of her walk seems unusual, for though Dorothy was young and strong, she did not habitually take long walks, particularly on cold, icy December days.

Outside the bookstore, Dorothy bumped into a friend named Gladys King. As Gladys later recalled, the two chatted for a few moments about the party they were both supposed to attend. Then Gladys said she had to meet her mother, that it was almost two o'clock and she was already late. When Gladys crossed the street, she turned to wave to Dorothy. That was the last time anyone ever reported seeing Dorothy Arnold.

Dorothy didn't return home for dinner, and she didn't call, which was quite unlike her. The family was worried, and they telephoned friends to see if they knew anything. No one did. It was at this point that the Arnold family began acting oddly. They insisted that her friends not tell anyone that Dorothy was missing. Later that evening, when a friend called back to ask if Dorothy had returned, her father lied and said she had.

The family seemed obsessed with respectability, with keeping the news of the girl's disappearance quiet. The next morning, when Dorothy had still not returned, the family didn't go to the police, but they did call a lawyer and family friend named John S. Keith. Keith, along with Dorothy's father, Francis Arnold, searched her room. All her clothes were there except those she had worn on her walk down Fifth Avenue. Only two things were out of the ordinary: on Dorothy's desk were a couple of transatlantic steamship folders and in the fireplace was a pile of burned papers.

Keith checked the morgues, hospitals, and jails, and when he found nothing in New York, he went on to Boston and Philadelphia. No trace of her was found, yet the family still did not go to the police. Francis Arnold hired the famous Pinkerton Detective Agency, which expanded the search for Dorothy throughout the country. The family quietly offered a reward of five thousand dollars for any information on the missing girl. Still there was nothing.

On January 24, six weeks after Dorothy disappeared, the Arnold family finally officially went to the police. Of course, the New York police already knew about the disappearance, because the Pinkertons had been circulating Dorothy's picture all over the country. The police couldn't do anything officially until they were notified by the family.

The man who handled the disappearance for the New York police was Deputy Police Commissioner William J. Flynn. Flynn advised Francis Arnold to get the widest possible publicity about the disappearance, because someone who heard about it just might have a clue. But publicity is what the family had been trying to avoid all along. Ultimately, Flynn prevailed. On the afternoon of January 26, 1911, Francis Arnold called in newspaper reporters for a very curious news conference. He told the reporters that he was sure his daughter had been killed while walking through Central Park and that her body had been thrown into the reservoir. The reporters were not willing to passively accept that explanation. They began asking questions about Dorothy's personal life. Was she happy? What men did she know? Arnold, who was not used to having his authority challenged, flew into a rage and tossed the newsmen out of his office.

This impetuous act merely served to stimulate the reporters' natural curiosity, and they began digging, questioning friends, neighbors, and servants. Very soon they discovered that Dorothy Arnold had not been very happy. She had wanted to be a writer, and just a few months before her disappearance she told her family that she also wanted to move out of the family home and to take an apartment in Greenwich Village. The family wouldn't hear of it. Girls of her class were supposed to stay home until they were married, and they certainly were not supposed to move to Greenwich Village, which was filled with artists, writers, and other social undesirables.

Dorothy had written a story that had been rejected by one of the major magazines. When the members of her family found out about the rejection, they teased her mercilessly. They had no sympathy for her artistic goals.

In the matter of men, the reporters dug up even more interesting information. She was involved with a man named George Griscom, Jr. Everybody called him Junior, and the nickname was appropriate. He was a forty-year-old balding mama's boy. He still lived with his wealthy parents in Philadelphia, and traveled everywhere with them. He didn't work. He didn't seem to do anything—his mother even still picked out his shirts. For a while, Dorothy had been going around saying that she was engaged to Junior, but her family disapproved strongly.

While both Dorothy and Junior seemed very much under the control of their respective families, they did manage to slip away now and then. In September 1910, just four months before she disappeared, Dorothy told her parents that she was going to visit an old classmate, Theodora Bates, who lived near Boston. On September 16, she left New York, but instead of seeing Theodora, she went directly to Boston and checked into the Hotel Lenox. Junior Griscom had arrived in Boston a day earlier and was staying at the nearby Hotel Essex. He had reserved Dorothy's room at the Lenox.

For the next week, the couple went around Boston, looking very happy and making no particular attempt to hide their real identities. Before leaving Boston, Dorothy pawned some jewelry, using her own name and address. That's how reporters and police found out about the Boston trip.

Whether the Arnold family knew about Dorothy's Boston meeting with Junior is a matter of speculation. But when she asked to visit Theodora again, the family agreed. Theodora was now teaching in Washington, D.C., and Dorothy paid her a Thanksgiving visit.

Dorothy arrived in Washington the day before Thanksgiving. On Thanksgiving Day, she said she did not feel well and spent the morning in bed. Sometime during the day, a bulky envelope addressed to Dorothy Arnold arrived at the house. Theodora recalled that it came by regular mail. But there would have been no regular mail delivery on Thanksgiving Day. Besides, how could Dorothy have arranged to have her mail sent to Washington, since she only intended to stay a few days?

Theodora thought the envelope must have contained another of Dorothy's stories being returned by a magazine. When Dorothy was given the envelope, she didn't even bother to open it. It was as if she knew what it contained. Theodora was dying to know, but Dorothy didn't volunteer any information and Theodora didn't dare ask. Dorothy left the day after Thanksgiving, though she had originally planned to stay through the weekend.

It was now the end of November, less than two weeks before Dorothy Arnold took her final walk down Fifth Avenue. She got some letters from Junior, who was in Italy with his parents, and she wrote to him. Her letter was cheerful and noncommittal but contained one troubling and possibly significant paragraph:

"Well, it has come back. *McClure's* [the magazine] has turned me down. All I can see ahead is a long road with no turning. Mother will always think an accident has happened."

As soon as Dorothy disappeared, her family immediately thought of Junior. The lawyer John Keith sent him a cable in Italy. He immediately cabled back, "KNOW ABSOLUTELY NOTHING. JUNIOR." There were several other letters exchanged between Junior and the Arnold family.

On January 16, Junior got some visitors. One was a young man, the other a woman wearing a heavy veil that completely obscured her face. According to reports that appeared in the newspapers, there was an argument, perhaps even a fight. The two visitors left with a packet of letters.

The young man was quickly identified as John W. Arnold, Dorothy's older brother. At first there was speculation that the veiled woman was Dorothy herself, but she turned out to be Dorothy's mother. The family had said that Mrs. Arnold had been so upset by her daughter's disappearance that she had to enter a rest home, but, actually, she had gone to Italy with her son. John Arnold came back to America; Mrs. Arnold stayed in Europe. Again there was speculation that she thought Dorothy would come looking for Junior and she wanted to be close at hand. More probably she just wanted to avoid American reporters. Junior Griscom himself returned to America in February. He put ads in the papers begging Dorothy to return. She never did, and no new information on the disappearance has ever turned up.

What happened to Dorothy Arnold? Today we can only guess. She might have been murdered and dumped into the reservoir, as her father had claimed. But no body was ever found.

Perhaps she ran away and took on a new identity. It's always possible, but Dorothy had very little money with her when she vanished. She had always led a sheltered life, so how could she have survived on her own without help? Inevitably, there were reports of Dorothy's having been spotted in different parts of the country, but none of these leads ever amounted to anything. This attractive and romantic solution seems highly unlikely.

It is far more probable that Dorothy, despondent over the way her life was going, had decided to kill herself. There was that telling phrase in the letter to Junior: "Mother will always think an accident has happened."

She knew that one of Junior's cousins had killed himself because his family would not allow him to marry a poor woman. That young man had jumped from a transatlantic ship. Steamship folders had been found in Dorothy's room. However, had she jumped from a transatlantic ship, it would have been known immediately that a young woman passenger was missing, since transatlantic ships kept careful passenger lists. It would not have taken long to connect the missing passenger to Dorothy Arnold, no matter what name she traveled under. It is more likely that Dorothy jumped from one of the many short-haul ships in New York Harbor, where no passenger lists were kept. But even that explanation is not entirely credible. Why did no one notice the fashionably dressed young lady on board? What happened to the body? Why did the last person to see her alive say she seemed cheerful? If she wanted her death to appear to be an accident, then she would not have left a suicide note; Could a would-be writer have resisted the temptation to write that final note?

One can't escape the feeling that some people knew a lot more about the disappearance of Dorothy Arnold than they would say. From the beginning, her family always was so sure that she was dead. Perhaps they knew she killed herself, perhaps the body had even been found, but the family had tried to cover up this fact because suicide was considered so shameful. The Arnold family was certainly influential enough to mount an effective cover-up.

In 1921, Captain J. J. Ayers, head of the New York City Department of Missing Persons, gave a speech in which, according to many who heard it, he said that the family and the police had always known the truth about the disappearance. Later, Ayers denied that he ever said any such thing. He insisted it was all a misunderstanding. But was it?

1921

"TERRIBLE TOMMY" O'CONNER   Somewhere in a basement storeroom of the Chicago Criminal Courts Building there is
(or was until fairly recently) a dismantled but potentially operative
gallows waiting for the return of "Terrible Tommy" O'Conner.
O'Conner escaped just a few days before his scheduled execution
by hanging in 1921, and he was never caught. In 1928, the electric
chair replaced hanging as the method of execution in Illinois. But
O'Conner had been condemned to hang, and by law the state had
to keep the gallows ready until O'Conner's fate had definitely been
determined. Now it's doubtful if Tommy O'Conner will ever be
found alive—if he is still alive, he would be over a hundred. Court
decisions restricting the use of the death penalty make it highly
unlikely that any state would try to hang a man after so long—
particularly a one hundred-year-old man. But the tale of the gallows' being kept all those years for O'Conner has given his story
a certain sort of immortality.

O'Conner, born in Ireland in 1886, came to the United States
around 1900. Settling in Chicago, he embarked on a career of
robbery and violence. In June 1921, the police were looking for
O'Conner in connection with an earlier robbery at the Illinois
Central downtown railroad station in which a night watchman was
killed. When police tried to arrest him at his sister's home, there
was a shootout in which one officer was killed. While there may
have been some doubt about O'Conner's part in killing the watchman, there was no doubt he had killed a policeman, and he was
found guilty of murder and sentenced to hang on December 15.

Accounts of the details of Terrible Tommy's escape vary.
Some say he feigned illness and then pulled out a gun that had
been smuggled to him while he was being taken to the medical
office. Another account, one less flattering to the police, holds
that O'Conner was mingling with other prisoners in the bullpen

247

of the jail located in the Criminal Courts Building, when he was able to wrestle a gun away from one of the guards.

Whatever the exact sequence of events, O'Conner and three other inmates rode the elevator from the fourth floor down to the basement, disarmed another guard, unlocked the basement door leading to the jailyard, and then somehow scaled a twenty-foot wall and jumped down into the street. One of the escapees, who weighed over two hundred pounds, broke his ankles in the jump and was found by the police within minutes. The others, including O'Conner, made a clean getaway.

In his escape, gun-waving O'Conner commandeered a number of cars and cut a crazy pattern through the city, until he completely disappeared.

Terrible Tommy's escape generated a tremendous amount of publicity, and for a while he was one of the best known criminals in America. The hunt for him was intensive. Not only was he a cop killer, but his escape had embarrassed prison authorities. There were even proposals made that the Army should be used to hunt him down.

O'Conner's family was delighted. "We're going to have a merry Christmas," his father said. Another brother, "Darling Dave" O'Conner, who was in jail on a minor offense, just laughed when reporters tried to question him. "I suppose you think you ought to have some O'Conner around here," he said.

Rewards were offered, and it was thought that eventually some informer would turn Tommy in—but no one did. O'Conner was reportedly seen in a variety of places. According to one story, he returned to Ireland and was killed during the Black and Tan wars the year after his daring escape.

1925

COLONEL PERCY FAWCETT   Colonel Percy Harrison Fawcett was an adventurer in all senses of that term. A former British Army man, Colonel Fawcett had spent a lot of time as a surveyor in the then uncharted jungles of Brazil. In the early years of this century, he wandered all over South America, and when he came back from his expeditions he told colorful and often highly embroidered tales of his experiences.

At some point during his travels, he said that he picked up accounts of the remains of a lost civilization deep in the Amazon jungles. He said he had met Indians in the jungle who he was convinced were "survivors from a once great civilization. Many of them tell stories of a lost city rich in treasure, which was destroyed by some natural calamity and has been cut off from the outside world for centuries."

But Colonel Fawcett didn't just rely on rumors; he said he had "psychic" information as well. He had been given a small, strangely inscribed stone statue by his friend, the fantasy-adventure writer H. Rider Haggard. The statue was reputed to have "strange" powers and everyone who held it experienced a "tingling sensation," but there was no clue as to where it had come from.

Colonel Fawcett took the statue to a professional psychic, who held it for a few seconds and said, "It comes from South America." The psychic then went on to describe a magnificent civilization that had existed long before that of Egypt. That was the clincher as far as Colonel Fawcett was concerned. He decided to lead an expedition in search of the "lost civilization." Scientific societies, which distrusted Fawcett anyway, thought that his search was a mad one and refused to have anything to do with it. But the adventurer was able to get financing through the North American Newspaper Alliance in return for exclusive rights to his story. So in April 1925, Colonel Fawcett, his son Jack, and a young friend,

Raleigh Rimell, started off into the interior of the dense Amazon jungle. The small party reached a place called Dead Horse Camp on May 29. From there Colonel Fawcett sent back by a messenger an account of the expedition so far to the newspaper syndicate and a letter to his wife that contained the sentence, "You need have no fear of any failure." Colonel Fawcett was a poor prophet, for those were the last authentic words anyone ever heard from him. Colonel Fawcett and the two young men marched off into the jungle and disappeared.

The disappearance of so colorful a character as Colonel Percy H. Fawcett while on a jungle expedition to find a lost civilization was bound to capture public attention and excite a lot of speculation. In one form or another, the story kept popping up in the news for years.

In 1927, a French engineer said that he had encountered an elderly white man in Lima, Peru, who seemed to have suffered some terrible hardship and was slightly deranged. When the Frenchman asked the man's name, he said it was "Fawcett." Colonel Fawcett's younger son, who was living in Peru at the time, tried to track down this story, but to no avail.

In 1928, the newspaper syndicate sent out another expedition to search for Colonel Fawcett. They were able to trace him to a remote Indian village, but no farther. The leader of the search expedition suggested that the two Fawcetts and Rimell had been murdered. It was a reasonable suggestion, since the tribes in that region were not excessively friendly to strangers.

There were more rumors. A Swiss hunter named Stefan Rattin emerged from the jungle with a story about a "half-crazy English colonel" and his son who were being held captive by the Indians. A Brazilian expedition came back with stories of three white men being held captive by the Indians. All of these rumors were dismissed as absurd by son Brian Fawcett.

In 1937, the Fawcett disappearance story was again in the news. Missionaries in the jungle found a white boy who, it was said, was really Colonel Fawcett's grandson. It ultimately turned out the boy was an albino Indian who was an outcast from his tribe because of his skin color.

In 1952, a chief of one of the jungle tribes confessed before his death that he had Colonel Fawcett and the other two men clubbed to death for insulting him. "The bodies of the young ones were thrown into a river, but we buried the old man in a grave."

This rumor seemed credible enough to move Brian Fawcett, who was by then living in England, to make an expedition into the Brazilian jungle. He found the grave, but when the remains were taken back to England for examination, the experts determined that they were not those of Colonel Fawcett.

Three more skeletons turned up in the region where Fawcett disappeared in 1964, but again the remains did not seem to belong to the three explorers.

Since that time there has been no further news of Colonel Fawcett, and if he managed to survive he would certainly be dead by now. The real fate of Colonel Fawcett and his companions may never be known.

And what of his quest for the "lost civilization"? No evidence that such a civilization ever existed has turned up to date, and it seems unlikely that any ever will. But one should keep a small reserve of hope, for the Amazon jungle is still the least thoroughly explored area on the face of the earth, and it is just possible that the jungle may still hold a few surprises.

1930

JUDGE CRATER   At one time, Judge (really Justice) Joseph Force Crater was the most famous missing man in America, perhaps in the world. For years people investigated the case, speculated on it, and argued over it. Memories of the case were regularly revived in newspapers and magazines. So much work and so many words had been poured into the search for Judge Crater with so little success—Judge Crater had been "found" so many times— that finally the case became a joke.

As late as the 1960s, there were still cartoons about Judge Crater. One showed an astronaut stepping out of a space capsule on the moon and being greeted by a man in an old-fashioned business suit. The caption read: "Hello there, I'm Judge Crater." Another pictured a startled scientist looking through a microscope and saying to a colleague, "I think I've just discovered Judge Crater."

Judge Crater's final known appearance on this earth took place in New York City on the evening of August 6, 1930. Crater had dinner with some friends at the Billy Haas restaurant at 332 West Forty-fifth Street. It was in the heart of the theater district, and the judge announced his intention of going over to the Belasco Theater to see the hit show *Dancing Partner*. He had a ticket waiting for him at the box office. He was seen leaving the restaurant, hailing a cab, and getting in, though the theater was only a block away. Someone picked up the ticket that had been left in Crater's name, but the man at the box office could not recall whether it was Crater or not, so we don't know if Judge Crater ever saw *Dancing Partner*. We do know that no one ever saw Judge Crater again—certainly not anyone who was willing to talk about it.

What made the disappearance so sensational was that Judge Crater was really an important man. He had been born in Easton,

Judge Crater (*UPI*)

Pennsylvania, and studied law at Columbia University in New York City. He set up practice in the city and he prospered, partly through his legal skill but more significantly through his political skill. Crater was fascinated by the rough-and-tumble world of New York City politics, and he was able to play the game as well as anyone. While he taught law at Fordham University and served as law clerk to Supreme Court Justice and later senator Robert Wagner,

Tammany Hall

Crater's real power came from being president of the Cayuga Dem-
ocratic Club, an Upper West Side Manhattan bulwark of Tammany
Hall, the political power center of the city.

For years, Tammany had been flying high. Times had been
good, and if the politicians stole a bit here and there, no one seemed
to mind very much. But in October 1929, the stock market collapsed and the Great Depression gathered steam. As prosperity
disappeared, so did some of the easygoing tolerance for crooked
politics. Investigations began, and several Tammany stalwarts found
themselves out of office and in jail.

Early in 1930, a justice of the Supreme Court retired, and it
was up to Governor Franklin D. Roosevelt to appoint a temporary
successor. It was a ticklish problem in scandal-tainted New York
City, and Roosevelt turned to Senator Wagner for advice. Wagner
recommended his former clerk, Joseph Force Crater. Though Crater was a loyal Tammany man, the appointment was generally
applauded, for no scandal had touched Crater—yet.

In November 1930, Crater would have had to stand for election to a full fourteen-year term on the state Supreme Court bench,

and he was fully prepared to do so. It was said that he had his eye on ultimate appointment to the United States Supreme Court. He was only forty-one, and that was not an impossible dream—if he had not disappeared.

Summer in New York City can be unbearably hot. It threatened to become even hotter for the newly appointed justice, because the press had uncovered the fact that Crater had been the main speaker at a dinner for a man who was suspected of buying appointment to the post of magistrate in New York City's traffic court. It wasn't a major scandal, but it was an embarrassment. Crater and his wife Stella moved up to their summer cottage near Augusta, Maine. From time to time during the summer, Crater made trips back to the city.

He returned from one of those trips on August 1, and was expected to stay at the cottage until the end of the month, when the fall term of the court was to begin. The day after he got back, he received a phone call—from whom we do not know. He mumbled something to his wife like, "I've got to straighten those fellows out," and then told her he would have to go back to New York again the next day, but that he would return to Maine on August 9.

Crater arrived back in the city by train on the fourth and went to his apartment on Fifth Avenue, one of the two he rented in the city. There Crater found the sleep-in maid and suggested that she take a four-day vacation until August 8, the day he planned to leave for Maine. Later that day, he visited his doctor. The reason for this visit has never been made public.

He spent most of the following day in his judicial chambers, apparently doing routine work.

The following day—the fatal sixth of August—Judge Crater again went to his chambers. He did behave in a rather unusual manner. He asked one of his two assistants to cash a couple of checks for him. These checks totaled $5,100, a far more substantial sum in 1930 than today. He told the assistant to get large bills, and when given the money in an envelope, he slipped it into his pocket without bothering to count the cash. He also removed a large number of papers from his personal files. There were so many papers that they overflowed his briefcase. He borrowed an assistant's briefcase, but that still wasn't enough, and some of the papers had to be tied together in a bundle.

Crater then asked his assistant, Joseph L. Mara, to help him get the papers to his Fifth Avenue apartment. Later, Mara told investigators that the usually cheerful Crater seemed "very blue and moody, evidently depressed and worried about something." But during the cab ride, he told Mara that he was going to West-chester for a swim that afternoon, and that he would see him the next day.

Whether Crater actually went for a swim that afternoon we do not know, for there is no trace of his movements from noon to 7:00 P.M. Nor is there any indication what happened to the papers that he removed from his files.

At approximately 7:00 P.M., Crater appeared at the Arrow Theater ticket agency and asked for a single seat to that night's performance of *Dancing Partner*. He was told that tickets were scarce, but that if he went to the box office shortly before curtain time, he would find a ticket waiting in his name.

Crater then strolled over to the popular Billy Haas restaurant, where he ran into a friend, William Klein, a lawyer who worked for major Broadway producers. With Klein was a showgirl named Sally-Lou Ritz. Klein asked the judge to join them for dinner. Later, Klein said the dinner was unmemorable. Crater seemed to be in a good mood, and mentioned that he would be going back to Maine in a day or two.

After dinner, Crater announced that he was going to see *Dancing Partner*. And here is one of the many oddities of the case. Crater left the restaurant at nine-fifteen. The curtain for *Dancing Partner* had already gone up, yet he had been told to arrive before curtain time to pick up his ticket.

If Crater himself had picked up the ticket, then he would have done so nearly an hour *after* curtain time. In that case, the man at the box office would probably have remembered him. The cab driver who had taken Judge Crater around the block to the Belasco Theater, or to somewhere else, could not be located, despite numerous appeals by the police and the newspapers.

Crater was a very distinctive-looking man, six feet tall and heavyset, with an absurdly small head and neck. He looked, one writer said, "something like a turtle walking upright." He had false teeth and a bandage on his hand, for he had injured a finger earlier in the summer. He was quite a well-known figure around New York City, certainly not the sort of person who could easily melt into a crowd. Yet he disappeared, though it took a while before anyone seemed to realize this.

Up in Maine, Mrs. Stella Crater began to worry when her husband didn't return as scheduled. Still, she waited six days, before doing anything, and what she finally did do was send the family chauffeur to New York to see what he could find out. He found nothing, and drove back to Maine.

Rumors about Crater's disappearance began to circulate and became worse when he failed to show up for the opening of court on August 26. His political cronies began informal investigations, but it wasn't until September 3, nearly a month after he disappeared, that the police were officially notified.

The police and the press began digging into Crater's background. Among his colleagues, he was known as "good old Joe Crater," a hearty backslapper who loved a good time. He had had affairs with a string of showgirls and a longtime mistress named Constance Braemer Marcus. Crater was also a regular customer at a Broadway speakeasy called Club Abbey, which was also a favorite hangout of such Prohibition-era gangsters as "Dutch" Schultz and "Legs" Diamond.

An investigation of Crater's financial affairs turned up nothing unusual. He didn't seem to have any more money than he could have acquired more or less legally as a lawyer and judge.

Mrs. Crater complained that the police had bungled the investigation because of political interference. Yet she had not reported the disappearance for nearly a month, allowing the trail to grow cold, and either she knew incredibly little about her husband's life and work or did not choose to tell all she knew.

The result was that there was no result. The disappearance of Judge Crater remains a mystery. But in the absence of hard facts, there are plenty of theories. The most obvious is that Crater disappeared because he wanted to. Law enforcement officials have often stated that most mysterious disappearances are voluntary.

Some of his actions make a voluntary disappearance seem

likely. He got money, purged his personal papers, and seemed to be trying to set up some sort of alibi with the theater. But why would he have disappeared? His personal life was not revealed until after his disappearance. The corruption investigators didn't seem to be after him. He didn't seem to be in any immediate danger of disgrace.

Another theory put forth by a sensationalist tabloid was that Crater, disgusted with the empty life he was leading, had undergone some sort of religious conversion and run off to join a monastery in Mexico. An intriguing notion, but one for which there is no supporting evidence whatever.

Most people feel Crater's disappearance was involuntary—that he was murdered. He may have been killed in a holdup—but then what happened to the body? He may have been killed by some of the gangsters he knew from the Club Abbey. They were very good at getting rid of bodies. But why would they have taken the risk of killing a justice of the state Supreme Court? Such murders inevitably attract unwelcome publicity.

The theory that makes the most sense is that Crater went to meet some of his crooked associates on an important matter, perhaps blackmail. That fits with destroying papers, getting money, and preparing an alibi. During the meeting, there could have been an argument in which Crater was killed. But who were the associates? What was the meeting about?

The disappearance of Judge Crater is one of those cases in which one feels that evidence may still possibly be revealed, even though it took place over half a century ago. If, as appears likely, there was some sort of cover-up involved, then memoirs, diaries, letters, or perhaps even official files may yet turn up. By now, all those involved are certainly beyond punishment or censure.

1934

JOHN DILLINGER   One of the truly mythic scenes in the annals of American crime took place outside of the Biograph Theater in Chicago on the evening of July 22, 1934. The daring bank robber John Dillinger, who had escaped from jail and humiliated the FBI by slipping out of a carefully set trap, had been in hiding in Chicago under the name of "Jimmy Lawrence." Though he was the most wanted man in America, Dillinger had undergone plastic surgery, and he felt confident enough to show himself openly on the street.

On that fateful evening, Dillinger had gone to the movies with two women, Polly Hamilton, a Chicago waitress, and a forty-two-year-old madam, Anna Sage. Unknown to Dillinger, Sage had betrayed him, perhaps to collect the ten-thousand-dollar reward that was offered for his capture, perhaps because she faced deportation to her native Rumania. She made a deal with the FBI. Sage called to tell them where Dillinger was going. The FBI staked out the theater. Sage was wearing a red dress so that the FBI would recognize her. (She was the famous "woman in red," but in reality, not at all the young and beautiful figure of later legend.) The agents saw Dillinger and the two women enter the Biograph, but decided it would be too dangerous to try to capture him inside the theater. In a previous attempt to capture Dillinger, several innocent bystanders had been shot and one was killed. That time Dillinger himself escaped. When Dillinger left the theater, agent Melvin Purvis lit his cigar—that was the signal to move in on the gangster. Purvis called on Dillinger to halt. Dillinger looked around. The two women were gone, and he must have realized that he had been betrayed. He grabbed for his gun and ran for the alley alongside the movie house. The FBI agents let loose with a barrage of bullets—once again innocent bystanders were wounded—but this time Dillinger was hit as well. One bullet went right through his head.

The death of John Dillinger from the 1973 film *Dillinger*.

So John Dillinger was shot down by the FBI on July 22, 1934—right? There are some people who don't think so. They believe that the FBI agents shot the wrong man, and then when they discovered their error, they engaged in a massive cover-up to hide their embarrassment. Certainly Dillinger had embarrassed the FBI before, and Bureau director J. Edgar Hoover was obsessed with public image. Humorist Will Rogers had written, "Dillinger is going to accidentally get with some innocent bystanders some time, then he will get shot." That sort of ridicule drove Hoover wild.

Though everyone closely connected with Dillinger, including the members of his own family, were convinced the gangster was dead, there were others who refused to believe it. The most influential current proponent of the Dillinger-didn't-die theory is the knowledgeable Chicago-area crime writer Jay Robert Nash. His 1970 book *Dillinger Dead or Alive?* (written in conjunction with Ron Offen) makes the case that it really was Jimmy Lawrence, a minor hoodlum with an obscure background, who was gunned down by the FBI that July evening.

The most compelling evidence for the fake Dillinger theory lies in the massive discrepancies and contradictions found in the report of the autopsy performed on Dillinger by the Cook County coroner. For example, the dead man's eyes were listed as brown, while it is known that Dillinger's eyes were blue.

The problem with using this evidence to support the fake Dillinger theory is that even today autopsy reports are full of errors, and back in the 1930s, particularly in Cook County, coroner's reports were notoriously lax. Add to the usual incompetence and confusion the fact that this particular autopsy was performed in a circus atmosphere with reporters and others crawling all over the place, and the many errors do not seem so surprising or so sinister.

If there was a conspiracy to cover up the misidentification, an awful lot of people had to have been in on it. Not one of them ever confessed, not even Anna Sage. Despite the agreement she thought she had with the FBI, she was sent back to Rumania anyway. She certainly had no reason to keep quiet.

If Dillinger survived, how did he live? He didn't have a great deal of cash available. He was no sophisticated international criminal who could easily have fled the country and assumed a new identity. He almost certainly would have had to stay in America —or at best go to Mexico. Ultimately he would have had to turn back to the only profession he really knew—crime—and he would have been caught or identified.

Legends aside, Dillinger was no criminal mastermind. He was violent, daring, and lucky, at least for a while. Yet the spectacular part of his criminal career lasted a mere eleven months, and most of that time he was on the run.

So, while one would have to admit the possibility that the man shot down in front of the Biograph was not John Dillinger, it is a very faint possibility indeed. Rather than being based on any solid evidence, the persistent belief that Dillinger survived is based primarily on the human reaction that folk heroes—that is what John Dillinger had become—could not die. King Arthur was not supposed to be dead but merely "sleeping." After the death in

1250 of the Holy Roman Emperor Frederic II, several impostors claiming to be the "real" Frederic appeared and gathered huge followings because people refused to believe Frederic was dead. The historical examples can be multiplied. In more modern times, it has often been said that Jesse James was not shot, it was someone else. And for decades, impostors claiming to be the "real" Jesse James kept showing up and getting more publicity than they deserved.

Dillinger became a folk hero because of his daring, and because he seemed to be sort of a modern Robin Hood. He robbed banks, not people, and though he didn't give his loot to the poor, he was generally courteous to those who happened to be unlucky enough to be caught in the middle of one of his holdups. It was the Depression, and a lot of people hated banks and bankers. The fact that Dillinger also killed ten people was conveniently forgotten. Even during his lifetime, the real Dillinger had been replaced by a myth, and myths are very hard to kill.

1941

THE PEKING MAN BONES   In 1941, the most valuable bones in the world disappeared mysteriously into the chaos of war-torn China. Even today, there are those who still have hope that the priceless fossils have not been destroyed, that they still remain hidden somewhere.

The bones are those of Peking man, discovered in the 1920s in caves at Chou Kou Tien, a town about thirty miles from the capital of China, then called Peking in the West. The bones from about forty beetle-browed but distinctly human individuals, who had lived some five hundred thousand years ago, had been carefully dug from the caves by an international team of scientists.

The remains of our prehuman ancestors are rare. A jawbone and a couple of teeth have sometimes been enough to drastically alter our view of the human family tree. There had never been a fossil site remotely as rich as the one found at Chou Kou Tien, and there hasn't been one since. Naturally, the discovery created a sensation in scientific circles and beyond.

In the years following the original discovery, the site produced a series of sensations. The attention of the scientific world had been focused on the caves, but from the very beginning of the excavations there had been trouble. The government of China was weak, and a long-running civil war between the Chinese Communists and Nationalists was being fought. More seriously, the Japanese had invaded China, and slowly but relentlessly were taking over ever-larger chunks of Chinese territory. The Japanese invaders were moving in on the site at Chou Kou Tien.

For years the scientists simply tried to ignore the war; they just kept on working and steered clear of politics. But by 1937, it became impossible to ignore. There was fighting on all sides of Chou Kou Tien, and at any moment control of the area might fall to the Japanese invaders. The digging itself had stopped, but in a

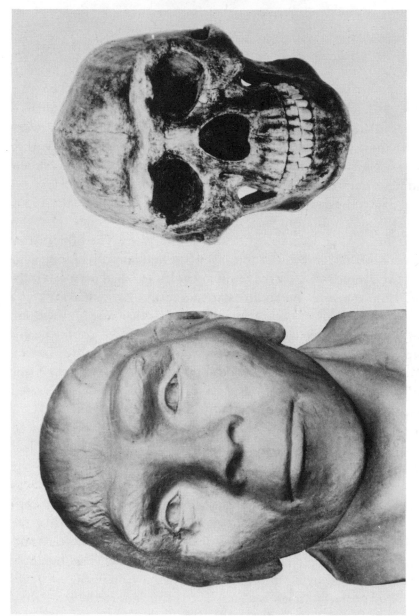

Reconstruction of Peking man and skull of Peking man. (*American Museum of Natural History*)

special laboratory at the Peking Union Medical College, the work of cleaning and classifying the enormous number of fossils that had been found continued.

Though the situation was chaotic, the fossils were officially still under control of the government of China. But the government had lost control of Peking itself. The medical college where the bones were kept had been founded and was supported by American interests. The Chinese were afraid that the Japanese would simply confiscate the fossils and ship them to Japan. There was a passion for fossil collecting in Japan, and the Japanese had already confiscated fossil collections from other conquered areas. However, the Japanese were still careful about interfering with American interests. Even if the bones were not taken outright, there was often fighting in the city, and a careless shell or bomb could destroy or seriously damage the fossils. Scientists working on the project felt that something had to be done.

The first thing they did—and future generations of paleontologists are eternally grateful for this—was to make careful models of all of the Peking man fossils. The models were then sent to the United States. The Chinese, however, were very reluctant to allow the original fossils to leave the country. For a while, Chinese officials considered trying to hide the fossils somewhere in China beyond the reach of the Japanese—but conditions were so unstable that this plan was finally deemed to be impractical.

Tensions between the United States and Japan were growing, and everyone in China assumed that war could break out at any moment. When that happened, there would be no protection for the fossils or for the American scientists who were working on them.

Early in 1941, American scientists began leaving China, and the Chinese authorities themselves had come to accept that the deteriorating political situation made it necessary to get the priceless fossils out of China to a safer place, where they would be beyond the reach of the Japanese. They were to be sent to the United States for safekeeping, and after the war were to be returned to China.

That decision was long delayed and wasn't made finally until November of 1941. The bones were carefully packed into metal footlockers, the kind that soldiers normally use to store their clothes.

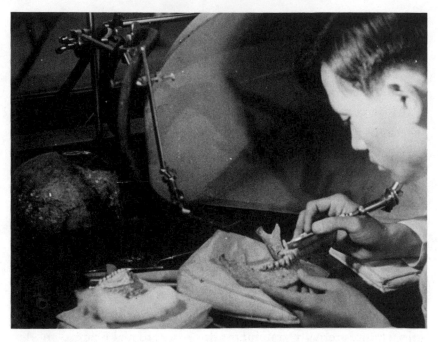

At work on the jaw of Peking man. (*American Museum of Natural History*)

The plan was to send the bones out of China on an American ship, the U.S.S. *President Harrison*, which was due in the port of Ching-wangtao on December 8, 1941, a very unfortunate date, as it turned out. The ship was due to take some United States Marines from the base at Camp Holcomb near Peking out of China. The bones were to be secretly smuggled out with them. The exact plan was known to very few. The footlockers were taken first to the American Embassy and then to the marine barracks, after which they were to travel by train with the Marines to the port where they were to be loaded aboard the *Harrison*.

The plan was never carried out, because on December 7 the Japanese bombed the American naval base at Pearl Harbor, and war was declared. All the Americans in Japanese-held areas of China were detained immediately. Early on the morning of December 8, the Japanese took over the Peking Union Medical College. One of the first things that they did was to open and examine the contents of the safe in the department of anatomy where the

Peking man fossils had been kept. Obviously, the bones were a high priority for the Japanese, but they found only casts of the originals in the safe, and were frustrated and angered by not finding the original material. All those Chinese who had been connected with the fossils were interrogated repeatedly. The marine barracks was also searched, without any success. The Marines themselves had been arrested. The U.S.S. *President Harrison* had never even reached port at Chingwangtao. It had run aground and been captured by the Japanese.

What happened to the footlockers containing the fossils? We must remember that this was a time of enormous confusion, and that many of those who might have known of the fate of the fossils did not survive the war. According to one report, the fossils had been sent to a warehouse at Chingwangtao to await the arrival of the *Harrison*. The warehouse, however, was ransacked by the Japanese, and they might have destroyed the fossils without ever knowing what they were. A box full of old bones would not have seemed interesting or significant to an ordinary soldier.

Another theory is that the footlockers containing the fossils actually got to the Marines, but when the Marines were detained and their baggage seized, the fossils were accidentally lost or destroyed.

There were some who believed that the Japanese found the fossils and spirited them off to Japan. At the end of the war, United States occupation forces in Japan searched for them. Not only were there no fossils to be found, there was no evidence at all that the Japanese ever had control of the fossils. Indeed, there was considerable evidence that the Japanese were searching for them in China throughout the war years.

The war with Japan ended, but China was still locked in a civil war, and chaotic conditions prevailed. The Chinese Communists were finally victorious in 1949, and their Nationalist opponents fled to the island of Taiwan. The new Chinese government was not absolutely convinced that the fossils had been destroyed. In some quarters, there was a suspicion that the fossils had been taken by the Nationalists to Taiwan, or that they might be in America after all. The reasoning was that the fossils had been under the control of the United States, and the United States had supported the Nationalists. Whoever had them, the new Chinese government certainly wanted them back.

United States authorities absolutely denied having any knowledge of the ultimate fate of the Peking man fossils. Indeed, it was rather surprising how little hard information actually existed about the final days of the fossils. Accounts differed widely; there wasn't even any general agreement as to how many footlockers had been packed with bones. One report said the bones had been packed in white wooden boxes, not footlockers. The whole incident was a mystery and a muddle.

In 1972, when the Chinese government was building a museum at Chou Kou Tien, they encouraged an American businessman, Christopher Janus, to try and ferret out information of the fossils in America. Janus offered a reward of a modest five thousand dollars for information on the fossils, and he got hundreds of responses, most of them from crackpots.

He did, however, get an interesting phone call from a woman who refused to give her name. She said that not only did she have information about the fossils, she had the fossils themselves. The woman was extremely nervous, but finally agreed to meet Janus in the observatory atop the Empire State Building.

Janus was more than half convinced that the whole thing was a hoax, and he really didn't expect anyone to show up. But someone did. He described the woman as being in her late forties and quite good-looking. The woman told him that her husband had been in China during the war, and when he came home he had a box filled with what he called "war booty." The box, she later learned, contained the Peking man fossils. Her husband said they were very valuable, but that they were also dangerous to possess. She did not explain how her husband obtained them or brought them over from China.

Then the woman told Janus that her husband had died recently and that she needed money. So when she found out he was interested, she decided to take the risk and contact him. She wanted five hundred thousand dollars for the fossils, a modest price if they were the priceless genuine article. In order to prove that she really did have the fossils, she showed Janus a photograph of what looked like bones inside a box. Janus was no expert, and he simply didn't know what to make of the photo.

Suddenly the mysterious woman became very agitated and claimed that someone was trying to take a picture of her. All Janus could see were groups of ordinary-looking tourists taking pictures at the top of the Empire State Building. Still, the woman bolted for the exit. On the way down in the elevator, the woman said that she would phone Janus again in a few days. Weeks went by, and he heard nothing. Finally he placed an ad in the personal column of *The New York Times* addressed to: "The lady who met me in the Empire State Building." The ad asked her to call, but Janus thought this was a long shot. Much to his surprise, she did call.

Janus wanted her to let some experts look at the fossils, or at a sample of them, to determine if they were genuine. This she absolutely refused to do. But she did agree to send him the picture. It wasn't a very clear photograph, but those who examined it admitted that the bones in the photo might belong to Peking man. But without examination of the bones themselves there would be no way of telling.

Unfortunately, the mysterious woman never contacted Janus again. All attempts to trace her failed. Did the woman really possess the fossils, or was her story all a joke, or, more likely, part of a confidence game that was never carried through? No one really knows. All that can be said is that her story, while highly implausible, was certainly not impossible.

Other promising leads have also run into dead ends. But those who are searching for the missing Peking man fossils have not entirely given up hope. Somewhere in China or America or Japan, or perhaps somewhere else in the world, the bones of Peking man may be awaiting yet another discovery.

1956

COMMANDER CRABB   In the murky world of international espionage, lying is the norm, and the truth usually beyond reach. No explanation, however plausible, can ever be fully believable. Thus, the fate of Lieutenant Commander Lionel Crabb will probably always remain a mystery.

The mystery began in April 1956, when the Royal Naval College at Greenwich, England, had a couple of distinguished and unusual visitors. They were N. A. Bulganin and N. S. Khrushchev, then joint rulers of the Soviet Union. Dictator Joseph Stalin had been dead for a few years, and the new Soviet leadership was trying to reestablish some ties with the West. B and K, as the press called them, had arrived in Portsmouth Harbor aboard a twelve-thousand-ton cruiser, *Ordzhonikidze*.

The ship's speed and easy maneuverability had raised eyebrows and interest among Western naval experts. They wondered if perhaps the Soviet warship had some new and better form of hull or rudder. Of course, to know that, one would have to examine the ship under water, and the Soviets were unlikely to allow anyone to go messing about with the bottom of their ship. So the Western observers could do nothing but stare and wonder what the ship looked like under water. At least, that is all they could do openly.

Another visitor to Portsmouth that April was a dapper little tweed-suited man who carried a distinctive ebony swordstick with a golden crab head. His name was Lieutenant Commander Lionel "Buster" Crabb, officially retired from the Royal Navy but still a fairly well-known figure around the naval headquarters in Portsmouth and the Royal Naval College in nearby Greenwich. Crabb had been one of Britain's pioneer frogmen, and a World War II hero. He had officially retired from the Navy, but those in a position to know suspected that he might still do a job now and then for the CID, British intelligence.

Commander Lionel "Buster" Crabb (*Keystone*)

Crabb registered at a Portsmouth hotel and was later joined by a "Mr. Smith." On April 19, Crabb left the hotel and never came back. "Smith" paid the bill, took Crabb's luggage, and disappeared. A few days later, the head of the Portsmouth CID came to the hotel, tore all the April pages out of the register, and told employees not to say anything about Messrs. Crabb and Smith.

But it was too late. Crabb's associates realized he was missing and began asking questions. Newspapers picked up the story. The most widely circulated rumor was that Crabb had been doing some underwater spying on the *Ordzhonikidze*, and had either been killed or captured.

The whole affair was an extreme embarrassment to the British and Soviet governments. At a moment when both nations were trying to establish better relations, the British would not want to admit that they were spying and the Soviets would not want to admit that they had killed or captured a British citizen in British waters, even if he *was* spying. So every official agency of both countries denied everything. The Soviet Embassy did say that one of the cruiser's lookouts had briefly seen a frogman, but no measures were taken against him.

The British government finally said that Commander Crabb was presumably carrying out "frogman tests" in the harbor, and was assumed to have lost his life during the tests. The government further admitted that Crabb probably was the frogman sighted by the Soviet lookout, but "his presence in the vicinity of the destroyer occurred without any permission whatever and Her Majesty's government expresses their regret for the incident."

No one really believed that story, though it was speculated that possibly Crabb had been working freelance for the CIA. But if Crabb had "lost his life," where was the body? Rumors began to circulate that Crabb had actually been captured and spirited back to the Soviet Union.

A little more than a year after Crabb's disappearance, a headless, handless body was washed up at Chichester Harbor, twelve miles from Portsmouth. The remains were encased in a frogman's suit of a type known to be owned by Crabb. The body also appeared to have some of the physical characteristics of the missing Crabb, and an inquest determined that the body was indeed the remains of the frogman. The body was buried at Portsmouth, though without any official honors or ceremony. It was a lonely burial if Crabb had died in the service of his country.

But the story did not end there, for everyone assumed that it is not beyond the technical capacities of the intelligence services, either of the East or West, to prepare a fake corpse. In 1959, a British journalist who had many Eastern European contacts and specialized in writing about Eastern European affairs published a sensational book. It was ostensibly based on a smuggled Soviet dossier.

According to this thesis, Crabb had indeed been captured while spying and spirited back to the Soviet Union. Then, realizing that he would be disowned by his own government and would never be allowed to return home, Crabb defected. He joined the Russian Navy as "L. L. Korablov," and quickly became a frogman instructor. The same journalist published a second book, which added accounts from individuals who said that they had actually seen Crabb in the Soviet Union.

The probability remains that Crabb was killed in Portsmouth Harbor while spying on the *Ordzhonikidze*, and that the body identified as his *was* his. The "dossier" about the defection might have been prepared by one or the other intelligence service and slipped to the journalist. Or the journalist may simply have faked the entire story. Most "true" espionage tales are not true at all.

On the other hand, there is at least a faint possibility that an aging "L. L. Korablov" may one day appear to reveal his true identity.

1971

D. B. COOPER   On November 24, 1971, a very ordinary-looking middle-aged man who came to be known as D. B. Cooper hijacked Northwest Orient Airlines Flight 305. After being given two hundred thousand dollars and two pairs of parachutes, he jumped from the plane into the black, cold night over Washington state, and into the realm of modern legend.

The legend of D. B. Cooper began at Portland, Oregon, International Airport on the Wednesday before Thanksgiving 1971. A man giving the name Dan Cooper bought a ticket on Northwest Orient's Flight 305. He paid cash. The flight had originated in Washington, D.C., that morning at 8:30. After several stops it had arrived in Portland, and was scheduled to take off for Seattle at 4:35 P.M. As the story unfolded, the man was mistakenly called D. B. Cooper by the press, and that is the name that stuck.

Cooper was a man of almost stunning ordinariness. Later, when witnesses, some of whom had a chance to observe him very closely, tried to describe him, they were vague. He seemed to have no distinguishing characteristics. Police artists' sketches made from descriptions are bland and unhelpful. D. B. Cooper, it seems, could have been any one of millions of men in their late thirties or early forties.

The airline agent at the boarding area recalled that Cooper carried a large attaché case and wore dark or tinted glasses. He was neatly dressed in a dark business suit. Some witnesses thought the suit was black, others that it was brown or gray. Some thought he was wearing loafers; others were not sure. Cooper did not talk to any of the other passengers waiting for the flight.

In 1971, there were no metal detectors, X-rays, or other extensive security checks at airports. The agent looked at your carry-on luggage just to see if it was small enough to be taken into the passenger cabin. Cooper's case was.

Artist's sketch of D.B. Cooper.

Flight 305 was a Boeing 727, a very popular three-engined plane that had an unusual feature—a rear entrance or exit with a set of stairs that could be lowered from the underside of the fuselage at the rear. It was for use in small airports that didn't even have mobile stairs. These stairs could also be lowered during flight, though they never were.

Cooper took seat 15D, an aisle seat near the rear of the aircraft. The craft was less than half full, and no one was sitting next to him. Flight 305 lifted off at 4:45 P.M., and a few minutes later the man in 15D motioned to stewardess Florence Schaffner, handed her a folded note, and said quietly, "Read that."

At first the stewardess thought it was a proposition, and took the note without reading it and walked away. A short time later, she looked back and the man was gesturing to her. So she read the note, and it was not at all what she expected.

The note itself has been lost, but the contents were clear enough. It was hand-printed in ink, and said that the man had a bomb in his case. He wanted four parachutes and two hundred thousand dollars in twenty-dollar bills. They were to be delivered to the plane when it landed in Seattle; otherwise, he was going to blow up the plane.

The stewardess took the note to Captain William W. Scott, who at first thought it was a hoax. He left the copilot at the controls and went back to talk to the passenger. Cooper opened his attaché case and showed the captain two red cylinders and a jumble of wires that looked like an explosive device. The man was calm and dead serious, and Captain Scott realized this was no joke.

Cooper told Captain Scott not to land at Seattle until the money and the parachutes were ready on the ground. Captain Scott contacted the airport, which in turn got in touch with the police, the FBI, and officials of Northwest Orient Airlines. The decision was made to cooperate fully with the hijacker's demands.

Cooper insisted on civilian parachutes—the kind with a rip cord that could be controlled by the jumper rather than military chutes that would open automatically. These were quickly obtained from a skydiving school near Seattle. Experts are divided on how much knowledge of parachuting Cooper seemed to possess, but it is safe to say that he was not a complete novice.

The ten thousand twenty-dollar bills were obtained from a Seattle bank. Before they were delivered to the airport, the bills were run through a high-speed Recordax machine that stored their images on microfilm. So there was a record of the bills sent to the airport. By 5:24, Captain Scott was told everything was ready.

The hijacker instructed the pilot to take the plane to an isolated but well-lit part of the airfield. The passengers were allowed to leave the plane, but the cockpit crew and one stewardess, Tina Mucklow, were told to remain. The passengers were not only unharmed, but barely aware of what had happened, and they had been delayed by a mere forty-five minutes.

The money and the parachutes were delivered to the plane, and it was refueled. The first officer then asked where they were going. Cooper asked if the plane could fly to Mexico City. He was told that it could but that another refueling stop at Reno would be necessary. That didn't seem to trouble the hijacker. Surprisingly, Cooper did not tell the crew what route they were to fly to Reno—several were available—but he did tell them to fly with the landing gear and flaps down, and very slowly—minimum speed for the 727 was about a hundred knots—and that they were not to exceed an altitude of ten thousand feet. At that altitude, the plane did not have to be pressurized.

After some anxious moments in getting the plane refueled, it took off from Seattle at 7:46 P.M. Captain Scott discovered that if he was to remain below ten thousand feet, there was essentially only one route he could take, and that was over the logging forests of Washington and Oregon. On any other southward route, the plane would have slammed into the Cascade Mountains at ten thousand feet. Whether Cooper had planned this, or it just worked out that way, is unknown.

Cooper ordered the stewardess and the flight crew to lock themselves in the cockpit. The door was solid, so the crew had no idea what the hijacker was doing. At about eight o'clock, a warning light indicating that one of the doors was open appeared on the engineer's panel. It didn't say which door, but everyone assumed that the hijacker was lowering the airstairs.

Captain Scott called out over the intercom, "Is there anything we can do for you?"

There was a pause of several seconds, and the reply came: "No." That was the last authenticated word ever heard from D. B. Cooper.

At 8:10 P.M., the plane was passing over the Lewis River in the southwest corner of Washington state, when it performed what has been described as an odd little "curtsey," possibly because a weight had been dropped out of it. The hijacked 727 was being followed by a variety of different aircraft from the police and the Air Force. No one saw any parachutist. Indeed, on this dark and rainy night, the trailing planes had trouble keeping Flight 305 itself in sight.

The airliner landed in Reno at 10:51 P.M. FBI agents rushed to the scene. Some law enforcement authorities felt that the idea of jumping was just a bluff, and that the hijacker's real plan was to sneak off the plane as soon as it landed in Reno. But when the plane was searched, no hijacker was found. D. B. Cooper had jumped.

At first many in the aviation field believed this must have been the act of a madman or a fool. No one could—or at least no one ever had—jumped from a commercial airliner. But the more they investigated, the more they realized that D. B. Cooper had planned carefully. Tests determined that an individual could step down the lowered airstairs and jump without being blown away or barbecued by the 727's engines. It would not have been an easy or safe jump, particularly since it was being made over rugged terrain in the dark, but it would have been possible. In requesting two hundred thousand dollars in twenty-dollar bills, Cooper got cash that would not only have been easily spendable, but made a convenient package of about twenty-five pounds. A heavier package would have made jumping more difficult. By asking for four chutes, Cooper would give the impression that he might have wanted a hostage to jump with him. This would exclude the possibility of deliberately giving him chutes that would not open. Actually, one of the chutes delivered to Cooper was a dummy, but this was an accident and it wasn't one that he used.

Still, most authorities felt that it was unlikely that the jumper would have survived the experience, so an immediate search was launched in the vicinity of the Lewis River to find what they assumed would be the body of D. B. Cooper. The likely landing area was searched intensively, but no trace of the hijacker was found, and the longer the search came up empty, the more people began to feel that the hijacker just might have survived the jump and walked away with the money. The legend of D. B. Cooper began to grow rapidly.

There had been a couple of unsuccessful airline hijacking attempts before Cooper—but air piracy was not a major concern in 1971, so ordinary people did not feel threatened by the crime as they do today. No one was hurt, or even seriously frightened, during the hijacking. Cooper was always polite and businesslike. He didn't ask for an enormous amount of money, or make any other unreasonable demands. Today, airplane hijackers are hated and feared by the American public, but back in 1971, Cooper could seem romantic, even heroic.

What contributes most to the legend of D. B. Cooper is that not only has he never been found, but no one has the faintest notion who he really was. His name certainly wasn't D. B. (or Dan) Cooper. Whoever he was, a lot of people believed he had "beaten the system." He "got away with it." And they were all for him.

T-shirts bearing the words D. B. COOPER—WHERE ARE YOU? became popular items. The case has been the subject of several books, innumerable articles, even a fictionalized film. Despite all the interest, no authentic trace of the hijacker was found until early 1980. A family picnicking on the Washington bank of the Columbia River near Vancouver, Washington, found a package of worn, waterlogged twenty-dollar bills sticking up out of the sand. The bills proved to be $5,800 of the $200,000 given to D. B. Cooper. The money was found well south of the main search area. Another search was conducted. But again no trace of a body or any other sign of the hijacker was found nearby. The packet of money could have been washed downriver a considerable distance. But why had one packet of money become separated from all the rest? Did the find make it more or less likely that Cooper survived? No one knows.

The discovery of the money does seem to sink one theory popular with law enforcement officials—that Cooper had parachuted into a large lake in the area and drowned. The rivers that flow from the lake do not drain into the region where the find was made.

A writer named Max Gunther says he was contacted by letter by a man claiming to be D. B. Cooper. Later, he was contacted (also by letter) by a woman calling herself Clara who said that she had met the hijacker after he stumbled out of the woods, and that the two had lived together for many years until Cooper's death from natural causes. In his book *D. B. Cooper: What Really Happened*, Gunther pieces together what he says is a picture of the hijacker's life. He is portrayed as a very ordinary man indeed. Gunther's theory is intriguing and not entirely farfetched, but the details are uncheckable.

The best guess of law enforcement officials and others who have studied the case is still that Cooper was killed in the jump, or was badly injured and died of exposure in the woods. Why hasn't his body been found? The terrain is extremely rugged, and he might have landed outside of the primary search area. In fact, during the search for D. B. Cooper, the remains of three other bodies—completely unconnected with the hijacking—were discovered in the woods.

Why hasn't Cooper's real identity ever been established? The fact is that thousands of people "vanish" in the United States every year. That is, they walk away from family, friends, job, and often debts. Some later return, but many others go to new areas, take new names, and some join the large and largely anonymous population of drifters. Cooper might have been one of the "vanished." Gunther thinks he was. Cooper might have had some parachute experience in World War II—he was old enough. Or he may have done some skydiving. He seemed to know a fair amount about planes. But attempts to run him down through war records or skydiving clubs have been unsuccessful. He must have been a secretive man, secretive at least about his plans. Many who have followed the case feel he was probably an ex-convict. There may be those who actually know who D. B. Cooper is, but for reasons of their own will not reveal his identity. Or maybe they've done a lot of talking, but no one believes them.

Perhaps, as these words are being written or next week or

next year, a skeleton with a tattered parachute nearby will be found in the Washington pine forests. Perhaps an elderly man will step forward and announce that he is D. B. Cooper and produce an incriminating packet of twenty-dollar bills to prove his claim. (Cooper, by the way, would still face indictment on the charge of air piracy.) If something like this happens, then part or all of the mystery will be solved.

If nothing ever turns up, the legend of D. B. Cooper will continue to flourish. In reality, the story is probably a sad one— the hijacking must have been the act of a desperate and lonely man. The case also publicized and romanticized the act of air piracy, and it changed the way we all feel about flying. The metal detectors, X-ray machines, and other security devices that slow air travel and make us feel insecure are part of his legacy. So D. B. Cooper is no romantic hero—no Robin Hood. He didn't do us any favors.

Still, so long as his identity and fate remain unknown, the aura of heroic romance will persist.

1974

LORD LUCAN   Practically everybody but his closest friends and a few reporters are convinced that Richard John Bingham Lucan, seventh earl of Lucan, is a murderer. The evidence is strong that on the chilly night of November 7, 1974, John Lucan burst into the expensive London townhouse occupied by his estranged wife and children, attacked and injured his wife, and killed, probably by accident, the children's nanny, Sandra Rivett. The mystery is that Lord Lucan then disappeared, and though he was one of the most sought-after men in the world, no trace of him has ever been found.

Lord Lucan was not a model English gentleman. Gambling and poor management of his large estate and his personal life had left him near bankruptcy. If anything, his personal life was worse than his finances. He was married to his wife Veronica in 1963, and the couple had two children. But the marriage had gone downhill swiftly and badly. By 1974, the couple was living apart, and there was enormous bitterness between them. Much of the bitterness centered around the children. Lucan had tried to gain custody of the children, but after a brutal court case, his suit was denied and they were living with their mother. Lord Lucan had an apartment near his wife's home, and he saw his children often. He did more than see them—he once tried to have them snatched, but the attempt was not successful. Lord Lucan had taken to sometimes watching his wife's house secretly in the hopes of finding something that could be used against her. Lady Lucan, who was highly excitable, had even accused her husband of having "a contract out on her life." Lord Lucan insisted that his wife was mentally unstable.

At about 11 P.M. on this particular November night, Lord Lucan suddenly and unexpectedly showed up on the doorstep of his friends, the Maxwell-Scotts, in Sussex. Ian Maxwell-Scott was

Lord Lucan

not at home, but his wife was. She thought the old family friend John Lucan looked a bit distracted and rumpled, and she gave him a drink.

It was then that Lucan told her an incredible story. He said that he had been walking by his wife's house in Belgravia, when he happened to look through the basement window and saw his wife Veronica struggling with a man.

He still had a front-door key, so he rushed into the house and down into the cellar. On his way down, he slipped in a pool of blood. The man who attacked his wife was nowhere to be seen, and his wife was both hysterical and injured. There was blood everywhere. On the floor was a sack containing the body of the nanny, Sandra Rivett.

Lucan said he persuaded his distraught wife to come upstairs. In her bedroom he found their eldest daughter Frances watching television. He told Frances that her mother had had a "slight accident" and sent her to bed. He then went to get some damp towels to wipe the blood from her face and get some tranquilizers to calm her. By the time he returned to the bedroom, Lady Lucan had fled. She ran, bloodstained and barefooted, to the local pub, shouting, "Help me . . . murder . . . he's murdered the nanny!"

Lucan said that he panicked and fled. But he was not entirely out of control. From a telephone booth he called his mother, told her his version of what had happened, and asked her to take care of the children. His mother also called the police, as had the pub owner. Lord Lucan then drove to the house of the Maxwell-Scotts in Sussex.

The story he told Mrs. Maxwell-Scott sounds incredible. Lucan insisted the murder must have been committed by a maniac. There is no indication that Mrs. Maxwell-Scott questioned the story. Lucan again called his mother to check on the children. The police were at her house, and she asked if he would like to speak to them. He said no, that he would call them in the morning. He wrote a couple of letters to friends about his children and business affairs. Mrs. Maxwell-Scott tried to persuade him to stay the night, but he refused. At about 1:00 A.M., he got into his car and drove away. As far as we know, that is the last that anyone has seen of John Lucan.

Ian Maxwell-Scott arrived home the next morning. His wife told him about the strange visit. He suggested that Lucan was exaggerating or even imagining things. The Maxwell-Scotts insist that they did not read the papers or watch television that entire day, and so did not discover that their friend had not been exaggerating or imagining and that he was a wanted man. The police were furious that they had not been contacted at once.

Three days after the murder, the police found an old Ford Corsair that had been left on a side street in the seaport town of Newhaven. The car was traced to a Michael Stoop, a friend of Lucan. Stoop admitted that he had lent Lucan the car several weeks earlier. It was an inconspicuous-looking vehicle, and apparently Lucan had used it to spy on his wife. Bloodstains and other clues found in the Ford linked it to the murder. Why hadn't Stoop immediately informed the police about the car? He said he didn't think it was important.

The next day, Stoop actually got a letter from Lord Lucan. He apologized to Stoop for not returning the car, and told him where it could be found. By that time it had already been found by the police. He told Stoop to keep an eye on his children, and he was convinced that no judge would believe his story. This time, Stoop did call the police. He gave them the letter, but the envelope, which would have contained a postmark that might have helped in the police search, had somehow been destroyed. This act merely deepened official suspicion of Lucan's friends.

The search for the missing earl was concentrated on Newhaven, a port city where he could have taken a ferry to France. Lucan was known to have friends in France. Despite a careful check, there was no evidence that he had fled the country. Lucan's passport was still in London, and apparently he had very little cash with him when he disappeared.

Lucan's friends insisted that he didn't possess either the cash or the cunning to successfully flee the country or go into hiding. They thought he must have committed suicide rather than face the disgrace of a murder trial. Yet, despite careful searching, no corpse has ever turned up.

Inevitably, there have been reports that Lord Lucan has been sighted in various parts of the world—France, South America,

South Africa, Las Vegas, Dublin, and elsewhere. Some of these "sightings" turned out to be deliberate hoaxes. None of them resulted in any solid evidence.

While no trial was ever held in the death of Sandra Rivett, there was an inquest. Usually such inquests result in a finding of murder by "person or persons unknown." But the evidence seemed so overwhelming in this case that the coroner's jury named Lord Lucan as the guilty party. Lucan's mother tried to have the verdict overturned. It wasn't, but the law has since been changed, and coroner's juries are no longer allowed to name a person as a murderer.

Many policemen who investigated the case are extremely bitter. They feel that because of deliberate delays, Lucan had enough time to find a boat and sail to France, and that their entire investigation had been stymied by a massive cover-up engineered by the earl's aristocratic friends. After his retirement, Detective Chief Superintendent Roy Ransdon, who had been in charge of the case, denounced what he called the "Lucan set" as "living in their own world, quite apart from the rest of us."

As for Lord Lucan's guilt or innocence, those who believe he did not commit the crime point out that if he had killed the nanny by accident, why did he then not also kill his wife when he had the chance? Because, reply those who believe in his guilt, after committing one murder, and actually injuring his wife, he lost his nerve. No evidence connecting anyone else with the crime has ever been found.

So Lord Lucan is most probably guilty. Did he get away with murder and is he now living quietly in some obscure place? That is the real mystery.

1975

JIMMY HOFFA   On the afternoon of July 30, 1975, former
Teamster boss James R. (Jimmy) Hoffa was seen getting into a car
with several other men in the parking lot of Manchus Red Fox, a
Detroit-area restaurant. He was never seen again. Officially, Hoffa's disappearance is listed as unsolved. Unofficially, the FBI and
other law enforcement authorities are absolutely convinced that
Hoffa was murdered by underworld associates, though there is
still some dispute as to exactly how and why.

Hoffa had been a powerful leader of the huge Teamsters union,
and like other Teamster bosses both before and since, he had close
ties to organized crime. For years the tough and arrogant Hoffa
seemed immune to prosecution, but he became the special target
of Robert F. Kennedy, first as chief counsel to the Senate Select
Committee on Improper Activities in the Labor or Management
Field, and later, and more significantly, as attorney general in the
administration of his brother, President John F. Kennedy.

Critics of Robert Kennedy have claimed that his pursuit of
Hoffa became more of a personal vendetta, that he went way
beyond the normal procedures of law enforcement in order to "get"
Hoffa. Ultimately, however, he did "get" the Teamster boss. Hoffa
went to jail for jury tampering and tax evasion in 1967. In 1971,
Hoffa's sentence was commuted by President Richard Nixon. The
Teamsters had been one of the few unions to support Nixon.

One of the provisions of Hoffa's release was that he not engage
in Teamster politics for ten years. Hoffa challenged the restriction
in the courts, and most of the time he simply ignored it. By 1975,
Hoffa was locked in a serious power struggle with the new Teamster president, Frank Fitzsimmons, who had once been his protégé
and had been handpicked by Hoffa to run the union while he was
in jail. Fitzsimmons apparently did not wish to surrender the power
now that it was in his hands. He had also reached a comfortable

Jimmy Hoffa (*Wide World*)

accommodation with the mobsters, who were not enthusiastic about having to deal with the strong and independent Hoffa once again, though he had previously been their ally.

On the fatal day in 1975, Hoffa left his home in suburban Detroit at 2:00 P.M. to drive to the popular restaurant, allegedly for a meeting with a Detroit underworld figure. At 2:30, Hoffa called his wife to say that the others hadn't shown up yet. Fifteen minutes later he was seen getting into a car—and never seen again.

One of Hoffa's enemies in the Teamsters union told police that Hoffa had run off to Brazil with a go-go dancer. Police, however, believe otherwise. The abduction car was located and traces of Hoffa's hair and blood were found on the back seat. The man suspected of masterminding the abduction and murder plot was well-known mob figure Anthony "Tony Pro" Provenzano. Hoffa had told his friends that it was Tony Pro who set up the meeting at the Red Fox restaurant. Tony Pro denied everything and said that he wasn't even in Detroit at the time. No one could prove otherwise. Another suspect was shot to death in New York City in March 1978.

A popular police theory is that Hoffa was killed in the car, and then his body destroyed in a mob-controlled fat-rendering plant. Other theories have Hoffa's body encased in cement in the foundation of a building, put in an old car and run through a car crusher, or buried in any one of a number of garbage dumps that serve as mob burial grounds. No one seriously believes that Jimmy Hoffa is still alive. But barring some completely unforeseen development, it is doubtful if anyone will ever be brought to trial for his murder.

6

Getting Away With It

1810

THE DUKE OF CUMBERLAND　　King George III's son, the Duke of Cumberland, was never a popular figure at court. Ugly and savage-tempered, he was ignored and avoided as much as it was possible to ignore and avoid the son of a reigning monarch.

The duke lived in the red brick St. James's Palace in London. At about three o'clock in the morning of Thursday, May 3, 1810, screams and the sounds of a struggle were heard coming from the duke's apartments in the palace. Strange noises in the duke's quarters were not unknown, and the servants who heard the noises at first ignored them.

The duke had two valets, Yew and Sellis, and after a while, when things had quieted down, the duke called for Yew. The valet found his master standing in his room "cool and composed," but the front of his shirt was covered with blood and his bloody sword was lying on the floor. The duke calmly announced that he had been attacked and severely wounded. He told Yew to send for his physician, Sir Henry Halford. Sir Henry answered the summons within a few minutes, and upon examining the duke found that none of his wounds was serious, the worst being a deep cut on his sword hand.

The duke had gone out to the opera that evening, and some two hours had passed since he had returned to the palace. Now, with his wounds dressed and his room straightened up, the duke told Yew to "call Sellis." According to Yew's sworn statement, he went directly to Sellis's room as ordered, but he found that the door was locked and had to be broken down. Sellis was in his bed lying perfectly straight with his head propped up against the headboard. His throat had been cut through to the bone; he had been dead well over an hour. A razor covered with blood was found across the room, too far from the body to have been dropped by Sellis if he had cut his own throat, and if he had inflicted such a severe wound upon himself he would certainly never have had the strength to throw the razor across the room.

An inquest into the death was held. The duke stated that for some inexplicable reason, Sellis had attacked him, hence his wounds, then run back to his own room and, overcome by what he had just done, committed suicide by cutting his own throat with his razor. In light of the available evidence, this story was absurd, but it was officially accepted—for it was not prudent to doubt the word of the king's son. However, everyone at court believed that the Duke of Cumberland had murdered his valet, and the duke became more of a pariah at court than he had ever been. The people of London took to openly booing him in the street, and it was unsafe for him to appear in public for many months.

What probably happened is that the duke attacked his valet while the poor man was in bed, cut his throat with a sword, and then inflicted a few superficial wounds upon himself with Sellis's razor in order to give the appearance of having been attacked.

A number of possible reasons for this brutal murder have been advanced. One holds that the duke had an affair with Sellis's daughter, who either had a child by him or committed suicide. In order to silence the valet, the duke killed him. A contradictory theory was that Sellis was killed because he was about to expose a homosexual affair between the duke and one of his other servants.

Over twenty years after the murder, this latter theory was printed in a publication called *The Satirist*. The publisher, Josiah Phillipps, was charged with slander by the duke and sent to prison.

The ghost of the murdered valet is said to still haunt St. James's Palace, and is one of London's best-known ghosts.

1885

ADELAIDE BARTLETT   At first glance, this case seems to be just another dreary Victorian domestic crime. The characters sound familiar: spirited young wife caught in a loveless and perhaps sexless marriage with a dim-witted and boring older man. Add a young man entering the household, and some poison. But on closer examination there are some distinctly odd and quite mysterious elements in the drama as it was played out in the Bartlett household.

Adelaide herself has a mysterious background. She was probably the illegitimate daughter of a wealthy Englishman and an aristocratic French woman. Born in Orléans, France, in 1856, Adelaide was raised in France by the family of her mother. But facts are lacking, and all that is known for certain is that she spent her early years in a convent. It has been suggested that her father was part of the entourage of Victoria and Albert, when they made a state visit to France in 1855. Adelaide's unknown father must have taken some interest in her welfare, for when she was brought to trial for murder in 1886, her counsel was Edward Clarke, a man whose services Adelaide certainly could not have afforded on her own. Later Clarke said she was "the unacknowledged daughter of an Englishman in good social position," but he didn't say who.

In the 1870s, she came to England with a guardian to complete her education. In the same rented house in which she had rooms there lived the Bartlett family. Charles Bartlett, who was married to a widow, dealt in real estate. His youngest brother, unmarried and essentially unemployed Frederick, lived with them. Adelaide appears to have been attracted to Frederick, but since he had no possible way of supporting her, no thought of marriage could be entertained.

There was, however, a middle brother, Edwin, who lived some distance away. He was a hardworking and moderately successful grocer with excellent prospects. Edwin Bartlett was good-

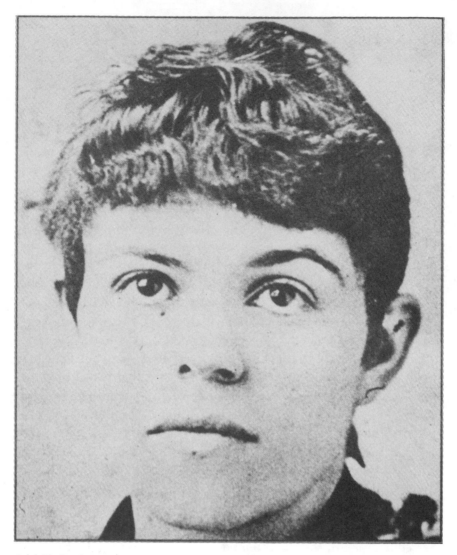

Adelaide Bartlett

looking, but rather shy, and outside of his business an inexperienced man. He was a regular churchgoer, whose only hobby was
breeding Saint Bernard dogs.

Adelaide was later to claim that she had only met her husband
once before her wedding day. Like so much that Adelaide said,
this was probably a self-serving exaggeration, but the couple certainly did not meet often, and the marriage had been arranged by

her guardian, doubtless an agent of her unknown father. It was a perfect marriage as far as her father was concerned. The inconvenient child could be placed in a respectable yet modest situation, where she would not attract attention, and there would be little chance of embarrassing revelations at some future date. Edwin received not only an attractive and well-educated bride but a substantial dowry, more than he might otherwise have expected, which allowed him to expand his business. The arrangements for the marriage allowed Adelaide to continue her education, part of the time in Europe. Edwin, who was poorly educated, appears to have held any form of learning in awe.

In 1878, when Adelaide was twenty-two, she returned to Edwin to set up housekeeping. It was a life for which she was not suited. She made few friends and Edwin worked long hours. Most of the time she was alone, bored, and unhappy.

At her trial, Adelaide said that Edwin had very "peculiar" ideas about sex; that their relationship, except for one occasion, was totally nonsexual. They had what she called a "platonic compact." The single occasion on which the compact was broken was when they wanted to have a child. Adelaide became pregnant, but the child was stillborn. Once again it is reasonable to assume that Adelaide was exaggerating, but certainly the couple did not have a very satisfactory sex life. It is also probable that at some point early in her marriage to Edwin, Adelaide had an affair with his younger brother Frederick. This affair created a great deal of tension with the entire Bartlett family, and Frederick left England for America.

Into this scene came, in 1885, a young Wesleyan clergyman named Reverend Mr. George Dyson. Edwin engaged him as a tutor for Adelaide in Latin, history, and geography. George soon became practically a fixture in the Bartlett house. Edwin was impressed by the young clergyman's education (educated he may have been, but in other ways Dyson seems to have been rather a dim fellow). For his part, the poor-as-a-churchmouse clergyman was impressed by the successful man of business.

How George felt toward Adelaide, and how she felt toward him, is a matter of dispute. Adelaide later claimed that Edwin actually "gave" her to George. George claimed the relationship, though close, was purely platonic, and Adelaide echoed that claim. The clergyman did spend a lot of time at the Bartlett house when Edwin was at work. Edwin not only did not object, he seemed genuinely grateful to the young clergyman for paying so much attention to his wife.

In December 1885, Edwin Bartlett fell ill with a confusing collection of symptoms. Not only did he feel ill and weak, he was overcome with fits of weeping and prey to irrational fears. A young physician, Dr. Leach, thought he detected signs of mercury poisoning. There was some suggestion that Edwin was dosing himself with mercury as a treatment for venereal disease—a suggestion Edwin hotly denied. Adelaide may have told George that her husband knew he was suffering from a fatal disease, and that was why he was so despondent. Adelaide later denied making such a statement. Mercury was used as a treatment for Edwin's Saint Bernards, so there was plenty around. By the end of December, Edwin seemed to be improving. His most serious remaining medical problem was the result of remarkably incompetent dental work. Edwin needed false teeth, so the dentist simply sawed his remaining teeth off at the gum line! No wonder he was in agony. Dr. Leach was able to have the extractions completed, and to ease the pain the doctor used hypnosis. This is a point to be remembered.

After the extractions, Edwin seemed to be on his way back to normally robust health. On New Year's Eve, 1885, a revived Edwin Bartlett ate a huge dinner, and said that he was going back to work on New Year's Day. He didn't, because the next morning he was dead.

An autopsy revealed that Edwin had died from drinking a large quantity of liquid chloroform. George Dyson was horrified, for he had quite openly purchased liquid chloroform for Adelaide just a few days before Edwin's death. He insisted that Adelaide had persuaded him to buy the chloroform for Edwin to help ease his pain during his final "fatal" illness.

To Dr. Leach, however, Adelaide told a quite different story. She said that Edwin had decided to abandon his "platonic compact" with her, and had begun to demand his sexual rights. She needed the chloroform to ward him off. This suggestion played very well in court, for in Victorian times it was considered both proper and normal for respectable women to dislike sex, even with their husbands.

In order to portray Edwin as a man with "peculiar" sexual tastes, Adelaide's lawyer pointed out that in the Bartletts' house was a copy of a book by an American doctor and free-love advocate, Thomas Low Nichols. Merely reading such a book, in the words of the judge, would cause a woman to abandon "a woman's natural instincts."

Liquid chloroform is a very unusual choice of poison. It would burn the mouth and throat on contact. The obvious strong odor makes it unlikely that it could ever be secretly administered to anyone. This was the first known case tried in which liquid chloroform was the poison cited. Adelaide's lawyer suggested that Edwin had downed the substance deliberately in order to hasten the time that Adelaide and George could be together. Even Adelaide's supporters thought that was a bit farfetched. The judge suggested the more moderate theory that Edwin may have downed the chloroform in the hope that it would dull the pain in his jaw. In any event, by trial's end Edwin Bartlett had been portrayed as such a strange character that he seemed capable of anything.

Adelaide was acquitted, and there was cheering in the Old Bailey when the verdict was announced. Though the verdict was popular, not everyone was convinced of Adelaide's innocence. The Reverend George Dyson had turned on her and was sometimes cast as the villain of the piece. Surgeon Sir James Paget was reported to have said after the trial that now that Adelaide was free and beyond further prosecution, she should tell the world how she did it, in the interests of science!

Public sympathy and a fine lawyer were working for her. It certainly wasn't the facts, for there are gaping holes in Adelaide's story. There was, for example, no evidence except for Adelaide's own word that Edwin had ever suggested a "platonic compact" or that they abstained from sex on all but one occasion. It is far more plausible to suggest that Adelaide simply found her husband repulsive, and she was the one who avoided sexual activity, at least with him.

Edwin undoubtedly had invited a young minister into his home, but there is no evidence that he "gave" Adelaide to him in any sense. He may simply have believed that George Dyson would keep his wife company, and since he was a man of God, keep her out of trouble. The belief may have been stupid, but it was not necessarily "peculiar."

The free-love book by Thomas Low Nichols was not Edwin's but Adelaide's, and there was much more to it than a book. Thomas Nichols's wife was an Englishwoman, Mary Nichols, who shared his views and spent much of her time counseling unhappy married women, of whom Adelaide Bartlett was one.

The term "free love" sounds as if it advocated unlimited and uninhibited sexuality, but in Victorian times the term could have many meanings. In the case of the Nicholses, it meant a woman's right to abstain from unwanted sex, even with her husband. This advice was in clear conflict with prevailing ideas about a husband's "rights." By the time Adelaide encountered Mary Nichols and her doctrines, both the Nichols had become Roman Catholics and advocated that sexual intercourse should be reserved exclusively for procreation. Though Adelaide was Protestant, she had been brought up in a Catholic convent, and such views may have been congenial to her. If there was any "platonic compact" in the Bartlett household, it was almost certainly initiated by Adelaide, not Edwin.

The most puzzling part of the case has always been how Adelaide managed to administer a lethal dose of chloroform to her husband. Some who have examined the events argue that the secret was hypnotism. Hypnotism, commonly called mesmerism or animal magnetism in the nineteenth century, was very fashionable in Victorian London. Edwin was known to be interested in the subject, and according to Dr. Leach he was a good—that meant easily hypnotized—subject. The doctor had used hypnotism to work on Edwin's sawed-off teeth. Edwin also told the doctor that he sometimes believed he was under a mesmeric spell, which he claimed had been cast on him by a friend through his wife. Leach tried to talk him out of the belief, and Adelaide said the notion was "absurd." Yet Edwin does seem to have been under his wife's influence. About fourteen months before his death, he changed his will so that she was given full control of her inheritance in case of his death. This was a somewhat unusual arrangement for Victorian wives.

Historian Mary S. Hartman writes, "Then there were the other reported symptoms—the crying, despondency, fear of leaving his bed, fear of death—all of which were consistent with the hypnotic state and suggestion. And if Edwin were mesmerized, murder by means of liquid chloroform presented no serious difficulties. In an appropriate solvent the poison might be downed with some ease by a suitably prepared victim." Brandy was an appropriate solvent, and Adelaide had ordered some brandy for a "holiday celebration."

Hartman goes on to suggest that Adelaide had learned her mesmerism from Mary Nichols, for along with free love, vegetarianism, and water cures, fashionable mesmerism was one of Mrs. Nichols's enthusiasms.

Writes Hartman, "The technique of mesmerism was ideal for [Adelaide] maintaining her fantasy of being a mere victim, long after Adelaide had become an active victimizer. It permitted her to kill Edwin as surely as if she had pulled the trigger of a gun, but it left her free to deny responsibility. Edwin, after all, had raised the glass to his own lips."

There is, however, something almost Victorian about this view of the power of hypnotism. Most studies of hypnotism make it seem highly unlikely that a person could be induced to knowingly drink a substance like chloroform while in a hypnotic state. It is much more likely that Adelaide told her husband that the concoction would dull the pain and help him sleep—and the foolish man believed her.

Adelaide Bartlett never explained anything. After her trial, she simply dropped from sight. Did she run off with her first love, Frederick Bartlett? He had come back from America, and two days after Edwin's death he called on his sister-in-law. Had the whole thing been prearranged? Had there been a deadline that drove Adelaide to use the unlikely weapon of chloroform? We shall never know.

See also: *Gabrielle Bompard.*

1896

MATE BRAM   The saga of the *Herbert Fuller* sounds as if it were conceived by Alfred Hitchcock. Nine men are aboard a small sailing vessel and one of them is a killer, perhaps an insane killer, but no one is sure who among them is the murderer. All are armed, suspicious of one another, and fearful that the killer may strike again. In this state, they are forced to spend six days sailing back to port.

On July 3, 1896, the *Herbert Fuller*, a three-masted sailing vessel, set out from Boston with a load of lumber bound for South America. The captain of the *Fuller* was Charles I. Nash, a man in his mid-forties, an experienced and stable officer and part owner of the ship. He was accompanied by his wife, Laura. They had been married for many years, and she sailed with him on most of his voyages.

The crew who signed on at Boston were strangers to the captain and to one another. The only man who had sailed with Captain Nash before was the steward, Jonathan Spencer, a native of the island of St. Vincent in the British West Indies.

There was one passenger on board, twenty-year-old Lester Hawthorne Monks of Brookline, Massachusetts, a student from the Lawrence Scientific School of Harvard University. He was going on the voyage for his health, for he had been suffering from bronchial troubles.

The rest of the crew were a mixed bag, from France, Germany, Sweden, Russia, and Holland. They were not a criminal bunch, but apart from the steward they were not very bright. The man who became central to this mystery of the sea was the first mate, thirty-two-year-old Thomas Mead Chambers Bram, or Mate Bram, as he was most commonly called. Bram had been born on the island of St. Kitts in the British West Indies. He had run away to sea when he was a boy, but some time later appeared in New

York as a waiter in one of the Dennett restaurants, a chain of eating places that mixed Christian piety with wholesome food. Evangelistic services were often held in Dennett establishments, and they much affected the emotional young Bram. His interest in religion continued even after his return to the sea. He was always attending or conducting services as a lay preacher. He was married with two or three children, but apparently had not lived with his family for over a year.

On the night of July 13, everything seemed normal aboard the *Fuller*. The passenger, Monks, had gone to bed in his cabin. He locked his door to prevent it from rattling when the ship rolled, not because he feared anything. Next to the passenger's cabin was Mrs. Nash's cabin. The captain customarily slept in the chart room nearby. In the same area were both the first and second mates' cabins.

At about 2:00 A.M., Monks was awakened by a woman's scream. At first he wasn't quite sure if the scream was real, or something from a nightmare. Then he heard what was described as a "gurgling noise" coming from the chart room. He called out for the captain, but there was no answer. He then loaded the revolver that he kept under his pillow, unlocked his door, and stepped into the chart room. The captain was on the floor, making strange gasping noises. Captain Nash seemed to be dying. Monks went to call his wife; she could not be seen, but on her bunk were what appeared to be splashes of blood.

Monks was terrified; for all he knew, the murderer was still lurking in some dark corner of the poorly lit cabin. He crept toward the forward companionway, looked up, and saw Mate Bram walking the deck. He pointed his revolver toward the mate and called his name. Bram reacted by grabbing a plank and throwing it at him, perhaps a natural reaction when you see someone pointing a gun at you. But the passenger shouted that the captain had been murdered, and that Bram should come below. Bram did descend into the cabin and looked at the captain, who was dying but not yet dead. He did nothing to help the captain; he wouldn't even go near him. Bram then went into his own room and got his revolver. Both Bram and Monks returned to the deck.

Bram insisted there had been a mutiny led by the second mate.

He began crying, and said someone had tried to poison him. The frightened passenger and tearful seaman sat there, revolvers in hand, until daybreak. The first person they told of the murders was the steward, and he didn't believe them. Steward Spencer went below to see for himself, and found not two bodies, but three—the second mate was lying on his bunk with a huge gash in his skull.

Bram spotted a bloody axe on deck, half hidden under some planks.

"There is an axe. There is the axe that did it," he cried. He was practically hysterical, and then said they should throw it overboard, "for the crew may use it against us." The steward objected, but it was too late, since the frantic first mate had already cast the weapon into the sea. The steward commented ruefully that this was a mistake.

Slowly the crew began to appear on the deck, and it became apparent that there had been no mutiny. The killing of Captain Nash, his wife, and the second mate, had been the act of a single man. But who? And why? Monks must have frequently speculated over the possibility that if he had not locked his door that night, he, too, could have been a victim.

Mate Bram began whimpering about how both he and the captain were Freemasons, and something about his "poor old mother." He started praying. And then he made an astonishing suggestion. Throw the bodies overboard and clean up the blood, because no one alive was guilty of anything. He said that the captain and the mate must have been killed in a fight over Mrs. Nash.

"We must not blame the living for the dead; the dead can't speak for themselves."

The whole idea was absurd. Had the second mate killed the captain and his wife, then hit himself in the head with the axe, run up on deck, hidden the axe, and then returned to his cabin to die? If there had been a fight on deck, why hadn't Bram or the helmsman seen it?

The crew decided to place the bodies in the lifeboat and cover it with canvas. They also made a decision to sail to the nearest port. Mate Bram said that was French Guiana—some fifteen hundred miles away. Though he was technically in command of the *Fuller*, and was the only experienced navigator on board, Bram did not

try to press his opinion. The decision was made to sail to Halifax,
Nova Scotia, the easiest port to reach because of the currents and
prevailing winds. Meekly, Mate Bram went along with the decision.

The voyage was anything but normal. The cabins were all
shut up and everybody had to stay on deck, where they could
keep an eye on one another. Bram had been acting oddly, but one
of the seamen, who was nicknamed Charley Brown (his real name
was long and German), had also begun to act oddly. Bram and
some of the others decided that Charley Brown might be dangerous
and should be put in irons. The seaman offered little resistance.
Mate Bram's reaction was that now they had the murderer in chains
and everything was fine. Monks and the steward were not so sure.
In fact, the steward had told Monks directly: "The mate killed
them people."

After a few days, some of the crewmen began talking to the
manacled Charley Brown. He had an amazing story. He said that
he had been at the wheel at the time of the murders, and through
a window in the chart room he had actually seen Bram kill the
captain. He was in mortal fear for his own life, and that is why
he had acted so strangely.

Other crew members, led by the steward, seized Bram and
manacled him as well. He protested that he was innocent, but he
made no resistance.

On July 20, while there was a thick fog, the *Fuller* sailed into
the middle of a fishing fleet out of Halifax. They picked up a pilot,
who guided them into Halifax the next day. When the story of
what had happened aboard the *Fuller* came out, it was sensational
news, particularly along the waterfronts.

Bram was indicted and finally brought to trial in December
1896. During the trial, his defense brought out the information
that a few years earlier, Charley Brown had suffered some sort of
mental attack while he was in Holland. For two weeks he was
completely out of his head and had to be put in a hospital after a
bout of shouting that unknown people were out to kill him or steal
his money. Later he told the story that he had actually killed a
man during that mad period. The story of the killing was an idle
though strange boast.

A good deal of time was spent disputing whether Brown could

Mate Bram in court at the second trial.

have actually seen the murder being committed, as he had claimed. There was also dispute over whether Brown could have left the wheel unattended for the ten minutes or so it would have taken to commit the crime himself, without the ship going completely, and obviously, out of control. In general, the conclusions were that Brown could have seen the murders, and could not have left the wheel. In short, that he was telling the truth.

Evidence weighed heavily against Mate Bram. The prosecution's greatest difficulty was to establish a motive for the killings. What was Bram trying to accomplish? He had complained to some of his shipmates about Captain Nash being tight-fisted, and had argued openly with the second mate, but such activity was common, indeed inevitable, aboard ship. There was nothing to indicate that Mate Bram nursed any sort of murderous hatred toward Captain Nash, his wife, or the second mate. The prosecution made no direct attempt to establish a motive, but outside the court it was freely speculated that Mate Bram possessed the soul of a pirate. The theory was that he intended to seize the ship and sell it, possibly to Cuban insurgents. Bram had previously served as second mate on the schooner *White Wings*. The first mate on the voyage, a man named Nicklas, said Bram had proposed that they kill the captain and seize the cargo. Nicklas laughed at the suggestion. Bram then proposed that they go on board a Norwegian vessel where there were fewer men, and kill the captain and drug the crew. Nicklas was still unimpressed by the scheme. To prove he was serious, Bram then told him how he had stolen the cargo of two previous ships he had been on, though neither of these plots involved murder. Nicklas's evidence was not allowed in court. Nor was a certificate from the American vice-consul at Rio saying that Bram had been discharged at that port "on complaint of the Master, R.E.M. Davisson, that he had well founded suspicions of said Bram having intentions to steal the vessel." That happened just a few months before the sailing of the *Fuller*. Why the court did not allow the introduction of this evidence is unclear.

If Bram planned to kill the captain and steal the *Fuller*, the plan was a mad one. He may have been drunk during the killings, and when he sobered up, completely lost his nerve. There is really no rational way of explaining his actions.

Bram testified in his own defense, and according to reports of the trial, made an excellent witness. Many doubted the jury could bring in a guilty verdict on a man who looked and sounded so sincere. But on March 9, the jury, after long deliberation, did declare Mate Bram guilty of three murders, and he was sentenced to be hanged. This was by no means the end of the story.

Bram's lawyers brought the case before the United States Supreme Court, arguing that a number of serious errors had been committed in the original trial. The Supreme Court set aside the verdict and ordered a new trial. The whole *Herbert Fuller* drama was replayed once again between March 16 and April 20, 1898, and once again Bram was convicted. This time, however, Bram was not sentenced to death, but to life imprisonment.

Bram was released on parole August 27, 1913. He had spent about fifteen years in prison after having been convicted twice of three atrocious murders on the high seas, at a time when draconian punishments even for less serious crimes were the rule. Bram was on parole for a little over five years, and in 1919 was granted a full and unconditional pardon by President Woodrow Wilson. Throughout it all, Bram continued to proclaim his innocence, and often signed letters to his lawyer "Your Innocent Victim."

Mystery writer Mary Roberts Rinehart wrote a story, "The After House," about a triple murder on a private yacht, that was clearly based on the murders aboard *Herbert Fuller*. In the story, the mate turns out to be innocent and blame is placed on "Charley Jones," a mad, homicidal helmsman. It was sometimes said that President Wilson was moved to pardon Bram after reading the Reinhart story, but Edmund Pearson in his *Studies in Murder* notes, "This sounds too much a campaign slander, invented by the President's political opponents."

After his release from prison and even before his pardon, Bram prospered, first in the peanut business in Georgia, then reputedly as a speculator in a Florida land boom. But his ambition was always to have a ship of his own, and finally he got one, the *Alvena*. In January 1928, the *Alvena* was reported lost at sea, and that revived stories of the *Herbert Fuller* in the press. Some of Bram's old shipmates from the *Fuller* were interviewed, but were not convinced Mate Bram was dead. "That fellow had nine lives," one remarked. Sure enough, the *Alvena* turned up unharmed. Bram didn't want to talk about the past. "That's dead and gone now."

Five years later, Bram was reported in Bermuda, still captain of the *Alvena*. He did not hide his past. He would tell just about anyone who would listen that he had been imprisoned for someone else's crimes, but that he had been completely exonerated by the "death-bed confession" of another member of the ship's company. Indeed, every time a member of the crew of the *Fuller* died, there were rumors of a "death-bed confession." There was not a bit of solid evidence to support a single one of these rumors, and several were demonstrably false. There is, however, no hint that when Mate Bram died he uttered any "death-bed confession."

1934

GEORGE W. ROGERS   The most difficult sort of criminal for society to deal with or understand is the psychopath. Utterly without what we call conscience, the psychopath can seem outwardly normal, even friendly and charming, yet is capable of committing the most horrifying acts and feeling not a twinge of remorse. The psychopath is never tormented by guilt feelings, and will go on committing crimes until he is caught.

Such a person was George W. Rogers. But he first burst onto the public scene as a hero. Rogers was radioman on the luxury liner *Morro Castle* when, on September 8, 1934, there was a fire aboard. Rogers was on duty when the fire broke out, and he remained at his post, until the flames were quite literally licking at his ankles, sending out the distress signals that finally brought help. He received painful, though not serious, burns because of his actions. One hundred and thirty-four passengers died as a result of the fire, but had it not been for Rogers's diligence at the radio, help might not have arrived as swiftly as it did, and the death toll could have been much worse.

The ship, which had been en route back from Havana, Cuba, to New York, caught fire off the New Jersey coast, and it continued to burn even after the hulk was beached at Asbury Park, New Jersey. While not one of the worst maritime disasters in history, it was certainly one of the most spectacular. The *Morro Castle* fire received a tremendous amount of press coverage, and Rogers became famous.

There were villains in the tragedy, as well. The acting captain, William Warms, and the chief engineer were both tried for negligence. They were convicted, at least in part, on Rogers's testimony. (Later the convictions of both men were reversed, and they were released from prison.)

When Rogers got back to his hometown of Bayonne, New Jersey, the mayor gave him a gold medal, and he got a job. He joined the Bayonne police force as an assistant to Lieutenant Vincent J. Doyle, chief of the police radio bureau. Four years later, someone tried to kill Lieutenant Doyle with a bomb. It was quickly established that the attempted killer was the former hero George Rogers. Rogers had wanted his chief's job. He was given a psychiatric examination and was diagnosed as having a "psychopathic personality." The judge in the case put it a little more strongly, saying Rogers had "the mind of a fiend," and sentenced him to from twelve to twenty years.

In 1942, Rogers was released from prison, because it was felt that his skills as a radio operator would be needed in the war effort. However, the armed services took one look at his record and decided they didn't need radio operators that badly. Still, Rogers was allowed to remain free.

Rogers remained in the Bayonne area, and somehow he managed to borrow over seven thousand dollars from eighty-three-year-old William Hummel. In 1953, Hummel decided he wanted to move to Florida, so he pressed Rogers for repayment of the debt. Instead, Rogers crushed his skull with a footstool. He then went upstairs and killed Hummel's daughter the same way.

Hummel had twenty-five hundred dollars in cash in his house when Rogers killed him. Rogers pocketed the money and then, apparently having lost the traditional psychopath's cunning, went on a spending spree. The police knew Rogers well, and they also knew he had no money and no way of getting any legitimately. Once the Hummel murders were discovered, Rogers was an immediate suspect. He was sent back to prison, where he died in 1958.

A nagging question remains. Could an undoubted villain like George Rogers also have been a hero? Writers Gordon Thomas and Max Morgan Witts reexamined the circumstances surrounding the *Morro Castle* disaster in their 1972 book *Shipwreck: The Strange Fate of the Morro Castle*. They concluded that, far from being the hero of the disaster, Rogers may very well have been the villain there, too.

The authors suggested that he poisoned the captain and then started the fire with a small time bomb. His heroics at the radio, they said, were merely an attempt to divert attention from his crimes.

1954

DR. SAM SHEPPARD   The trial of Dr. Samuel H. Sheppard for the murder of his wife was to become one of the most sensational and well-publicized criminal trials of the 1950s in America.

Dr. Sam, as the papers liked to call him, was a respected and very successful osteopath in the Cleveland, Ohio, area. According to Dr. Sam, he had been asleep in his suburban Cleveland home fronting Lake Erie, on July 4, 1954, when he heard the sounds of a violent struggle and his wife screaming for help. He rushed to the upstairs bedroom, where he was confronted with a "bushy-haired" intruder, who knocked him unconscious. When Dr. Sam awoke, he found his wife's battered and bloody body.

Police were quickly suspicious of the story. No trace of the "bushy-haired" man could be found. Marilyn Sheppard had been struck over twenty-five times with a blunt surgical instrument, presumably belonging to the doctor. Nothing was taken from the house except one of Dr. Sam's T-shirts. Dr. Sam said the killer must have stolen the shirt to replace his own bloodstained shirt.

More suspicious still was an investigation of Dr. Sam's private life. Marilyn Sheppard was thirty-one years old at the time of her death and four months pregnant. She had been Dr. Sam's childhood sweetheart, but at the time of her death the doctor was carrying on an affair with Susan Hays, a young, attractive medical technician at Bay View Hospital, where the doctor worked.

Dr. Sam went to his wife's funeral in a wheelchair, and wearing a neck brace. He said that this was the result of the injuries caused by the "bushy-haired" man. He kept the neck brace on during the trial, but it did him no good. Dr. Sam was a terrible witness in his own defense, and both he and Miss Hays admitted their affair on the witness stand. That as much as anything else contributed to a conviction on second-degree murder and a life sentence.

But it wasn't over. A lot of newspapers and magazines took

up a crusade to have Dr. Sam's conviction reversed. A notable champion of the imprisoned osteopath was mystery writer Erle Stanley Gardner. Dr. Sam got a new lawyer, F. Lee Bailey, who already had a reputation as a courtroom magician. Bailey petitioned the Ohio Supreme Court for a new trial, citing "prejudicial publicity" and a "carnival atmosphere" at the first trial. Bailey had a good case, and in 1964 Dr. Sam was released from the Ohio State Penitentiary to await his second trial.

The second trial did not take place until 1966, and the publicity-charged atmosphere of the first trial was entirely absent. The truth was the public didn't really care one way or another about Dr. Sam anymore. This time Bailey didn't put his client on the stand, and the doctor was acquitted.

During his imprisonment, Dr. Sam got many letters from women who said they believed in his innocence. He continued his correspondence with one of them, and after his release from prison she married him. Less than two years after their marriage, Dr. Sam's second wife left him, saying that she feared for her safety. Dr. Sam briefly turned professional wrestler, but his health was failing, and in 1970 he died.

Officially the case remains unsolved, but many still believe that there really was no "bushy-haired" intruder. As one well-known columnist who covered the trials said, "I never was sure about Dr. Sam."

1964

CANDACE MOSSLER   Candy Mossler was a tabloid journalist's dream. She'd grown up in a hardscrabble Georgia family
and had run away at fifteen to become a model—shoes and tooth-
paste. Pretty, bright, and tough, she was running her own modeling
agency within ten years. She had married young, and had two
children before the marriage broke up. Then, in 1948, when she
was in her late thirties, she met and married Texas millionaire
Jacques Mossler, a man twenty-four years her senior. The couple
adopted four more children.

The marriage was not a conventional one. Mossler was very
much the indulgent father, while Candy looked and acted a lot
younger than she really was. And sometimes she acted very oddly.
Once, while driving between Atlanta and Houston, she simply
disappeared. Police from several counties searched for her. The
rented auto she had been driving was found smashed into a tree in
a rural county in Georgia, but Candy herself was missing. Three
days later, barefoot and bruised, she staggered up to a farmhouse
in central Georgia. What had happened to her? Candy said she
didn't know because the accident had given her amnesia and she
couldn't remember a thing.

At 1:00 A.M. on June 30, 1964, Candy Mossler put four of
her children into her car and drove away from the luxurious
Mossler apartment in Key Biscayne, Florida. For several hours she
drove around, apparently without any purpose. Later, Candy was
to claim that she had a severe migraine and was looking for a
hospital.

When Candy returned home at 4:30 A.M., she found the beaten
and stabbed corpse of her husband on the living-room floor. The
family dog, a boxer, was chained to the kitchen doorknob, barking
furiously.

Neighbors said that they heard shouting in the apartment at

Candace Mossler (*Wide World*)

about 2:00 A.M., and after that the barking started. A man's heavy footsteps were heard running down the hall. At first the police rounded up the usual suspects, but had to release them for lack of evidence.

The investigation continued, and on July 4, there was a bombshell. Police arrested twenty-four-year-old Melvin Lane Powers, Candy Mossler's nephew. They said that Powers had flown from Houston to Florida, and in a bizarre twist, obtained a giant Coke bottle from a bar with which he crushed Mossler's skull. He had also stabbed the old man repeatedly. Moreover, police said, Candy and her nephew were lovers, thus raising the specter of incest. Investigators found a note from Mossler stating, "If Mel and Candace don't kill me first, I'll kill them."

Candy leaped to her nephew's defense, but soon found herself under arrest. She hired the colorful and expensive Texas lawyer Percy Forman for the defense. Forman had the reputation of having lost only one client to the electric chair.

Powers said nothing, and fought extraditon to Florida. Candy talked almost obsessively to reporters, denying everything and telling one strange contradictory story after another. At one point, she said that she knew the real killer was a man named Ted, and that he would step forward and admit his guilt if "things get bad."

It was over a year before the authorities managed to get Powers back to Florida, and when the eagerly awaited trial finally began, it was everything the press and public had hoped for. All sorts of details, real and suggested, about Candy's love life were discussed in the courtroom and reported at great length in the papers.

The prosecution case was that Candy wanted her husband dead so that she could inherit his millions and marry Powers. The prosecutor said that Mossler had found out about the affair between his wife and Powers, and had threatened to divorce her and cut her off without a dime. The state put a prisoner named Frank Mulvey on the stand who said that Candy had given him seventy-five hundred dollars to kill Mossler, but that he just took the money and did nothing. Later, he was arrested on another charge, and when he met Powers in prison, Powers had boasted of the killing. The prosecution even said that Powers's bloody handprint had been found in the Mossler apartment after the murder.

Percy Forman wisely declined to put either the stolid Powers or the irrepressible Candy on the stand. Instead, he tried to put Jacques Mossler on trial. He said that Mossler was, among other things, a homosexual, and was probably killed by one of the men he had picked up. There wasn't much evidence to back up this assertion, but it had an impact on the jury. As for Mulvey, he was a drug addict and jailbird who would say anything to get out of prison.

The sensational but exhausting trial (one of the longest criminal trials in Florida history) finally ended on March 6, 1966, when the jury returned a verdict of not guilty. Candy immediately rushed the jury box and kissed all of the male jurors, thanking them "for my little children."

Candy inherited the Mossler money, but never did marry Powers. Instead she married a Texas electrician named Barnett Wade Garrison, who was eighteen years her junior. On the night of August 12, 1977, Garrison came home to the Mossler mansion in Houston, only to find that he had been locked out. He tried to climb in through an unlocked third-floor window, but he lost his grip, which wasn't too secure because in one hand he was clutching a gun. The fall put him in a coma for two weeks and permanently affected his mind, and he never did say why he was carrying that gun. Barnett was taken to his parents' home, and one night Candy showed up wearing a fur coat over her nightgown and pounding on the door and shouting that her husband had been kidnapped.

The couple was divorced in a bitter case in 1975. Percy Forman didn't represent Candy this time. In fact, he was suing her to collect his fee from the murder trial.

Melvin Powers went on to become a millionaire real estate broker in Houston. Candy Mossler died at the Fontainebleau Hotel in Miami, on October 26, 1976, from an overdose of sedatives. She was sixty-two years old. Her death probably wasn't suicide, since she had been addicted to a variety of drugs for years. This time she had simply taken too many at one time. Candace Mossler was buried in Arlington National Cemetery, next to the remains of the husband she had been tried for murdering. Powers did not attend the services.

1969

JOAN HILL   The death, possibly murder, of wealthy Joan
Robinson Hill blew up into a gigantic Texas-style scandal with a
lot of additional violence. She was the adored daughter of Texas
oil millionaire Ash Robinson, and a champion horsewoman. In
1958, when she was twenty-six, Joan Robinson married for the
third time, to a young Houston plastic surgeon, John Hill. Ash
Robinson paid for the splashy wedding.

Joan and John didn't seem to be a particularly well-matched
pair. He worked long hours and was fond of literature and good
music; he had an expensive music room installed in their home.
She cared only for her horses. Yet for several years it all seemed
to be working out, and Ash Robinson was happy because his
daughter was happy.

But by 1968, the marriage was falling apart, and John Hill
began having affairs with other women. The couple argued frequently. On March 17, 1969, Joan became ill after eating breakfast.
For some reason, John delayed getting medical treatment for his
wife; it wasn't until the following day that he took her to the
hospital, which happened to be the small Sharpstown General Hospital, of which he was part owner. It was later alleged that the
hospital didn't have the facilities to treat her properly, and the next
morning, during the course of treatment, she died.

The events surrounding the death were curious, but by the
time the medical examiner was informed of the woman's death,
Joan's body had already been taken to a funeral home and partially
embalmed, thus making a thorough autopsy more difficult. Back
at the hospital, a brain said to be Joan Hill's was given to the
medical examiners. The brain showed signs of meningitis, but it
is possible that it wasn't Joan Hill's brain they examined. The body
was hastily buried.

From the moment of his daughter's death, Ash Robinson was

Dr. John Hill (*Wide World*)

convinced that her husband had been responsible. He used all his political clout, which was considerable, to have John Hill indicted for murder. When, three months after Joan's death, John married the woman to whom he had been linked while his marriage was breaking up, Robinson was further enraged. In August 1969, at the request of the district attorney, a friend of Ash Robinson, Joan's body was exhumed and reexamined. Robinson even brought in New York City's celebrated medical examiner, Dr. Milton Helpern. Still, no definite conclusions could be reached about the woman's death, and two grand juries refused to indict John Hill. Hill's lawyers threatened Robinson with a multimillion-dollar lawsuit for slander. Then Hill's second marriage broke up, and his second wife, Ann Kurth, said that Hill had confessed to her that he had killed Joan. Moreover, she said Hill had tried to kill her.

This time when a grand jury was convened, it indicted John Hill. But the charge was an odd one—murder by neglect, technically "murder by omission," in that he had failed to provide his wife with proper medical attention when she became ill. Hill's trial was filled with all sorts of intriguing but far-from-conclusive testimony about how the doctor may have been growing disease-causing bacteria that he tried to administer to his wife. But when his second wife, Ann, got on the stand and blurted out that John Hill had tried to kill her in a car accident, that was too much. The judge ruled that the testimony was inadmissible, because under the law she could only testify about the period before she married Hill. A mistrial was declared.

Another trial seemed inevitable but a conviction was not, and there was a great deal of legal wrangling. Undaunted by his troubles, John Hill married a third time, and just after returning from his honeymoon in September 1972, he was shot and killed by an unknown gunman who burst into his house wearing a Halloween mask. The assassin, however, was not very professional. He threw away his gun, which was traced by the police to a young Houston tough, Bobby Vandiver. Vandiver confessed that he had gotten five thousand dollars for the hit from Lilla Paulus, a Houston madam. But he said the money for the contract killing originated with Ash Robinson, who let it be known that he was willing to pay for the murder of his hated ex–son-in-law. Paulus was indicted along with Vandiver, and the trial promised to be a sensational one. However, before the trial could take place, Bobby Vandiver was shot by police, apparently while attempting to escape. Lilla Paulus was convicted and given a life sentence, but refused to implicate anyone else in the murder plot. Ash Robinson, then seventy-nine years old and reputedly in poor health, insisted he had nothing to do with the killing and was never indicted. He also said that a lie detector test had absolved him of any involvement in the murder of John Hill.

This bizarre and explosive case refused to die. John Hill's family tried unsuccessfully to sue Robinson. The case was the subject of a best-selling book, *Blood and Money*, by Thomas Thompson. In the book, Thompson virtually accused Robinson of setting up the Hill murder. Robinson sued, but that simply gave the book publicity and made it more popular. In 1981, there was a four-hour TV miniseries based on the case. Joan Robinson was played by the glamorous Farrah Fawcett, who was far more attractive than the real Joan. The actress's publicity agent let it be known that old Ash Robinson himself had given his "casting approval." There were rumors that it was Robinson who had originally suggested Farrah Fawcett for the part.

Since the miniseries, Ash Robinson has died, and so the strange deaths of John and Joan Hill are destined to remain officially unsolved.

See also: *Claus von Bülow*.

Selected Bibliography

The most prolific of today's true crime writers is Jay Robert Nash. His best-known book is *Bloodletters and Badmen* (Evans. N.Y., 1973), but there have been many others, including: *Look for the Woman* (Evans. N.Y., 1981), *The Almanac of World Crime* (Doubleday. N.Y., 1981), and *Murder Among the Mighty* (Delacorte. N.Y., 1983). Nash is most entertaining and most reliable when writing about what he knows best, the gangsters of Prohibition-era Chicago.

Englishman Colin Wilson writes on the occult as well as crime. His two best-known crime books are *The Encyclopedia of Murder*, co-authored by Patricia Pitman (Putnam. N.Y., 1961) and the followup, *The Encyclopedia of Modern Murder*, written with Donald Seeman (Putnam. N.Y., 1983). Wilson is most knowledgeable about English sex crimes, and they do not always make pleasant reading.

From an earlier and more elegant era of American crime writing comes Edmund Pearson's *Studies in Murder* (Macmillan. N.Y., 1924), followed by *Five Murders* (Doubleday. N.Y., 1928) and *More Studies in Murder* (H. Smith. N.Y., 1936). And from a more elegant time in England is Raymond Postgate's *Murder, Piracy and Treason* (Houghton Mifflin. Boston, n.d.)

The Encyclopedia of American Crime, by Carl Sifakia (Facts on File. N.Y., 1982), is massive and very readable.

Of the many Jack the Ripper books, the best is *The Complete Jack the Ripper*, by Donald Rumbelow (W. H. Allen. London, 1975). The Masonic cabal fantasy is spun out in *Jack the Ripper: The Final Solution*, by Stephen Knight (Grafton Books. London, 1977).

Good accounts of the cases of Oscar Slater and Madeleine Smith are found in *Famous Trials*, edited by John Mortimer (Dorset Press. N.Y., 1986).

Mary S. Hartman's *Victorian Murderesses* (Shocken Books. N.Y., 1976) looks at the killings and the society in which they took place.

If you like pictures, *A Pictorial History of Crime*, by Julian Symons (Crown. N.Y., 1966), is a good coffee-table crime volume.

A well-illustrated book of mysteries, though not necessarily crimes, is *Great Unsolved Mysteries*, edited by John Canning (Chartwell Books. Secaucus, N.J., 1984).

One of the finest reconstructions of an historic crime is *The Maul and the Pear Tree: The Ratcliffe Highway Murder 1811*, by P. D. James and T. A. Critchley (The Mysterious Press. N.Y., 1971).

There are lots of books on Mayerling. A couple of good ones are: Richard Barkeley, *The Road to Mayerling* (Macmillan. London, 1958), and Judith Listower, *A Hapsburg Tragedy* (Dorset Press. N.Y., 1978).

The case that Napoleon was poisoned is put forth effectively in *The Murder of Napoleon*, by Ben Weider and David Hapgood (Congdon & Lattes. N.Y., 1982).

Forgotten News: The Crime of the Century and Other Lost Stories, by Jack Finney (Simon & Schuster. N.Y., 1983), is an interesting attempt to reconstruct the Burdell case from newspaper accounts of the time.

Captain Kidd and the War Against the Pirates, by historian Robert C. Titchie (Harvard University Press. Cambridge, Mass., 1986), is a well-researched study that will change your view of pirates.

A fairly complete history of the murderer who never was can be found in Peter Haining's *Sweeney Todd, The Demon Barber of Fleet Street* (Frederick Miller, Ltd., London, 1979).

The Bog People, by P. V. Glob (Cornell University Press. Ithaca N.Y., 1965), gives the history of those remarkable mummies. The pictures must be seen to be believed.

The whole sordid Hill case was spelled out in Thomas Thompson's *Blood and Money* (Doubleday. N.Y., 1976).

A Cast of Killers, by Sidney D. Kirkpatrick (Dutton. N.Y., 1986), tells the story of the William Desmond Taylor killing from notes gathered by director King Vidor.

The lawyer who led Claus von Bülow's successful appeal gives his version of events in *Reversal of Fortunes*, by Alan Dershowitz (Random House. N.Y., 1986).

Evil Angels (Summit Books. N.Y., 1987), by John Bryson, is an angry book about the Dingo Baby Murder Case. Austrialian society is really on trial in this one.

Judgment Day, by Bob Lancaster and B.C. Hall (Seaview/G.P.S. Putnam's. N.Y., 1983), is a bit melodramatic, but basically a sound and interesting account of the killing of rural bully Ken Rex McElroy.

Who Killed Sir Harry Oakes?, by James Leasor (Houghton Mifflin. Boston, 1983) asks the question, but does not fully answer it.

Michael M. Mooney's *The Hindenberg* (Dodd, Mead. N.Y., 1972) is an excellent reconstruction of the events leading up to the disaster.

Zodiac, by Robert Graysmith (St. Martin's/Marek. N.Y., 1986), gives a very full account of the most mysterious mass killer of modern times.

D.B. Cooper, What Really Happened, by Max Gunther (Contemporary Books. Chicago, 1985), may not tell you what really happened, but it is a good retelling of what is known, and presents an intriguing possibility of what might have happened.

Peking Man, by Harry L. Shapiro (Simon & Schuster. N.Y., 1974), looks at one fossil mystery, while *The Piltdown Inquest*, by Charles Blinderman (Prometheus. Buffalo, N.Y., 1986), looks at another.

For devotees of history as well as mystery, I strongly recommend *The Historian as a Detective, Essays on Evidence*, edited by Robin W. Winks (Harper & Row, N.Y., 1969).